CORONAVIRUS CRIMINALS
AND PANDEMIC PROFITEERS

CORONAVIRUS CRIMINALS
AND PANDEMIC PROFITEERS

ACCOUNTABILITY FOR THOSE
WHO CAUSED THE CRISIS

John Nichols

VERSO

London • New York

First published by Verso 2022
© John Nichols 2022

1 3 5 7 9 10 8 6 4 2

Verso
UK: 6 Meard Street, London W1F 0EG
US: 20 Jay Street, Suite 1010, Brooklyn, NY 11201
versobooks.com

Verso is the imprint of New Left Books

ISBN-13: 978-1-83976-377-9
ISBN-13: 978-1-83976-425-7 (UK EBK)
ISBN-13: 978-1-83976-424-0 (US EBK)

British Library Cataloguing in Publication Data
A catalogue record for this book is available from the British Library

Library of Congress Cataloging-in-Publication Data
A catalog record for this book is available from the Library of Congress

Typeset in Garamond by Biblichor Ltd, Edinburgh
Printed and bound by CPI Group (UK) Ltd, Croydon CR0 4YY

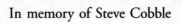

In memory of Steve Cobble

Contents

PREFACE

Accountability Is a Dish
Best Served Fresh, and Hot

When I interviewed New York Assemblyman Ron Kim, a hero of this book, he told me, "There's no justice without accountability." The legislator was not merely suggesting that accountability for coronavirus criminals and pandemic profiteers equaled justice. Rather, he was explaining that the systemic change that might assure a more humane and equitable response to the next catastrophe will never come if the wrongdoers of this epoch are let off the hook. "We need accountability to get to the justice that we need, whether it's systemic changes or anything. But if we don't have accountability at the front end, we can't get to any of the changes."

Kim's reference to getting accountability at the front end reminds us of an essential premise in the struggle for social progress. It is best to demand change when memories of callousness and cruelty are fresh. The passage of time dulls the appetite for necessary action to address fundamental flaws in the organization of any society, and that is especially true in Western democracies that make a great show of the peaceful transfer of power. There is a pressure to forgive and forget, to reshuffle and rehabilitate the personalities who possess great political and economic power. As a result, we often get the theater of change without the reality. A game of musical chairs may put different individuals in different seats. But, without accountability, it is the same game, with the same people sitting in the same chairs.

The only way transformative change occurs is if the bad players are told they can't play the game anymore. And that only happens if their lying, cheating, and stealing is called out at the point when anger over this wrongdoing is intense enough to write a new set of rules. This isn't an untested concept. It is as old as the story of man's inhumanity to man. But in the political sphere, it is a notion that must be regularly reintroduced.

The greatest polemicist of the past century, the British writer and parliamentarian Michael Foot, understood the power of an immediate demand for accountability. When Britain found itself in the worst of all circumstances, at the beginning of a world war in which victory was far from assured, Foot and a pair of his fellow journalists at the *London Evening Standard* asked the essential question: How did we get into this mess? They answered that question with a short book, *Guilty Men*, which called out the British political leaders who had appeased Hitler and the Nazis during the 1930s.

Their enormously influential book made a fierce assertion about the war effort in which everyone had become engaged. The fight would not be won if the appeasers were allowed to return to positions of power. Accountability was not, in Foot's view, a narrow project involving the settling of partisan or ideological scores. It was a vital struggle—a *J'Accuse . . . !*—that sought to dismiss from the political stage the weak and compromising leaders of the past so that a new and bolder generation might save Britain and the world.

To that end, Foot and his compatriots, Frank Owen and Peter Howard, opened their book with a seventy-six word preface:

> On a spring day in 1793, a crowd of angry men burst their way through the doors of the assembly room where the French Convention was in session. A discomforted figure addressed them from the rostrum. "What do the people desire?" he asked. "The Convention has only their welfare at heart." The leader of the angry crowd replied, "The people haven't come here to be given a lot of phrases. They demand a dozen guilty men."

The book *Guilty Men* was slightly more ambitious than the Jacobins. It identified a "cast" of fifteen of the worst players, most of them Tories, all of them men. The names were named. The crimes were charged. Yet, Foot and his co-writers did not merely call out the "ignoramuses or poltroons or cowards." They proposed a "cleansing liberation."

Foot's biographer, Kenneth Morgan, explained that the publication of *Guilty Men* assured that "everyone knew who the villains of the thirties were, and why they could never be forgiven." Foot admitted that the book, written "in a rush and a rage," aimed, simply, "to secure changes in the men running the war." Yet, eighty years on, it seemed to me the most relevant reading during the long months of the coronavirus pandemic.

This book, inspired by Foot and the pamphleteering tradition he embraced, casts a somewhat wider net. It features guilty men and guilty women. Instead of twelve, or fifteen, there are eighteen offenders—reflecting, I would argue, the wider array of wrongdoing during the course of the pandemic. The focus is, primarily, on the political class that, in a democratic republic, is supposed to be able to set things right. But it does not stop there. It considers, as well, the most egregious offenders among the economic and social elites.

The point, which I will return to in the concluding chapter, is to demand accountability in our moment as Michael Foot did in his. "It will make you fiercely angry as you read," declared a review of *Guilty Men* in 1940. "And it is anger that is needed to sweep these relics of appeasement, incompetence and muddle out of public life."

It is this justified anger, this righteous fury at those who caused thousands of unnecessary deaths, and at those who enriched themselves in a time of crisis, that remains America's best hope for achieving accountability—and for the justice that extends from it.

ACKNOWLEDGMENTS

In February of 2020, I was on the campaign trail, covering the race for the Democratic presidential nomination. March was going to be a busy month—with a book festival and union events in Tucson, then the mad rush of rallies, town hall meetings, caucuses, and primary elections that would lead to the Democratic National Convention in Milwaukee and the Republican National Convention in Charlotte. But March didn't go as planned. After a speech to the Ohio Federation of Teachers in Columbus, and a last dinner with my friend and comrade Amy Hanauer, I was off the road. The country was locking down. People started getting sick, and dying, from Covid-19. The economy stalled. The stock market crashed.

Suddenly, I found myself covering a different story. Some of the first articles I wrote were on transit workers who were dying at a shocking rate as the coronavirus pandemic overtook New York and other cities. Then I wrote about machinists working around the clock to produce ventilators. And members of Congress passing massive spending bills to deal with an overwhelming crisis. And a president denying the crisis. While the pandemic may have been unprecedented in some senses, the predictable patterns of political chicanery and corporate profiteering quickly emerged. I recognized that nothing would change unless, this time, we kept a record of the ways in which even the most challenging moments are corrupted by those who refuse to recognize the common good. My longtime editor Andy Hsiao was seeing what I was seeing. We started talking about this book. Andy and I have worked together for two decades and I cherish our partnership. I also value the rest of the team at Verso, my publisher for many years, which embraced this project from the start. I want to extend special thanks to Mark Martin, for his patience and support, and to Jeffrey Klein, for wise suggestions regarding the manuscript.

I cover politics for the *Nation* magazine, and I am eternally grateful to Katrina vanden Heuvel, my longtime editor, for her insights, support, and enthusiasm. She is the strongest person I know. I also valued every conversation with Anna Hiatt, a brilliant editor and friend, with whom I spoke on pretty much a daily basis throughout the pandemic. Many of the chapters in this book had their roots in discussions with Katrina and Anna, and in articles for the *Nation* that extended from those discussions. I also want to thank Don Guttenplan, a friend and wise editor, who maintained the *Nation*'s dissenting tradition and radical mission throughout the pandemic. Thanks, as well, to Dave Zweifel, my longtime editor at the *Capital Times* in Madison, Wisconsin; to Bill Lueders and Norm Stockwell at the *Progressive*; to colleagues such as Joan Walsh, Sasha Abramsky, and Jessica Opoien; and to radio friends and wise counselors Amy Goodman, Santita Jackson, Chip Franklin, Michelangelo Signorile, Jeff Santos, Mitch Jeserich and all the folks at KPFA, and, of course, John "Sly" Sylvester.

Conversations with Bernie Sanders, Noam Chomsky, Jesse Jackson, Mark Pocan, Ro Khanna, Ilhan Omar, Pramila Jayapal, Gwen Moore, Sherrod Brown, Francesca Hong, and Ron Kim, among others, framed and extended my thinking as I was writing this book. I also benefitted from many conversations with union members who guided me through the essential work they were doing—especially the folks at National Nurses United and the Amalgamated Transit Union. And, as always, I valued the tremendous work of Public Citizen, the Institute for Policy Studies and other watchdog groups and think tanks that informed my writing.

My mother, Mary Nichols, who is a wise and healthy ninety, provided me with firsthand recollections of past pandemics and health scares. I cherished every one of our conversations. I will also cherish the memory of lockdown days because I got to spend them with two of the smartest and bravest and best people in the world, Mary Bottari and Whitman Bottari, as well as the funniest person in the world, Laura Dresser. They made a challenging time not just tolerable but enlightening and hopeful, as did friends and neighbors in Madison's Tenney-Lapham neighborhood. Finally, I want to acknowledge the memory of my dear friend and comrade Steve Cobble, with whom I spent long hours on the phone during the pandemic. Steve died early in 2021, leaving this country without its ablest and most humane political strategist and seer. This book is dedicated to his memory.

Love and Solidarity,
John Nichols,
October 2021

INTRODUCTION

In the Name of Mike Jackson

Let us then do honor to revolutions by justice.
— Thomas Paine, *Agrarian Justice*, 1797

Mike Jackson was a working man with a big family to support. He showed up every day for his job on the assembly line at the Briggs & Stratton manufacturing plant in Wauwatosa, Wisconsin. Classified as an "essential worker" when the coronavirus pandemic hit, he kept busy on the line, producing lawn-mower engines and pressure washers. He worked his normal shifts. He worked mandatory overtime shifts. And the forty-five-year-old father of eight worried. Mike Jackson didn't think the company was doing what was necessary to protect workers against the deadly virus that was spreading rapidly in and around his hometown of Milwaukee. The protocols for protection were clear enough: wear masks, avoid face-to-face contact, keep a six-foot distance, don't touch surfaces touched by others. But Briggs & Stratton seemed to be more interested in turning a profit than in following the commonsense rules of a pandemic moment. Workers at the plant complained that they were required to do their jobs facing one another on the assembly line. Managers were casual about mask requirements; sometimes they didn't wear them at all.

A month after the state of Wisconsin locked down in mid-March, Jackson and his fellow workers were so concerned that they walked off the job in hopes of forcing the company to take the threat seriously. They weren't asking for much. They just wanted Briggs & Stratton to follow guidelines issued by the Centers for Disease Control and the Occupational Safety and Health Administration for protecting workers from the spread of Covid-19. "Mike and a bunch of people in the area came to me and said they were concerned about safety; one of the guys told me he was on medication," Chance Zombor, the grievance representative for United Steelworkers Local 2-232 at Briggs & Stratton, explained to a labor publication, the *Bellows*. "The first person in Milwaukee to die was the father of a worker who actually worked together with them on that same assembly line. They wanted to know what would happen if they walked off the line." Zombor continued: "They walked out on the job and called the manager. The manager perceived it as an unauthorized strike, called the union to complain, and coerced them back to work."

So Jackson kept working, even as he started to feel ill. On a Saturday in mid-May, he was covering a mandatory overtime shift. His co-workers saw Jackson slump and collapse along the assembly line. By the time Zombor arrived at the scene, Jackson was being walked out of the plant by a manager. But Jackson was back on the line the following Monday. It wasn't long before he slumped again. An EMT took Jackson to a local emergency room, where he tested positive for Covid-19. Instead of being hospitalized, he was discharged and told to quarantine at home—another working-class African-American who was sent home without the urgent care that saves lives.

By May 22, Jackson was having so much trouble breathing that he was finally admitted to the hospital. Six days later, he stopped breathing for the last time. A visitation and service were held for him at Milwaukee's Paradise Memorial Funeral Home. Then he was buried up on the North Side at Graceland Cemetery. People cried on the day of the funeral, and they kept crying. Weeks later, his mother, Virl Newsom, teared up when she said: "What hurts so bad, I wasn't there with him. When he passed, he died by himself."

Virl Newsom said her son felt he had to go to work because, if he didn't, "they will fire you." Jackson's son Kavonte said of his father, "All he wanted to do was take care of his kids."

On the night before Michael Donell Jackson died, the coronavirus death total for the United States surpassed 100,000. "One hundred thousand Americans are gone. They were our brothers and sisters. Our friends and neighbors," said Massachusetts senator Elizabeth Warren. "And too many of them could have been saved if our federal government had just done more." "It is a grim milestone," declared Josh Michaud, associate director of global health policy with the Kaiser Family Foundation in Washington, as commentators discussed the fact that the 100,000 figure was roughly equal to the combined US battle deaths in the invasions of Iraq and Afghanistan, and Vietnam and Korea, and the Spanish-American War and the Mexican-American War, and the War of 1812 and the Revolutionary War. "There are moments in our history so grim, so heart-rending, that they're forever fixed in each of our hearts as shared grief," observed Joe Biden, then the presumptive Democratic nominee for the presidency. "Today is one of those moments."

President Donald Trump had briefly toyed with framing the battle against Covid-19 as "our big war" (in mid-March 2020 he proclaimed, "It's a medical war. We have to win this war. It's very important") before going back to denying the consequences of the fight. In keeping with that denial, the president did not respond immediately to the stark numbers. Instead, he spent the day when the United States recorded its 100,000th coronavirus death spinning conspiracy theories about cable TV host Joe Scarborough that were so vile and false that Twitter had to add a warning label to the presidential pronouncements.

The next morning, Trump finally got around to saying something. He tapped off a tweet that described the 100,000 figure as "a very sad milestone." And he extended "heartfelt sympathy & love for everything that these great people stood for & represent."

That was all the president had to say on the day Mike Jackson died.

But the people who knew the factory worker had a lot they wanted to say. Chance Zombor was furious. "The company did absolutely nothing when Mike died," he told the *Bellows*. "And after that, several more people got it. People were self-quarantining; they didn't have enough people to run that assembly line. The company claimed they benevolently shut the whole line down so everyone could be tested. That was a load of bullshit. Everyone was infected, exposed, or dead. They didn't test people because they gave a shit if we lived or died, they did it so they could prove nothing was wrong and have people go back to work."

At a memorial march organized by Voces de la Frontera, a group that refused to let the deaths of workers like Jackson go un-noted and unaddressed, Zombor declared, "Give corporations a choice between workers' safety and profits, they're going to choose profits every time." That was a common sentiment among the Americans who were working, getting sick and dying in the spring and summer of 2020. "One thing that needs to be addressed is these companies and these corporations who are putting pressure on these workers for profit," Jackson's cousin Adebisi Agoro told a reporter. "Capitalism is moving toward this new system of 'isms': Essentialism, where they're putting the essence of the worker before the existence of the worker."

Mike Jackson's family and friends, co-workers and union brothers and sisters refused to let his death be in vain. They kept making noise through the summer following his death. On July 2, members of the Industrial Workers of the World marched from a nearby church to the Briggs & Stratton plant with signs featuring Jackson's image and the message "People Over Profit." They started to get noticed. The *Milwaukee Independent* news magazine noted, "While Briggs & Stratton executives were working from the safety of their homes during the pandemic, negotiating millions of dollars in bonuses for themselves, and finalizing plans to move hundreds of jobs out of the Milwaukee area, Mike Jackson was being worked to death in the company's Wauwatosa plant to make products that consumers could not buy for months." The *Milwaukee Journal Sentinel* newspaper reported on a complaint filed by Voces de la Frontera with the regional Occupational Safety and Health Administration office. In it, the group presented a list of demands for testing of employees at the plant where Jackson died, for a mandatory mask requirement, for policies and practices that would maintain a six-foot distance between workers on the production lines. Eventually, CBS News picked up the story and used it to illustrate a report on corporations that were trying to avoid liability for working employees to their deaths— and the politicians who were scheming to help them do so.

"Tonight, not much progress to report in negotiations over a new Covid relief bill," announced CBS News anchor Norah O'Donnell. "Among the sticking points, Republicans insist that in order to fully reopen, businesses need to be protected from lawsuits if employees or customers are exposed to the virus.

Workers say that puts them at risk. And our CBS News investigation found that, at one company, the consequences may have been deadly."

Chance Zombor said his piece: "The company doesn't care whether we live or die."

Briggs & Stratton "insisted it follows CDC guidelines and said workers can apply for paid leave to self-quarantine. They also provided a photo showing plastic barriers between workers at their Wisconsin plant," reported CBS. "But another photo provided by an employee a day later appears to show those same barriers rolled up."

Jackson's mother wasn't buying the company line. "If they were to protect the workers, I think my son probably would still have been here," she said quietly.

The report aired in the first week of August, when the death toll surged past 150,000 and Trump told interviewer Jonathan Swan that the virus was "under control."

"How?" asked Swan. "A thousand Americans are dying a day."

"They are dying. That's true. And you—it is what it is," the president mused. "But that doesn't mean we aren't doing everything we can. It's under control as much as you can control it."

That was a lie. It was never as under control as it could have been if the president had given a damn, or if the Senate had given a damn, or if Wall Street had given a damn, or if corporate CEOs had given a damn about workers like Mike Jackson.

But no one who mattered gave a damn because, for the most part, they didn't have to. They had been trained to stop caring by a country that claimed to be egalitarian but always let its elites off the hook—until, finally, a broken political system produced a sociopathic president. On the day after the CBS report on Mike Jackson aired, novelist Don Winslow produced a video titled #ConsequencesForTrump. It recounted how, throughout his life, Donald Trump had avoided duty and responsibility: five deferments during the Vietnam War, familial forgiveness for his cheating, bankruptcy protection for his collapsing business ventures, absolution from "his army of enablers" for high crimes and misdemeanors. "Donald Trump is seventy-four years old and he has never faced any consequences."

But, of course, there were consequences for the country he was supposed to serve as president. A commander-in-chief who had no sense of duty or responsibility was destined to fail his country in a time of crisis. And so he did. What was striking was the extent to which everyone around him went along with the crime. "When Donald Trump repeatedly lied to the American people about the coronavirus, deliberately spreading lies that caused over 155,000 Americans to die agonizing deaths alone," noted the narrator of Winslow's recounting of the crisis, "not one single doctor ever stood up in the White House briefing room and had the courage to say, 'Do not listen to the president, he's lying to you.' Instead, they praised him."

"Time and time again, people have stepped in and covered for Donald Trump," the narrator explained, as the music soared. "For seventy-four years, Donald Trump has gotten away with one crime after another. But on November 3, you can take away Donald Trump's power. And when he's not 'President Trump,' he can face charges for the crimes he's committed."

Trump was voted out of office on November 3, 2020, even if he refused to acknowledge his rejection by the American electorate. But more than a year after the voting was completed, the former president was lounging at Mar-a-Lago—untouched by anything more than an election defeat of the sort that presidents from John Adams to Jimmy Carter had experienced.

Will there ever be consequences along the lines Winslow's narrator proposed? For Trump? For his enablers? For the

Cabinet members who failed a sick and dying nation in its moment of greatest peril? For the senators? For the CEO's? For all the guilty men and women who failed to protect Michael Donell Jackson and left him to die alone?

This book explores that question by considering the culprits: naming names and describing crimes, conspiracies and corruptions. It rejects the claims of the apologists and revisionists who would have us believe that the pandemic was the healthcare equivalent of a "natural disaster" that would have gone badly no matter who was in charge. It argues that during the period from early 2020 to early 2021 choices were made, decisions were taken, lies were told that cost not a few lives, but hundreds and hundreds of thousands of lives that did not need to be lost. It does not pretend to present an encyclopedic list of all the wrongdoers. Rather, it presents examples of the kinds of wrongdoing that occurred, with the purpose of steering the discussion—in its concluding chapters—toward a recognition of why holding to account those who failed us in a time of crisis is the only way to assure that the next crisis will not see a repeat of their infamy.

Throughout this book, readers will encounter the stories not just of the guilty people who allowed an American carnage to play out on their watch but, also, the stories of the victims of a system that cared more about preserving political power and profit than the lives and livelihoods of the great mass of Americans. Mike Jackson was just one of those victims. He didn't know Donald Trump, and Donald Trump didn't know him. But their stories intersected on a day in October 2020.

Recovered from his own bout with Covid-19, for which he received literally the best care in the world, Trump was campaigning for re-election in the 2020 battleground state of Wisconsin. The polls were close, and Trump was desperate. Against the advice of doctors and public health officers, Republicans organized an October 27 rally where thousands of the president's backers crowded at the La Crosse County Fairgrounds Speedway. "There was little social distancing in the crowd, most of whom went without masks only a few hours after state officials reported a record 5,262 new cases of Covid-19, including eighty-four in La Crosse County, and sixty-four deaths," reported the local paper, the *La Crosse Tribune*. "But as in other recent appearances, Trump insisted the pandemic was on the wane."

"You know with the fake news, everything is Covid, Covid, Covid, Covid," the unmasked president declared. "You turn on the news, Covid, Covid. You know when they're going to stop talking about it so much? November 4th. November 4th. I know. It's a whole crazy thing. I mean, it's too complicated to explain. These people are very corrupt, very dishonest, but they've got a lot of problems. On November 4th, you'll hear we're doing extremely well and you'll see. You'll see . . . I'll tell you all they want to talk about is Covid. But the good news on the fourth, they'll stop talking. You watch. They'll stop talking."

Trump's claim that he was a victim—of a conspiracy to inflate virus fears before Election Day—was typical of the president's self-serving and dishonest responses to a pandemic that continued to surge at a terrifying rate. Johns Hopkins University had just reported that the seven-day average of daily new cases reached an all-time high of 68,767, a far higher figure than in the jarring early days of the pandemic. On the very day that Trump appeared at the speedway in West Salem, Wisconsin reported a record number of new Covid cases and deaths.

Across the state from where Trump was complaining that "everything is Covid," officials and advocates gathered at MacArthur Park outside the Milwaukee County Courthouse to mark a grim milestone: the 600th death in the county from the virus. Milwaukee mayor Tom Barrett, recalling a childhood friend, Carley Ann Gallun, who was one of the lost 600, said: "I still see the stories of people who say, 'It's fake, it's fake, it's fake.' I don't know how many times we have to read the stories or see the television news reports of someone who's lost their father or their mother until people realize you've got to wear these masks, you've got to keep the social distance. This is real, and it's very, very serious in our state right now."

Six hundred chairs had been arranged in the park to recall each one of the dead Milwaukeeans. "This virus is serious," said Pastor Greg Lewis, a local Souls to the Polls voting rights activist who had himself been hospitalized with Covid-19 earlier in the year. "Look at those chairs; that's how serious it is."

One of those chairs was placed in memory of Mike Jackson.

Looking at that chair, and all the others that had been arranged as part of the vigil, Representative Gwen Moore said, "As we remember the 600 people here in our own city, and the 1,800 people statewide, let us remember them with a resolve . . . to believe in our own humanity and the rights of everyone to be safe."

That is what this book seeks to do. In the name of Michael Donell Jackson, born April 14, 1975, a son, a brother, a husband, a father, a worker, a union member who fought for safety on the job, a man who collapsed at the machine he was operating and who died on May 28, 2020. And in the name of the hundreds of thousands of Americans who died unnecessarily, and unfairly, from a virus that politicians and profiteers could have battled righteously but instead chose to downplay, dismiss and deny.

The Killing Presidency of Donald Trump

If the impeachment provision in the Constitution of the United States will not reach the offenses charged here, then perhaps that eighteenth-century Constitution should be abandoned to a twentieth-century paper shredder!

—US Representative Barbara Jordan,
to the House Judiciary Committee, 1974

Donald Trump was appropriately impeached seven days before the end of a debauched presidency for his incitement of insurrection on January 6, 2021, just as he was appropriately impeached a little over a year earlier for his solicitation of foreign influence to disrupt the election of 2020. Only an excess of Republican partisanship spared him conviction for those high crimes in the Senate trials that followed his impeachments. Yet, history, if it is accurately written, will record that the forty-fifth president's highest crime was not an incitement or a foreign intrigue. It was his lethal failure to respond to the coronavirus pandemic that killed 400,000 Americans during the final year of his presidency—and that, because of patterns set in place by Trump's deliberate distortions and steady rejections of science, continued to cause thousands of unnecessary deaths after he left the position from which he was removed by the American people.

No American should forget that as Trump finished his presidential term, the United States experienced its highest single-day level of Covid-19 deaths since the beginning of a pandemic he consistently refused to combat with the full power of his office. No American should forgive the former president who acknowledged to journalist Bob Woodward that he deliberately downplayed the threat posed by a deadly virus. No American should casually "move on" after Trump lied, peddled conspiracies and mismanaged the coronavirus response so horribly that tens of thousands of preventable deaths occurred on his watch.

When Trump exited the White House on January 20, 2021, he did so "with blood on his hands," according to presidential historian Thomas Whalen, who said of Covid-19, "He knew this was a threat and really did not do what was necessary to respond to it in a thoughtful and resourceful way."

That is a polite way of saying that Trump failed the country he was duty-bound to protect and serve—and that this failure was particularly devastating to the people of color and immigrants Trump so frequently disparaged. This is one of the reasons why the Republican president was voted out of office after a campaign in which Joe Biden said, "Anyone who's responsible for that many deaths should not remain as president of the United States of America." Yet too many Americans imagine that Trump cannot—or, worse yet, should not—face investigation, prosecution and punishment for willfully mismanaging a catastrophe that caused the largest number of deaths from a single event on a president's watch in more than a century.

That's wrong. Trump and his co-conspirators should face accountability for their Covid crimes.

But political accountability is never guaranteed. It has to be achieved.

Some years ago, I wrote a book on the genius of impeachment. In the process, I became something of an expert on the failure of contemporary Congresses to effectively employ impeachment as an accountability tool. That put an end to any naivete I might have retained from Mrs. Stanek's eighth-grade civics class about the US Constitution as a protection against the most serious maladministrations of presidents in general and Donald Trump in particular. It was entirely predictable that the Congress that failed to remove Trump after he had provoked a deadly riot inside the US Capitol would fail to address Trump's high crime of presiding over a mass casualty event. As Dr. Steven Woolf, director emeritus of the Center on Society and Health at Virginia Commonwealth University, explained: "What's so troubling about this loss of life is it was preventable. This is an infectious disease we knew how to prevent, and as difficult as it is, far easier to solve than defeating Nazi Germany. And yet, we did not mount a response to wage war against this virus as we have in these other situations."

The failure of congressional duty and imagination ought not diminish our understanding of Trump's criminality and his guilt. Nor should it discourage us from seeking accountability in all of the legal and logical forms available to an American people who must protect themselves and their future. Americans cannot let their sense of outrage be numbed by the multitude of Trump's sins. They cannot allow themselves to be distracted by the fertilizing propaganda spewed from the mouths of the former president's desperate defenders, who continue to claim that the election of 2020 was stolen and that Trump had no role in sending a seditious mob into the citadel of democracy.

This is about much more than hating on Donald Trump. This is about future presidencies, and future pandemics. Constitutional scholars were right to argue that if a defeated president could not be held to account for seeking to overturn the results of an election in which voters chose to remove him from office, then the precedent would be set for future presidents to conspire to retain power by inspiring violence of the sort that on January 6 left hundreds injured and five people—including a Capitol Police officer—dead.

But it is equally dangerous to limit our definition of executive responsibility in a way that would have Americans believe that a former president cannot, or should not, be held to account for actions that left millions injured and hundreds of thousands dead. The genius of the impeachment power is that it is broad enough to encompass all high crimes and misdemeanors. There was a clear recognition at the founding of the American project—which extended from a revolt against the repeated "injuries and usurpations" of mad King George III—that officials could be penalized not merely for gross violations of their oaths of office but for gross damage to the republic and its people.

The purpose of the impeachment clauses that were added to the Constitution in the summer of 1787 was to answer the questions posed by George Mason after he explained to the Constitutional Convention, "No point is of more importance than that the right of impeachment should be continued." Mason demanded to know: "Shall any man be above Justice? Above all, shall that man be above it, who can commit the most extensive injustice?" The delegates to that convention responded by creating an instrument of accountability that was intended to be understood as former president Gerald Ford did, when he said, "An impeachable offense is whatever a majority of the House of Representatives considers it to be at a given moment in history;

conviction results from whatever offense or offenses two-thirds of the other body considers to be sufficiently serious to require removal of the accused from office."

Early in Trump's term, House Speaker Nancy Pelosi suggested that while the president had "acted in a way that is strategically incoherent, that is incompetent, that is reckless . . . that is not grounds for impeachment." In fact, incoherence, incompetence and recklessness have been recognized from the earliest days of the republic as credible grounds for impeachment. The first federal official to be removed from office after being impeached, New Hampshire federal judge John Pickering, became the target of congressional action in 1803 because of concerns about his erratic and irresponsible behavior. The following year, Supreme Court Justice Samuel Chase was impeached for, among other things, "intemperate and inflammatory . . . peculiarly indecent and unbecoming . . . [and] highly unwarrantable" behavior.

Those prosecutions occurred when the people who authored the Constitution were still active members of the Congress and presidential administrations. They understood that the impeachment power could be appropriately applied to a wide range of high crimes and misdemeanors. No doubt, incitement of insurrection is among the highest. But so, too, is deliberately failing to address the threat posed by a pandemic.

Each new commander-in-chief swears an oath pledging that they will "faithfully execute the office of President of the United States, and will to the best of my ability, preserve, protect and defend the Constitution of the United States." That Constitution begins with a commitment to "promote the general welfare" of the American people. Deliberately downplaying the danger of a deadly virus that is rapidly spreading through the land is not a faithful execution of the office of the presidency. Creating a circumstance in which hundreds of thousands of Americans are allowed to fall ill and die preventable deaths attacks the general welfare. These are truths that we should hold to be self-evident, and we should boldly apply them when assessing the high crimes of Donald Trump.

The most important point in seeking accountability is to understand that this is about more than punishing Trump as an individual. The same goes for the many other subjects of this book, whose criminal, civil and political wrongdoing will be detailed in ensuing chapters. The pursuit of accountability involves more than judging the moral character of our elites, or rebuking them for bad behaviors in personal relationships or business dealings. What's at stake is something far more vital than resolving individual grievances associated with politics. There must be a consideration of the deeper issue of systemic failure, and the deeper need for systemic change. Americans have to answer the question of whether anyone who is politically or economically powerful can be held to account in America, a subject that will be explored more thoroughly in a concluding chapter. The struggle to answer this question steers us toward the even more serious issue of whether we, as a people and as a nation, can reassemble ourselves so that the United States—and the world it so greatly influences—will never again be at the mercy of a president, Cabinet member, senator or CEO who would sacrifice the health and lives of Americans on the altar of his own ambition, or avarice, or remorseless brutality.

Trump sought and accepted a position of the greatest responsibility. He said that he understood what that entailed. Like presidents before him, Trump announced, "My first duty as president is to protect the American people." Yet when he was called upon to answer a threat so severe that it would in barely three months leave more Americans dead than were killed in World War I, Trump deliberately lied. He played down the danger of the disease in the critical early stages of the fight, and he continued to lie as the death toll ticked upward past 100,000, past 200,000, past 300,000, all the way to 400,000.

So many of those deaths were preventable. But Trump's lies made them inevitable. This is not hyperbole. This is not political exaggeration. It is the stark fact of Donald Trump's infamy—a deliberate dereliction of duty that in a time of declared war would be identified as treasonous.

On February 7, 2020, after he had been repeatedly briefed in detail on Covid-19, Trump spoke to the *Washington Post*'s Bob Woodward. "This is deadly stuff," he told Woodward. "You just breathe the air, and that's how it's passed."

A president who recognized his duty to protect the American people would have moved aggressively to address the threat, as leaders of other countries did. If international relations were strained, with China, with any other country, or with global organizations, this would have been the time to sort differences out. If the domestic infrastructure was insufficient, if bureaucrats were inattentive, a duty-bound president would have made urgent changes. He would have acted decisively. He would have leveled with the American people and built the trust necessary to overcome the threat. Instead, Donald Trump denied the danger in words and deeds, until the rates of infection and death surged during the course of 2020 to levels that at several points had the United States suffering with the worst coronavirus outbreak in the world.

On February 24, two weeks after he spoke to Woodward about "deadly stuff," Trump tweeted, "The Coronavirus is very much under control in the USA." On February 27, he said: "It's going to disappear. One day, it's like a miracle, it will disappear." On March 10, he said: "And we're prepared, and we're doing a great job with it. And it will go away. Just stay calm. It will go away." But it did not go away. It grew into a public health crisis of epic proportions that would rapidly leave tens of thousands of Americans dead, millions infected and tens of millions unemployed as the economy shut down.

If in March Trump had taken urgent action to enforce social distancing and other precautions instead of promising "it will go away," roughly 54,000 Covid-19 deaths would have been prevented in the early stages of the crisis, according to Columbia University analysts. Even as his failure became evident to all, including members of his own clueless cabal of aides and advisers, Trump continued to soft-pedal the danger. And people continued to die. At the conclusion of his presidency, a commission associated with the medical journal *Lancet* determined that had Covid-19 death rates in the US corresponded with those of other G7 countries during the period when Trump was in charge, 40 percent fewer Americans would have died.

On the day Trump left office, the Covid-19 death toll in the US stood at roughly 400,000. Forty percent of that figure is 160,000. The policies that Trump put in place—or failed to put in place—extended beyond his presidency. So if we wanted to blame all of the excess death rate in the US on Trump, the figure would actually be much higher. But, in fairness to Trump, policies that he inherited made both the crisis, and the prospects for his mismanagement of it, worse. "The US has fared so badly with this pandemic, but the bungling can't be attributed only to Mr. Trump; it also has to do with these societal failures," Dr. Mary T. Bassett, director of Harvard University's FXB Center for Health and Human Rights and a member of the *Lancet* commission, told the *Guardian*. The paper also reported that the commission report drew a line "from neoliberal policies pushed in the past forty years, such as those that intensified the drug war and resulted in mass incarceration, to health

inequities Trump exacerbated while in office. Many of the connections date back even further, to the colonization of the Americas
and the persistence of white supremacy in society."

This book recognizes these connections, which is one of the
reasons why it considers so many guilty men and women who
are not named Trump, including several who are not conservatives and not Republicans. There were Democrats who got things
horribly wrong. There were officials in other countries, including
but not exclusively China, whose actions merited concern at the
time and warrant continued scrutiny. There is plenty of blame,
historic and contemporary, to go around. The list of guilty parties
is long. But some parties are guiltier than others.

The Lancet Commission on Public Policy and Health in the
Trump Era put things in perspective by considering the global
pandemic and then focusing on the unique factors that made
Trump's presidency so dangerous in the crisis moment. The
commissioners recognized that the forty-fifth president had
assumed the office after Trump, as a 2016 contender, "stirred
up the underlying racial animus of US society to deflect attention from policies that abet billionaires' accretion of wealth and
power. His racist, anti-immigrant and nationalist appeals found
resonance in some middle-income and low-income white communities seeking scapegoats for their declining life prospects, even as
they retained some privileges denied to people of color."

With this in mind, the commissioners explained:

Although Trump's ascent to the presidency was propelled by
racism, nativism and fear of privation, his policies constituted
an intensified attack on the health and well-being of people
in the USA and elsewhere. His signature legislative achievement, a trillion-dollar tax cut for the wealthy, opened a budget
hole that served as justification for cuts to food and housing

subsidies that prevent malnutrition and homelessness for millions of people in the USA; the number of homeless school children increased by 150,000 in the first year of Trump's presidency. Trump's mismanagement of the Covid-19 pandemic—compounded by his efforts to dismantle the USA's already weakened public health infrastructure and the Affordable Care Act's (ACA) coverage expansions—has caused tens of thousands of unnecessary deaths. His elimination of the National Security Council's global health security team, and a 2017 hiring freeze that left almost 700 positions at the Centers for Disease Control and Prevention (CDC) unfilled, compromised preparedness. The number of people without health insurance had increased by 2–3 million during Trump's presidency, even before pandemic-driven losses of employment-based coverage increased the number of uninsured people by millions.

Then, of course, there was Trump's reaction to the pandemic itself. After detailing how "the global Covid-19 pandemic has had a disproportionate effect on the USA," the commissioners concluded: "Many of the cases and deaths were avoidable. Instead of galvanizing the US populace to fight the pandemic, President Trump publicly dismissed its threat (despite privately acknowledging it), discouraged action as infection spread and eschewed international cooperation. His refusal to develop a national strategy worsened shortages of personal protective equipment and diagnostic tests. President Trump politicized mask-wearing and school reopenings and convened indoor events attended by thousands, where masks were discouraged and physical distancing was impossible."

Disdain for science and cuts to global health programs and public health agencies, wrote the commissioners, "have impeded the response to the Covid-19 pandemic, causing tens of thousands of unnecessary deaths." That tracked with an assessment by the *Washington Post* in October 2020, when the US death toll was around 220,000. Noting the failures of the Trump administration, the *Post* concluded that "tens of thousands of those deaths, at least, were preventable," and that "tens of thousands of more deaths will occur, many of them also preventable." How many tens of thousands? The *Post* pointed to estimates by the Trump administration's coronavirus task force from March 2020, which suggested that "a successful pandemic response" by the government at that early point would result in a total of "only 100,000 to 240,000 deaths."

By the time Trump left the presidency, the death toll was at least 160,000 higher—perhaps 300,000 higher—than what his own task force had suggested a successful response would produce in a worst-case scenario. In other words, Trump and his associates failed, by a horrifyingly wide margin. And there was a general consensus that this failure resulted from deliberate actions by a president who admitted that he lied about the threat the pandemic posed, who ridiculed the advice and counsel of scientists who knew how to respond, and who modeled such bad behavior that his own schedule was packed with "superspreader events" at which close aides and allies got sick and he himself would fall seriously ill.

Why didn't the president of the United States protect the American people? "I wanted to always play it down," Trump told Woodward on March 19, 2020. "I still like playing it down, because I don't want to create a panic." That statement—which should have been reported immediately but wasn't—was not an acknowledgment of wrongdoing by a chastened president. It was a description of a deliberate strategy, employed by a president who was seeking re-election. Trump feared that a panic of any kind, health-related or economic, was likely to make his project of seeking a second term more difficult. His response was to lie to the American people about the threat they faced.

He would keep on lying. The president told Fox News viewers on March 24: "I brought some numbers here. We lose thousands and thousands of people a year to the flu. We don't turn the country off, I mean every year. Now when I heard the number— you know, we average 37,000 people a year. Can you believe that? And actually this year we're having a bad flu season. But we lose thousands of people a year to the flu. We never turn the country off. We lose much more than that to automobile accidents. We didn't call up the automobile companies, say, 'Stop making cars, we don't want any cars anymore.' We have to get back to work." Many people took the president seriously. They believed him as he minimized the pandemic, week after week, month after month, engaging in what he admitted was cheerleading.

One of the Americans who believed Trump was a sixty-five-year-old Arizonan who died June 30 after more than three weeks battling Covid-19. "My dad, Mark Anthony Urquiza, should be here today, but he isn't," his daughter, Kristin Urquiza, told the 2020 Democratic National Convention. "He had faith in Donald Trump. He voted for him, listened to him, believed him and his mouthpieces when they said that coronavirus was under control and going to disappear; that it was okay to end social distancing rules before it was safe; and that if you had no underlying health conditions, you'd probably be fine . . . My dad was a healthy sixty-five-year-old. His only pre-existing condition was trusting Donald Trump, and for that, he paid with his life."

Mark Anthony Urquiza was not alone. Trump's deliberate deception and dereliction of duty led thousands to their deaths. The toll rose with each passing day, yet Trump kept saying, months into the crisis, "Calm, no panic!" (his exact words in

September when his conversation with Woodward went public). America should have panicked.

Donald Trump made his presidency America's pre-existing condition. He lied, and Americans died. For that, he should be held to account—not as an act of personal animus or political vengeance, but as a practical and responsible intervention on behalf of the future. There is every reason to believe that there will be more pandemics, more overwhelming challenges, more crises of epic proportions, and it is quite likely that some of them will occur during the presidencies of flawed human beings who are motivated by ambition and avarice. If the precedent from the coronavirus pandemic tells them that they may act with the same remorseless brutality as Donald John Trump, then this country, and this planet, are doomed.

Mike Pence: Yes-Man of the Apocalypse

In following him, I follow but myself.
—William Shakespeare, *Othello*

As the coronavirus death toll in the United States surged past 100,000 in mid-June of 2020, with new cases being reported at ever more alarming rates and in more parts of the country, the chair of the White House Coronavirus Task Force raced to reassure the country that all hell was not breaking loose. With a *Wall Street Journal* op-ed piece headlined, "There Isn't a Coronavirus 'Second Wave,'" Mike Pence promised Americans that the crisis was well in hand.

The danger, the vice president explained, was not too much of a deadly virus. It was too much journalism: "In recent days, the media has taken to sounding the alarm bells over a 'second wave' of coronavirus infections," warned Pence. "Such panic is overblown. Thanks to the leadership of President Trump and the courage and compassion of the American people, our public health system is far stronger than it was four months ago, and we are winning the fight against the invisible enemy."

Along with the usual "dear leader" propagandizing and Trumpian media-blaming, the vice president argued that the whole "surge" thing was just a big misunderstanding:

While talk of an increase in cases dominates cable news coverage, more than half of states are actually seeing cases decline or remain stable. Every state, territory and major metropolitan area, with the exception of three, have positive test rates under 10 percent. And in the six states that have reached more than 1,000 new cases a day, increased testing has allowed public health officials to identify most of the outbreaks in particular settings—prisons, nursing homes and meatpacking facilities—and contain them.

Lost in the coverage is the fact that today less than 6 percent of Americans tested each week are found to have the virus. Cases have stabilized over the past two weeks, with the daily average case rate across the US dropping to 20,000—down from 30,000 in April and 25,000 in May . . .

The truth is that we've made great progress over the past four months, and it's a testament to the leadership of President Trump. When the president asked me to chair the White House Coronavirus Task Force at the end of February, he directed us to pursue not only a whole-of-government approach but a whole-of-America approach. The president brought together major commercial labs to expand our testing capacity, manufacturers to produce much-needed medical equipment, and major pharmaceutical companies to begin research on new medicines and vaccines. He rallied the American people to embrace social-distancing guidelines. And the progress we've made is remarkable.

Pence ended with another round of media-shaming: "The media has tried to scare the American people every step of the way, and these grim predictions of a second wave are no different. The truth is, whatever the media says, our whole-of-America approach has been a success. We've slowed the spread, we've cared for the most vulnerable, we've saved lives, and we've created a solid foundation for whatever challenges we may face in the future. That's a cause for celebration, not the media's fearmongering."

So, pop the champagne corks and celebrate a job well done, right? Wrong. On the night before Pence's *Journal* op-ed appeared on June 16, Covid trackers counted 2,102,051 diagnosed or probable cases nationwide, and the one-day increase in that number was 18,255. The death toll had increased that day by 385 to 111,834. Barely a week later, after the vice president reassured everyone there was no surge, there was a day when the increase in new cases surpassed 40,000. By mid-July, there were days when the total number of new cases topped 70,000. Within a month of the appearance of Pence's op-ed, the total number of cases in the US had spiked from a little over 2 million to more than 3.5 million.

The increase in the daily death toll was even more alarming—from 385 on June 15, to 698 on July 1, to 863 on July 15. And it kept surging upward. On some days in late July and early August, more than 1,500 lives were lost—a figure more than three times higher than the number of deaths on March 29, the day Donald Trump finally abandoned his "raring to go by Easter" happy talk and acknowledged that the pandemic had turned into a "nightmare."

Media outlets were not fear mongering. They were explaining with stark, desperately needed precision that things were getting worse—and that they were going to get a lot worse in the weeks and months to come. Whether reporters chose to call what was happening "a second wave" or a "surge," a "spike" or a "catastrophe," Americans were going to get sick and die at jarring rates if urgent actions were not taken. But there was no sense of urgency on the part of the Trump administration in general and the vice president in particular. Indeed, it was discouraged. What Pence offered, from his platform as chair of the task force that was supposed to be addressing the crisis, was false comfort. He encouraged Americans to imagine that the mid-April peak in cases and deaths—the crest of the first wave—was a bad memory fading in the rearview mirror as the country raced toward a summer in which it would "reopen in a safe and responsible manner." Those who trusted his counsel were dangerously unprepared for what was to come.

"By the end of June, the rolling average of new cases per day had far exceeded the April peak, prompting some states to pull back their reopening plans," explained *Time* magazine. "But the damage had been done. By mid-July, a second wave peaked at over twice the value of the first, exceeding 67,000 cases per day—more than 20 cases per capita." The virus remained an ongoing threat, and literally as Pence's piece was going to press, that threat was increasing. There were many reasons for the increase, as *Time* writers Chris Wilson and Jeffrey Kluger wrote in their astute assessment of what were described as first, second and third waves. But, they warned, one factor stood out—widespread and deliberate maladministration: "The politicization of mask-wearing; conflicting guidelines from the White House, the Centers for Disease Control and Prevention and the Food and Drug Administration; and state and local policies that contribute to viral transmission are helping to do the disease's work for it."

It is appropriate to blame Donald Trump for much of that politicization; the president set the tone for his administration and his party with a slurry of lies, conspiracy theories and cheerleading for his deadly "reopening" project. But Trump could not have done it on his own. Pence, who had replaced Secretary of Health and Human Services Alex Azar as chair of the White House Coronavirus Task Force on February 26, 2020, was literally the man in charge. He could have at least tried to lead. Or he could simply have gone silent and done no harm. Instead, he amplified the president's lies, and because he was the supposedly more responsible member of the Republican ticket, lent them a measure of "credibility" at precisely the points when it was most dangerous.

That's what happened at the Republican National Convention when Pence achieved the remarkable feat of delivering an address that was even more disingenuous than Trump's bizarre attempts to blame everyone but himself—Democrats, foreigners, the media—for the crisis. The president seemed to be furious with everyone. Except Mike Pence. In Trump's August 28 address to the convention, which was delivered via TV hookup from a White House superspreader event where the crowd disregarded public-health mandates and social-distancing protocols, Trump took time out from attacking Joe Biden to celebrate Pence as a heroic warrior on behalf of health and safety. "Good job heading the task force by our great vice president," the maskless president shouted. "Thank you very much, Mike. Please stand up. Please." A maskless Pence rose and accepted the applause.

There was nothing worthy of applause in the address the vice president had delivered to the convention two days earlier. In fact, it was more dangerously dishonest than anything Trump said. Speaking from Fort McHenry in Baltimore, Pence sought to put his remarks in historic context. "It is an honor to speak to you tonight from the hallowed grounds of Fort McHenry, the site of the very battle that inspired the words of our national anthem," he began. "Those words have inspired this land of heroes ever since. It was on this site 206 years ago when our young republic heroically withstood a ferocious naval bombardment from the most powerful empire on earth. They came to crush our revolution, to divide our nation, and to end the American experiment. The heroes who held this fort took their stand for life, liberty, freedom and the American flag. Those ideals have defined our nation. Yet they were hardly ever mentioned during last week's Democratic convention. Instead, Democrats spent four days attacking America. Joe Biden said we were living through a season of American darkness."

Then Pence launched into what the *New Yorker* magazine aptly identified as "the ultimate rewriting of history." Declaring that the administration had launched "the greatest national mobilization since World War II," Pence said:

> President Trump marshalled the full resources of the federal government and directed us to forge seamless partnerships with governors across America in both parties. We partnered with private industry to reinvent testing and produce supplies, and we're now conducting 800,000 tests per day, have coordinated the delivery of billions of pieces of personal protective equipment, and we saw to the manufacture of 100,000 ventilators in 100 days. And no one who required a ventilator was ever denied a ventilator in the United States. We built hospitals, we surged military medical personnel and enacted an economic rescue package that saved 50 million American jobs.

Fact checkers worked overtime throughout the 2020 Republican convention, but that section of Pence's address created an overwhelming burden. Every line contained a falsehood. Some lines were so packed with lies that they required paragraphs of explanation. Consider the claim about forging "seamless partnerships with governors across the United States in both parties." PolitiFact, the nonpartisan fact-checking operation run by the Poynter Institute, labeled it "revisionist history" and explained:

> After declaring a national emergency over the health crisis on March 13, Trump directed governors to order their own ventilators, respirators and supplies, saying the federal government is "not a shipping clerk." Governors say the disjointed response left states bidding against one another and the federal government for access to critical equipment. New York Gov. Andrew Cuomo said it was akin to competing on eBay with fifty other states and the Federal Emergency Management Agency. Maryland Gov. Larry Hogan, a Republican, pleaded for better coordination to ensure that supplies were distributed based on need. As late as July, some governors were calling on the feds for help and not getting what they needed. There were shortages of testing supplies, as well as personal protection gear. Washington state asked for 4.2 million N95 respirators. It got a bit under 500,000. It asked for about 300,000 gowns. It got about 160,000.

PolitiFact pointed out that Pence got timelines from the early days of the pandemic wrong, along with storylines from throughout the crisis. What of the claim that "As we speak we're developing a growing number of treatments, including convalescent plasma, that are saving lives all across the country"? Hold up, explained the fact-checker: "Although the Trump administration has said this treatment shows some encouraging early findings, the data they shared was based on a Mayo Clinic preliminary analysis that has not been peer reviewed. Clinicians and researchers have urged caution, maintaining that more research is necessary before a survival benefit is proven. They also question the timing of the authorization—which came on the eve of the Republican convention."

That last reference got to the heart of the matter, and to the real problem with Pence's approach to the crisis. The head of the coronavirus task force was not a scientist, nor even someone who had a history of working with scientists. A career politician—twice defeated for Congress as a young conservative activist, he spent the better part of a decade as a right-wing talk-radio host before finally winning a House seat in 2000 and the governorship of Indiana in the 2012—Pence was more than just a typical climate-denying, billionaire-coddling Republican. He had a checkered history of positioning himself on the wrong side of debates about public health. The dangerously wrong side.

In 2000, as a candidate for Congress, Pence attacked the American Cancer Society's "Great American Smokeout," a campaign to get people to give up cigarettes and other tobacco products with a screed about how

> in the coming weeks, Americans are going to be treated with the worst kind of Washington-speak regarding the tobacco legislation currently being considered by the Congress and attorney generals from forty different states. We will hear about the scourge of tobacco and the resultant premature deaths. We will hear about how this phalanx of government elates has suddenly grown a conscience after decades of subsidizing the product which, we are now told, kills millions of Americans each year.
>
> Time for a quick reality check. Despite the hysteria from the political class and the media, smoking doesn't kill. In fact, two out of every three smokers does not die from a smoking-related illness, and nine out of ten smokers do not contract lung cancer. This is not to say that smoking is good for you.

> News flash: smoking is not good for you. If you are reading
> this article through the blue haze of cigarette smoke, you
> should quit. The relevant question is, what is more harmful
> to the nation, secondhand smoke or backhanded big govern-
> ment disguised in do-gooder health care rhetoric.

Pence was factually wrong—two out of three smokers die of
smoking-related illnesses, the reverse of what he claimed—and
once he was elected to Congress he was wrong on policy. In
2009, for instance, he voted against the Family Smoking Prevention and Tobacco Control Act, a vital measure for regulating the
sale of tobacco products. Later, as Indiana's governor, Vox
reported, "He slashed funding for the Indiana Tobacco Prevention and Cessation office, and rejected a proposal from Republican
legislators to raise cigarette taxes to fund transportation."

As an anti-abortion crusader in the US House, Pence was for
many years the primary sponsor of legislation to defund Planned
Parenthood. When supporters of the health care provider explained
the broad range of services that its clinics provided, Pence
announced: "If Planned Parenthood wants to be involved in
providing counseling services and HIV testing, they ought not
be in the business of providing abortions. As long as they aspire
to do that, I'll be after them." He was true to his word. The
Republican-controlled Indiana state legislature had moved to cut
state support for Planned Parenthood the year before Pence was
elected governor, but court challenges stalled the initiative. Once
he took office in early 2013, the defunding push ramped up.

"Conservative political forces in Indiana were driven by religious
fervor to gut all public funding from Planned Parenthood," the
Chicago Tribune reported in 2015. "They led the nation in demonizing the organization because 3 percent of its services involved
reproductive services—abortion. To sterilize that contagion, the

remaining 97 percent of Planned Parenthood services would be expunged as necessary collateral damage. Private interest became public mandate." According to the *Huffington Post*: "In 2005, Planned Parenthood of Indiana received a total of $3.3 million in funding from government contracts and grants. By 2014, that funding had dropped to $1.9 million. Five of Planned Parenthood's smaller clinics in the state ... were unable to keep up with the growing technology costs that were necessary to remain competitive as a medical provider. All five clinics that were forced to close had offered HIV testing. None had offered abortions."

In rural southeast Indiana, Scott County's Planned Parenthood clinic had been the only place to go for HIV tests. It closed in the first year of Pence's governorship, and then things got ugly. Like many rural counties in that part of the state, Scott County was plagued by an opiate crisis. People used needles to shoot up, often reusing and even sharing them because the region had no needle-exchange program—Pence was opposed to them—and HIV spread quickly. In 2015, the *Tribune* reported that an HIV epidemic had struck the Scott County community of Austin, where a quarter of the 4,300 residents lived in poverty and a quarter more lived just barely above the poverty line. "Scott County has been without an HIV testing center for two years. That's how long it took the epidemic to flourish," explained the paper, noting that the 150 active HIV cases there constituted "a shocking epidemic inflicted on people who have little else but their addictions." Eventually, Dr. Tom Frieden, a former director of the CDC, reported that Austin, with less than 5,000 residents, was experiencing a higher HIV incidence than "any country in sub-Saharan Africa."

Only under pressure did Pence finally back off his opposition to needle-exchange programs and in early 2015 declare a public health emergency that allowed them in Austin and other communities. However, he also signed a bill that increased penalties for Indianans caught carrying needles from a mis-demeanor to a felony. That sent exactly the wrong signal, as Yale epidemiologists Gregg S. Gonsalves and Forrest W. Crawford, who examined the Scott County outbreak, noted in the *Lancet*. "Criminalizing possession of syringes, even clean ones, without a prescription undermines efforts to slow transmission of HIV among injection drug users, and may actually encourage needle sharing," they wrote. Moreover, Pence and his legislative allies refused to provide needed funding for the needle-exchange program or for reopening Planned Parenthood's HIV-testing program.

"The damage was done: by 2017, a total of 215 cases of HIV infection had been attributed to the outbreak," Gonsalves and Crawford found. "When we performed our analysis of the Indiana outbreak, we found that undiagnosed HIV infections peaked about two months before Pence declared a public health emergency—after the rise of HIV had been detected, but before the governor chose to act. Using a mathematical model of epidemic dynamics, we estimated that up to 127 HIV infections could have been averted if Pence had implemented public health measures like HIV testing and needle exchange proactively in 2013, when he had been urged to do so by experts in his state."

Gonsalves and Crawford called Pence's handling of the Indiana HIV outbreak "a case study in mismanagement of a public health crisis." Yet in February 2020, when Trump named Pence as head of the coronavirus task force, both the president and vice president spoke about his gubernatorial record as a justification for his selection. Trump told reporters that his vice president possessed "a certain talent" for handling public health issues. Pence told talk radio host Rush Limbaugh that his experience working on the HIV outbreak and other health concerns in Indiana "might be the main reason why President Trump asked me to do this. I think by putting me over the administration's response to the coronavirus, the president wanted to signal the priority that he's placed on this."

No one who was serious about combating Covid-19 saw it that way. "As governor, Mike Pence put ideology over science and contributed to one of the worst HIV crises his state had ever seen," wrote Senator Jeff Merkley, an Oregon Democrat and the ranking member of the subcommittee that oversaw the Food and Drug Administration. "In 2000, he wrote an op-ed arguing 'smoking doesn't kill.' We need competence and science driving our response—that's not the VP's record." Meanwhile, Representative Alexandria Ocasio-Cortez of New York noted that as governor: "Pence's science denial contributed to one of the worst HIV outbreaks in Indiana's history. He is not a medical doctor. He is not a health expert. He is not qualified nor positioned in any way to protect our public health . . . Mike Pence literally does not believe in science. It is utterly irresponsible to put him in charge of US coronavirus response as the world sits on the cusp of a pandemic. This decision could cost people their lives. Pence's past decisions already have."

Ocasio-Cortez was right to worry. Pence started on the wrong foot and never got onto the right one. Just days after his selection to head the task force, the vice president announced in his old talk-radio voice: "Let me be very clear. The average American does not need to go out and buy a mask." Long after it became clear that this was very bad advice, Pence kept sending the wrong signals. On a high-profile visit to the Mayo Clinic in late April, Pence was surrounded by mask-wearing patients, physicians and aides. But the vice president went maskless. "Yes, refusing to wear a mask is dangerous and disrespectful," Dr. Craig Spencer, the New York emergency room physician who served as director of Global Health in Emergency Medicine at New York-Presbyterian/Columbia University Medical Center, observed at the time. "But it represents something more concerning. It highlights a lack of understanding or respect of even the most basic principles of public health. And 'reopening' will ONLY succeed if built on public health principles."

It wasn't just Pence as public face of the task force that was a mess. Pence's management of it, while not so deliberately irresponsible as Trump's approach, was bumbling and ineffectual. Dan Diamond and Adam Cancryn of *Politico* interviewed twenty-one people who were involved with the task force during its first six months of operation. "Trump's mercurial behavior was not solely responsible for what amounted to a slow response to the deadliest pandemic in a century," Diamond and Cancryn found; rather, their sources pointed "to Pence's own leadership style as a force for delay." Many of those interviewed "said Pence's consensus-building approach drained urgency from the mission, pitted interests against each other and gave inappropriate weight to opinions outside the public health realm."

By the time of that *Politico* report, Pence had already lost control of the narrative. Trump's son-in-law, Jared Kushner, was stepping into a more prominent role in shaping the White House response to the virus, and the invariably maskless president was undermining the fight with his racist raving about "the China virus" and "Kung Flu."

As the presidential campaign ramped up after Labor Day, Pence checked out of task force meetings for weeks on end—"Pence absent from Covid-19 planning calls for more than a month," a *Politico* headline announced on October 29—and headed to events in battleground states such as Wisconsin and Georgia. Often without a mask, often speaking to crowds that made no attempt at social distancing, Pence acted as if the crisis had passed.

When it came time for the vice presidential debate on October 7, however, Pence's failure to get the focus or the facts right caught up with him. Pence had a big job going into his debate. Trump's performance in the initial presidential debate with Joe Biden was widely characterized as "deranged." As *Vanity Fair*'s Bess Levin mordantly observed: "For the people who were lucky enough to skip out on the first presidential debate, here are a few words that would describe it: Unwatchable. National embarrassment. A nightmare come to life. Like having periodontal surgery without anesthesia." Why was it so bad? Because Donald Trump came to the debate as himself. He spent ninety minutes incessantly interrupting Biden, arguing with moderator Chris Wallace as might a particularly naughty six-year-old with an indulgent babysitter, ranting about "antifa" and the "radical left," mocking Biden's son's struggle with substance abuse, and generally revealing his loathsomeness. So Pence had to clean things up, as he had done for Trump in 2016, when the Republican from Indiana held his own in a debate with Democratic vice presidential candidate Tim Kaine. But it would not be so easy with the 2020 Democratic vice presidential nominee, Senator Kamala Harris of California.

Harris came prepared to talk about Covid-19—and what should have been Pence's strong suit proved to be his undoing. Instead of showing up with a message about the seriousness of the administration's response to the pandemic, Pence arrived with talking points from the dear leader: "Under President Trump's leadership, we will always stand behind law enforcement." Pence then made wild claims that Harris's discussions of systemic racism should be seen as "a great insult to the men and women who serve in law enforcement." It was a transparently obvious attempt to distract from the real issues, and it came with a none-too-subtle racial bias. (As Representative Lisa Blunt Rochester, Democrat of Delaware, tweeted: "We just watched the first Black woman to ever be on a major party ticket be lectured on systemic racism by a White man. Unfortunately for Vice President Pence, Kamala Harris and Black people everywhere know the truth!") Pence's approach backfired at every turn. His attempts to steer the debate away from Covid concerns only served to highlight how unprepared he was for the moment when Harris, a courtroom veteran, began to prosecute him for the administration's disastrous response to a health care crisis that had already left close to a quarter million Americans dead.

The debate was over from the moment that moderator Susan Page announced, "Let's begin with the ongoing pandemic that has cost our country so much." That was all the invitation that Harris needed.

> The American people have witnessed what is the greatest failure of any presidential administration in the history of our country. And here are the facts. 210,000 dead people in our country in just the last several months. Over 7 million people who have contracted this disease. One in five businesses closed. We're looking at frontline workers who have been treated like sacrificial workers. We are looking at over 30 million people, who in the last several months, had to file for unemployment. And here's the thing, on January 28th, the vice president and the president were informed about the nature of this pandemic. They were informed that it's lethal in consequence, that it is airborne, that it will affect young people, and that it would be contracted because it is airborne. They knew what was happening, and they didn't tell you.
>
> Can you imagine if you knew on January 28th, as opposed to March 13th, what they knew, what you might've done to prepare? They knew, and they covered it up. The president said it was a hoax. They minimized the seriousness of it. The

president said, "You're on one side of his ledger if you wear a mask. You're on the other side of his ledger if you don't." And in spite of all of that, today, they still don't have a plan. They still don't have a plan. Well, Joe Biden does. And our plan is about what we need to do around a national strategy for contact tracing, for testing, for administration of the vaccine, and making sure that it will be free for all. That is the plan that Joe Biden has and that I have, knowing that we have to get a hold of what has been going on, and we need to save our country. And Joe Biden is the best leader to do that. And frankly, this administration has forfeited their right to re-election based on this.

Page then turned to the Republican. "Vice President Pence, more than 210,000 Americans have died of Covid-19 since February," she began. "The US death toll, as a percentage of our population, is higher than that of almost every other wealthy nation on Earth. For instance, our death rate is two and a half times that of Canada, next door. You head the administration's coronavirus task force. Why is the US death toll, as a percentage of our population, higher than that of almost every other wealthy country?"

Pence didn't even try to answer the question. Instead, he spoke as if he had been a spectator, rather than the head of the task force that was supposed to coordinate the response. He claimed that things were going swimmingly—making over-the-top pronouncements about the availability of testing, life-saving treatments and "Operation Warp Speed" vaccines. Finally, he chirped, "I think the American people know that this is a president who has put the health of America first."

The American people did not know that. They knew the opposite because, as Harris explained, they could see the evidence of the administration's malfeasance with their own eyes. "Whatever the vice president is claiming the administration has done, clearly, it hasn't worked," she said. "When you're looking at over 210,000 dead bodies in our country, American lives that have been lost, families that are grieving that loss, and the vice president is the head of the task force and knew on January 28th, how serious this was. And then, thanks to Bob Woodward, we learned that they knew about it. And then when that was exposed, the vice president said, when asked, 'Well, why didn't you all tell anybody?' he said, 'Because the president wanted people to remain calm.'"

At that point, a desperate Pence sought to interrupt Harris's indictment of the administration and of his own negligence. Appealing to the moderator, he said, "Susan, I have to weigh in here." Harris shut him down. "Mr. Vice President," she said, "I'm speaking." "I have to weigh in," insisted Pence. "I'm speaking," replied Harris, even more firmly this time. Then she turned her attention away from the sputtering man at her side. "So I want to ask the American people," said Harris, "how calm were you when you were panicked about where you were going to get your next roll of toilet paper? How calm were you when your kids were sent home from school and you didn't know when they could go back? How calm were you when your children couldn't see your parents because you were afraid they could kill them?"

Pence was given a chance to respond. But even at this critical juncture, he could not stay focused on Covid-19. "President Trump and I trust the American people to make choices in the best interest of their health," he said, before reaching back into the trick bag of talking points that he had hoped would see him through the debate. "Joe Biden and Kamala Harris consistently talk about mandates, and not just mandates with the coronavirus, but a government takeover of health care, the Green New Deal, all government control. We're about freedom and respecting the freedom of the American people."

An unwitting Pence, with his talk of trusting and respecting the American people, had invited Harris to pounce. And so she did:

> Let's talk about respecting the American people. You respect the American people when you tell them the truth. You respect the American people when you have the courage to be a leader, speaking of those things that you may not want people to hear, but they need to hear so they can protect themselves. But this administration stood on inform-ation that, if you had as a parent, if you had as a worker, knowing you didn't have enough money saved up, and now you're standing in a food line because of the ineptitude of an administration that was unwilling to speak the truth to the American people. So let's talk about caring about the American people. The American people have had to sacrifice far too much because of the incompetence of this administration.

Less than a month later, the American people would choose to replace Mike Pence with Kamala Harris. That should have been a cue for Pence, now an outgoing vice president free from the burden of seeking re-election, to return to the work of the task force. But it was not to be.

"Where has Vice President Mike Pence been for the past month?" asked *USA Today* columnist Suzette Hackney in early December. "As Covid-19 infections and deaths continue to surge nationally, I've been looking for Pence, the man tasked with guiding America through this public health crisis as head of the White House Coronavirus Task Force . . . What I've been looking for is public-facing leadership from Pence as America grapples with an out-of-control pandemic. Just because President Donald Trump won't do it doesn't mean that Pence shouldn't. He must."

He didn't. Pence spent much of December 2020 and early January 2021 doing the political work of a man who might run for president in 2024. He jetted off to Georgia to campaign for Republican candidates in runoffs that would decide which party controlled the US Senate. He flew to Florida to deliver a maskless address to young conservatives. He amplified Trump's lies about the election that the Republicans had lost, promising in mid-December that he and the president would keep fighting "until every legal vote is counted" and "until every illegal vote is thrown out." A consummate careerist, Pence focused on his own future, even as the futures of millions of Americans were imperiled by the pandemic and the economic devastation that extended from it.

Pence got a lot of credit on January 6, 2021, when he refused to go along with Trump's attempt to have Congress reject the electoral votes that would make Biden president and Harris vice president. But, even after the awful violence of that day, even after the threats that were targeted at him and his family, Pence refused to stand up to Trump by invoking the Twenty-fifth Amendment or supporting the president's impeachment for high crimes and misdemeanors. Pence was never willing to tell Trump he was wrong. He was never willing to speak the truth about the ongoing threat that Trump posed to democracy, or about the threat that Covid-19 posed to the American people. Had Pence done the right thing, he could have made more of a difference than anyone except Trump himself. Pence might even have gotten Trump to recognize the fundamental immorality and deadly danger of the administration's deliberately dishonest response to a pandemic. But he never put the lives of the American people ahead of his pandering project.

This is how Mike Pence should be remembered—not as any kind of hero, but as the desperate little man who could have saved so many lives but instead facilitated, in the words of the woman who defeated him at the debate, "the greatest failure of any presidential administration in the history of our country."

The Grounding of Jared Kushner

An aristocratic hand is without skills at the plow.

—Euripides

After years of deindustrialization and offshoring of industries, the United States was woefully unprepared for a pandemic that would require masks, gloves and all the other personal protective equipment needed by the nurses and doctors who care for the sick and the dying. By late March 2020, as the coronavirus infection rate was spiking and death tolls were rising at a horrifying rate, nurses at Mount Sinai Hospital in New York were photographed wearing trash bags for protection. Hospital officials tried to put the best spin on the images that flashed across social media. But their suggestion that it wasn't just a Mount Sinai problem ("the crisis is straining the resources of all New York–area hospitals") was hardly reassuring.

In the urgent first weeks of America's pandemic moment, the most haunting stories were those of the health care providers in New York and across the country who were being sent into battle against Covid-19 with little or no protection. In a mid-March survey of 8,200 nurses nationwide conducted by the National Nurses United union, only 24 percent reported their hospitals had sufficient PPE stock on hand to meet the challenge posed by a surge in coronavirus cases. Forty-five percent of the nurses surveyed reported that they did not have access to N95 respirator masks on their units. "Clearly, the nation's health facilities are still not ready and are in even worse shape than before in some respects to handle Covid-19," said National Nurses United executive director Bonnie Castillo, a registered nurse herself. "We need to act now and act fast. Priority number one is to protect the health and safety of our nurses and health care workers so that they can continue to take care of patients and keep our communities as healthy as possible through this pandemic. If our health facilities no longer stay as centers of healing and instead turn into disease vectors, many more people will needlessly suffer from this terrible disease."

Nurses were already dying on the front lines of a pandemic that would eventually claim more than 3,500 of America's most courageous caregivers. This was about more than individual hospitals or hotspots—it was a national crisis that demanded a national response. Even President Trump, who had been so slow and so dishonest in addressing the pandemic during its early stages, recognized the need to do something. Unfortunately, he defaulted to the most predictable response of his presidency: putting Jared Kushner in charge.

Kushner, a real estate heir, knew nothing about pandemics, health care or logistics. In fact, he was infamous for making bad circumstances worse—like the time he spent a then record-breaking $1.8 billion to buy the office tower at 666 Fifth Avenue in midtown Manhattan on the eve of the 2007 financial meltdown . . . and nearly bankrupted his family. That debacle set the tone for Kushner's career, which was ill planned, chaotic and unprofitable. Jared was never very good at business, so, of course, Jared did what failed businessmen invariably do. He went into politics.

Kushner's "qualification" to serve as a top government official was his marriage to Trump's daughter Ivanka, which made him a member of a presidential administration that embraced nepotism as a political sacrament. It is hard to imagine that Trump, a reality-TV star who made a career out of firing people who did not meet his standards, ever thought that Jared Kushner would do a good job at anything. But Jared could be trusted to put on a good show. And for a president who imagined that putting a family member in charge of a project would imply seriousness of intent, Jared was a convenient crutch.

As Trump burned bridges with competent conservatives in the corporate sector and government circles, he turned more and more to Kushner as a sort of Potemkin executive; he had the facade of a capable manager, if not the reality. During the 2016 campaign, it was Kushner who took charge of the vice-presidential selection process, pushing aside more competent Republicans (like Chris Christie, the former New Jersey governor) in order to make way for Mike Pence, a religious fanatic who had failed as governor of Indiana but could help Trump secure support from the Christian right. Once the new administration was sworn in, the president started putting Kushner in charge of things. Barely two months into Trump's tenure, Jared was shouldering most of the new administration's heavy burdens.

"Jared Kushner is a seemingly healthy thirty-six-year-old man with outstanding grooming habits," observed Judd Legum, founding editor-in-chief of ThinkProgress, in March 2017, but, he added, Kushner "seems to otherwise have no particular qualifications for any position in government. Prior to Donald Trump's campaign, Kushner had no experience working in policy or politics." Yet "Trump has given Kushner more responsibility than possibly anyone else in the US government. He is personally responsible for an astonishing variety of tasks, despite lacking any apparent knowledge or experience relevant to any of them."

Describing how "Trump's son-in-law has been put in charge of pretty much everything," Legum reviewed seven jobs Jared Kushner had been assigned to do for the United States of America:

"1. Jared Kushner is responsible for negotiating peace in the Middle East." (Trump tasked Kushner with brokering a peace agreement between Israel and the Palestinians. "If you can't produce peace in the Middle East, nobody can," Trump told Kushner at an inauguration event.)

"2. Jared Kushner is responsible for solving America's opioid epidemic." (Kushner was made responsible for crafting a strategy to combat an overdose epidemic.)

"3. Jared Kushner is responsible for diplomacy with Mexico." (After consulting with the Mexican foreign minister, Kushner persuaded Trump to soften a speech on the border wall to make it "less damaging" to relations with Mexico. Mexican officials told CBS News that "Kushner is now handling everything between the two countries, and personally trying to keep the relationship from disintegrating further.")

"4. Jared Kushner is responsible for diplomacy with China." (Kushner repeatedly met with Chinese diplomats, and according to the *New York Times* was heavily involved in planning the presidential visit of Xi Jinping and "took part in a National Security Council meeting . . . at which North Korea and China were discussed.")

"5. Jared Kushner is responsible for reforming care for veterans." (Kushner was given the task of "reimagining" the Department of Veterans Affairs.

"6. Jared Kushner is responsible for reforming the criminal justice system." (Kushner was dispatched to the Capitol to discuss mass incarceration and a host of other issues with senators.)

"7. Jared Kushner is responsible for reinventing the entire government and making it work like a business." (Trump put Kushner in charge of something called the "White House Office of American Innovation," which was meant "to infuse fresh thinking into Washington, float above the daily political grind and create a lasting legacy for a president." Kushner said the office's task was to make the entire US government "run like a great American company.")

As the long shadow of the Trump presidency stretched from 2017 to 2018 and 2019, Kushner took on more jobs. He did not do them well, but he stayed on Trump's good side. And he kept the jobs. "A lot of people in the administration don't like Jared and keep waiting for him to get his comeuppance. But it never happens," said WNYC journalist Andrea Bernstein, who wrote a book on the relationship between the Trump and Kushner families. "Jared's office is right next to Trump's in the Oval Office and he can go into the East Wing as well as the West Wing. So when everybody else leaves for the night, he can have family dinner with the president and that gives him enormous power. Trump also likes the sense that the family is running the business, and he trusts Ivanka and he trusts Jared."

At the start of 2020, Kushner's biggest responsibility was the president's re-election campaign, which, readers will note, did not end well. Before the first caucus vote was cast, however, the best laid plans of the president and his son-in-law were disrupted by the coronavirus pandemic. Trump's response was predictable. In March, as the pandemic surged, and as pleas for PPE poured in from nurses and doctors across the country, the president gave Jared another job: as head of Project Airbridge, a secretive initiative that Trump announced would move "massive amounts of medical supplies from other countries to the United States." This was a classic Trump exercise in showmanship and dim-wittery, with a little grift on the side. The pandemic had already been recognized as a global crisis. The idea that the rest of the world was going to have lots of masks to spare rested on a rejection of logic and logistics. But if common sense was going to be tossed aside, that meant this was just a job for Jared Kushner, who chirped, "At President Trump's direction we formed an unprecedented historic public-private partnership to ensure that massive amounts of masks, gear and other PPE will be brought to the United States immediately to better equip our health care workers on the front lines and to better serve the American people."

Things moved quickly for Jared. By April 1, the headline in *Politico* read, "Behind the scenes, Kushner takes charge of corona-virus response: Trump's son-in-law sets up shop at FEMA as his portfolio balloons to include manufacturing, supplies and long-term planning." The next day, *New York* magazine summed up the scope of Kushner's new responsibilities in a headline that read, "Trump Replaced White House Pandemic-Response Team With Jared Kushner."

The president's son-in-law was failing up. From the start of March, he had been getting pandemic responses wrong—often horribly so, as when he talked the president out of expanding testing as a means to figure out why and where the virus was spreading. At one especially chaotic point in mid-March, Gabriel Sherman of *Vanity Fair* reported that sources told him Trump was regretting that Kushner had swooped into the coronavirus response to encourage Trump to treat it as a P.R. problem when Dr. Anthony Fauci and others were calling for aggressive action. "This was Jared saying the world needs me to solve another problem," Sherman quoted an anonymous former White House official characterization of Trump's thinking. Another source told Sherman that Kushner advised Trump not to call a national emergency during his Oval Office address on March 11 because "it would tank the markets." The markets tanked anyway, and Trump announced the national emergency soon after. Still another source told Sherman that Trump was also angry that Kushner oversold Google's coronavirus testing website as a solution when it was actually nothing more than a fledgling effort, and Trump got slammed in the press. "Jared told Trump that Google was doing an entire website that would be up in seventy-two hours and had 1,100 people working on it 24/7," the source said. "That's just a lie."

Despite it all, Kushner's brief kept expanding. Why? Because he kept claiming expertise that he lacked, while playing to the myopic penchant of Trump and those around him to imagine that there was a "market solution" to the crisis. "Free markets will solve this," Kushner announced at a March 21 White House session, where tech executives pleaded with the government to take the lead in responding to PPE shortages. "That is not the role of government."

Dismissing urgent media reports about shortages in New York, the epicenter of the pandemic at that point, as "CNN bullshit," Kushner told the shocked executives, "They lie." He then blamed New York governor Andrew Cuomo for not pushing hard enough for PPE and reportedly announced, "His people are going to suffer and that's their problem."

"That's when I was like, 'We're screwed,'" one of the attendees told *Vanity Fair*, which reported that the group argued for invoking the Defense Production Act. "We were all saying, 'Mr. Kushner, if you want to fix this problem for PPE and ventilators, there's a path to do it, but you have to make a policy change.'" In response

Kushner got "very aggressive," the attendee recalled. "He kept invoking the markets" and told the group they "only understood how entrepreneurship works, but didn't understand how government worked . . . It felt like Kushner was the president. He sat in the chair and he was clearly making the decisions."

At precisely the point when the Trump administration should have been using all the power of the presidency to direct American factories to begin mass producing the gear that was needed, Kushner rejected the idea and began to implement his convoluted Project Airbridge scheme for getting PPE to the people.

Project Airbridge was a classic Trump scheme. It provided multinational corporations with no-bid contracts that guaranteed them federally funded air transportation and fast-tracked customs clearance in return for an agreement to sell some supplies to the government's Strategic National Stockpile and then accept counsel from the feds on sales of the remaining materials. The president loved everything about the initiative. "Through Project Airbridge, we have succeeded in bringing planeloads of vital supplies into the United States from overseas," Trump said at a briefing on April 7. "These are massive planes, by the way. The big planes—they are very big, very powerful—and they are loaded to the gills with supplies."

The president claimed the project was being run by "young geniuses," namely Kushner and the presidential son-in-law's college roommate, Adam Boehler, who had been installed as the chief executive officer of the administration's newly created US International Development Finance Corporation.

Jared seemed to agree. He described the administration's overall response to the crisis as a "great success story." The work he and his colleagues were doing was "truly extraordinary," if Jared didn't mind saying so himself. On Fox News, the son-in-law-in-chief bragged about "scaling supply chain really in a historic manner and pace." In the same interview, Kushner ripped critics who suggested that the Trump administration's rush to reopen was coming before essential steps had been taken to slow the spread of the virus. "The eternal-lockdown folks can make jokes on, uh, late-night television," he japed. "But the data is on our side."

The data wasn't on the administration's side. What it actually showed was that the administration lacked a coherent plan for much more than moving money into the accounts of multinational corporations, which accepted the free transportation, disregarded the counsel on where to sell their imported gear and gleefully bartered off what they could to the highest bidder. "The supply chain was broken to begin with, and they're putting [PPE] back into the supply chain with no idea where it's going," explained Representative Ted Deutch, Democrat of Florida.

The chaos made matters worse in many parts of the country. "We're bidding, unfortunately, for all of these items of equipment against the federal government and against the other states and against other countries," said Governor J. B. Pritzker of Illinois. "What the White House has done is created—you know, they call this the Airbridge—where they're bringing stuff back from China to the United States, and then they're delivering it to private companies in the United States, not to the states. And they're letting all of us bid against each other for those goods that are owned by the private companies."

Even by Kushner standards, Project Airbridge was incredibly convoluted. And shockingly costly. It burned through cash— close to $100 million in its first weeks of operation—and, as the *Washington Post* explained in early May, its impact was shrouded in secrecy: "The White House, the Federal Emergency Management Agency and the companies involved have declined to disclose where supplies have been delivered."

One detail did come out: even as Kushner was bragging about "historic" progress in the fight to save lives, the government had in April quietly ordered an additional 100,000 "human remains pouches." In its reporting on federal documents detailing the body-bag purchases, NBC News noted that "the biggest set was earmarked for purchase the day after President Donald Trump projected that the US death toll from the coronavirus might not exceed 50,000 or 60,000 people."

It did not take long for Project Airbridge to crash and burn. State and local officials were complaining within weeks of the program's inception that promised equipment was not being delivered. "From the start, Project Airbridge has done nothing to increase American manufacturing of [personal protective equipment] or even global production of PPE," asserted the office of Governor Jay Inslee of Washington. "It has only continued our reliance on foreign supply chains. It is both a public health and national security concern that we cannot manufacture the protective equipment necessary to keep Americans safe." Even as the administration was hailing its work in Michigan, that state's governor, Gretchen Whitmer, reported that Michigan hospitals were "running dangerously low" on protective gear for health care workers. Nurses in Ann Arbor organized a "PPE Over Profit" rally outside the University of Michigan's Rogel Cancer Center, where organizer Ann Jackson told reporters: "There are people that are still getting sick, health care workers getting sick. Our need for PPE is not going anywhere, and the most limited supply you have, you're lookin' at it, it's the health care workers." The American Federation of Teachers, a union that represented nurses in Michigan and other states, began running television ads that highlighted the administration's failure.

"We now know six to eight weeks of preparation were lost in the president's dismissal and denial of the pandemic," said AFT president Randi Weingarten. "The least he could do right now is use every lever of government to get health care professionals the PPE they desperately need, so they can help others. Trump calls himself a wartime president, but our states don't have the funds or testing they need, and our hospitals and health care professionals remain dangerously ill equipped to tackle this pandemic. His refusal to do his job means our heroes will remain exposed and at risk."

By mid-May, it was reported that Project Airbridge was "winding down." Kushner was still claiming it was a "success story." But according to Representative Angie Craig, a Minnesota Democrat, "We have literally wasted six weeks getting ourselves ramped up because we stood on the sidelines and allowed the private sector to manage itself instead of coming up with a centralized strategy."

The full measure of Kushner's failure would come in the weeks and months that followed. An investigation by two Democratic senators, Elizabeth Warren of Massachusetts and Richard Blumenthal of Connecticut, revealed evidence that Project Airbridge was awash in political favoritism, cronyism and price-gouging. Based on information gathered from medical supply companies that had cooperated with the senators, Warren announced in June that "our investigation found Project Airbridge—like the broader Trump Administration response to coronavirus—has been marked by delays, incompetence, confusion, ethics questions and secrecy across multiple Federal agencies and in the White House. Taxpayers have shelled out tens of millions of dollars on this secretive project, and they deserve to know whether it actually helped get critical supplies to the areas most in need."

It wasn't just the financial cost that worried the senators. It was the human toll. "Cronyism and incompetence seemingly led this taxpayer-funded boondoggle to tragically misallocate scarce medical supplies and PPE," Blumenthal said. "Jared Kushner's pet Airbridge project was a 'bridge to nowhere' for health providers most in need. Our investigation shows how secrecy and lies were Airbridge hallmarks, following faithfully the Trump model for pandemic response."

In July, the House Oversight and Government Reform Committee completed an investigation into Project Airbridge. It revealed that responsible firms had begun pleading with the Trump administration as early as January 2020 for guidance on how to meet the needs of hospital personnel who would be responding to Covid-19. According to the committee's report, "private sector companies were desperate for guidance from the federal government, but the Trump Administration failed to provide it." Finally, in March, the president of the Health Industry Distributors Association (HIDA), a trade group that represented medical supply firms, wrote a letter begging the administration "to provide the strategic direction needed to more effectively target PPE supplies based on greatest need." He concluded the letter by noting that "only the federal government" had the data and authority to provide that strategic direction.

"Unfortunately," noted House Oversight Committee chair Carolyn Maloney, "the Trump Administration decided not to lead a federal effort to procure PPE directly, forcing state and local governments, hospitals and others to compete for scarce supplies. One company told Committee staff that the failure to bring procurement efforts under a federal umbrella was 'one of the biggest missed opportunities.' The company explained that it proposed this federal umbrella approach directly to the administration, but that 'politics has gotten in the way of that.' As a result, the company explained that states have been forced into 'working through brokers in China, which has led to a series of problems,' and warned that there is 'way too much reliance on these Chinese brokers rather than a public-private partnership to procure necessary PPE.'"

Instead of procuring PPE directly, said Maloney, "the administration established Project Airbridge to provide transportation for PPE procured by private sector companies." The committee determined that contracts for Project Airbridge failed to "require distributors to report back information about the pricing of PPE [and] provided little guidance on how to prioritize specific end-users who need PPE most urgently." In other words, the Trump administration created a free-spending federal program with little or no oversight of what was done with "PPE imported at taxpayer expense."

Even as the evidence mounted for what the *New York Times* would eventually describe as Kushner's "fumbling hunt for medical supplies," the presidential son-in-law kept proclaiming himself to be a genius. "We created a control tower approach with the private company distributors in order to make sure that we can be as efficient as possible, and it's been quite successful," he told Fox News. That became the administration narrative. "Our administration," Vice President Mike Pence would claim in June "launched a partnership with private industry that, as of June 12, had delivered more than 143 million N95 masks, 598 million surgical and procedural masks, 20 million eye and face shields, 265 million gowns and coveralls, and 14 billion gloves."

In fact, explained the memorandum produced by the House Oversight Committee, "only about 7 percent of that PPE came through Project Airbridge." That memorandum detailed how, "In their June 18 briefing with Committee staff, FEMA officials confirmed that the Trump Administration has no involvement in directing PPE within hot spots. FEMA officials also explained that, for distributors other than those participating in Project

Airbridge, there (was) no industry-wide guidance on where the most urgent needs are—'aside from everyone watching the news.'" In perhaps the most damning revelation, the memorandum revealed that "going forward, FEMA officials conceded that 'the supply chain is still not stable,' but claimed that distributors can now 'do it on their own.'"

Jared Kushner's "great success" was dismissed as a lie by Representative Maloney. "The United States has had more cases and more deaths from coronavirus than any nation on Earth," she said. "Despite months of effort, there are still severe shortages of PPE and critical medical equipment, and the Trump Administration has no coherent national strategy to address these deficiencies."

Elizabeth Spiers, a veteran editor who once worked for Kushner, was a bit blunter. "Jared Kushner's coronavirus response team, we learned this week, is fumbling because it's largely staffed with inexperienced volunteers," she wrote in May 2020, as Project Airbridge was crashing. "Of course it is. It's being run by one." Spiers added: "Kushner's lack of experience and expertise has not been remedied in any way during his now three-plus years in the White House. After bungling many high-profile efforts to address various problems and often making them worse (see, Middle East, peace in), he keeps being handed more responsibilities with higher stakes. He has wasted taxpayer resources and endangered lives trying on policy roles usually reserved for the country's top experts with the sophistication of a child playing dress-up, cavalierly discarding them when he can't fit into them."

Unfortunately, observed Spiers, "Defining accomplishment down has deadly consequences in this case."

4

The Unmasking of Mark Meadows

Madman, thou errest. I say, there is no darkness but ignorance,
in which thou art more puzzled than the Egyptians in their fog.
—William Shakespeare, *Twelfth Night*

When the 1918 influenza pandemic surged in the United States, the message from Washington regarding masks was urgent and unequivocal. Surgeon General Rupert Blue informed the Senate Appropriations Committee, "Until we get a vaccine we have to rely upon careful treatment of the sick, keep away from crowds, and cover up the mouth and nose so that they will not spread the disease." Communities across the country got the message. From Iron River, Wisconsin, to Tucson, Arizona, local governments implemented strict orders for mask wearing. Newspaper advertisements endorsed by federal, state and local officials explained: "A gauze mask is 99 percent proof against influenza. Doctors wear them. Those who do not wear them get sick. The man or woman or child who will not wear a mask now is a dangerous slacker." Posters in California declared, "Wear a Mask or Go to Jail." That wasn't hyperbole. In San Francisco, according to review of the national response by the *Saturday Evening Post*, "the city's Board of Health, led by Dr. William C. Hassler, instituted a mask ordinance. The fine for disobedience was five dollars, which was then given to the Red Cross." The ordinance was aggressively enforced. When the mayor of San Francisco showed up at a boxing match without a mask, he was promptly cited and fined $50. The mayor got off easy. "In San Francisco, 100 people were arrested," recalled the *Post*, and according to the *Sacramento Bee* a Stockton, California, policeman "apparently found his own father to be a mask slacker, and he arrested him."

Mask mandates were controversial; local "Anti-Mask Leagues" objected. Yet, history would prove the rules and their strict enforcement to have been wise. "Today we can look back and see that they flattened the curve and the communities that did enforce much stricter regulations and for a longer period of time and began earlier had lower death rates," explained historian Nancy Bristow, author of the 2017 book *American Pandemic: The Lost Worlds of the 1918 Influenza Epidemic*.

But Americans did not have to look back a century for evidence of the importance of mask mandates. In the first stages of the 2020 coronavirus pandemic, a study funded by the World Health Organization determined that "face masks are associated with protection, even in non–health care settings." The *Lancet* reported, "Face mask use could result in a large reduction in risk of infection." When New Zealand announced in June 2020 that it had halted the spread of Covid-19, public health experts, researchers, policymakers and media outlets from around the world rushed to identify the strategies that had worked. In a widely circulated article for the *Conversation*, public health professors Michael Baker and Nick Wilson of the University of Otago proposed a list of "five key risk management approaches to achieve lasting protection" against Covid-19 and other serious public health threats. At the top of the list was a recommendation for making mask wearing mandatory in settings where the virus could spread. "Other personal hygiene measures (staying home if sick, washing hands, coughing into elbows) are insufficient when transmission is often from people who appear well and can spread the virus simply by breathing and talking," warned the professors. "The evidence base for the effectiveness of even simple fabric face masks is now strong."

Obituaries amplified the message. The *New York Times* explained poignantly: "As the death toll from the coronavirus in the United States grows steadily higher, families who have lost relatives to the disease are writing the pandemic more deeply into the death notices they submit to funeral homes and the materials they share with newspapers' obituary writers. They are crafting pleas for mask wearing, rebuking those who believe the virus is a hoax and describing, in blunt detail, the loneliness and physical suffering that the coronavirus inflicted on the dying." The *Times* report described Kim Miller, a retired college professor, who sat down in her Illinois house to compose an epitaph for her late husband. Miller, the *Times* explained, "could not hold back. Not about the coronavirus that had left Scott, her fit, healthy spouse who loved to swim, golf and putter in the garden, gasping for breath and unable to move his limbs as he stood at the kitchen counter. Not about what had killed him swiftly and cruelly in only a few days. 'This disease is real, it is serious and it is deadly,' she wrote in his obituary. 'Wear the mask, socially distance, if not for yourself then for others who may lose a loved one to the disease.'"

By the summer of 2020, the historic and contemporary data confirming the wisdom of mask mandates to protect against the spread of viruses was so complete, so compelling, so painfully clear, that only a fool or a charlatan would argue against it.

A fool? A charlatan?

Meet Mark Meadows, the scandal-plagued North Carolina real estate developer who, after a brief tenure as a Republican "Freedom Caucus" congressman who casually proposed shutting down the federal government, became Donald Trump's fourth White House chief of staff. After amending his official biography to acknowledge that he did not possess the bachelor's degree from the University of South Florida that he had previously claimed (he actually had an associate of arts degree from USF, the university reported, "similar to a degree an individual might earn after completing two years at a community college"), Meadows stepped into the thick of the coronavirus pandemic. He proceeded to get everything wrong.

Just as the United States appeared to be on the verge of implementing a mask mandate that could have saved hundreds of thousands of lives, Meadows pulled the brakes and derailed efforts to get President Trump to issue the order that the data argued was urgently necessary. "Making masks a culture war issue was the dumbest thing imaginable," a former senior adviser to Trump told the *New York Times*. Yet, that was precisely what Meadows, who was aided and abetted by veteran Trump aide Stephen Miller, succeeded in doing.

As infection rates and the death toll mounted in the spring, President Trump resisted not just a formal mask mandate but urging by the Centers for Disease Control that he and other top officials wear face coverings voluntarily. CDC strategists wanted the president and his aides to model best practices and, of course, to prevent infections and save lives. But that didn't happen. The president regularly appeared in public without a mask and ridiculed those who followed public health guidelines. When summer arrived and it became clear that warm weather would not end the pandemic, Trump came under increasing pressure to approve a national mask mandate. Democrats favored the move, with House Speaker Nancy Pelosi declaring the mandate was "long overdue." Even some of the president's closest aides were prodding him to embrace the idea. Jared Kushner, the presidential son-in-law, whom Trump had put in charge of many aspects of the pandemic response, was for it; so, too, was another senior aide to the president, Hope Hicks. Vice President Mike Pence was starting to talk up masks in media appearances, telling CBS's *Face the Nation* that "we believe people should wear masks wherever social distancing is not possible" and urging Americans to "defer" to orders that people mask up.

By late July, it looked as if a horrific period of presidential foot-dragging might finally be coming to an end—especially after Trump's favored pollster, Tony Fabrizio, delivered an Oval Office presentation during which he explained that an overwhelming majority of Americans favored mandatory mask-wearing in public. That was precisely the right way to appeal to Trump, whose obsession with his 2020 re-election campaign colored every decision regarding the pandemic response.

Fabrizio made a compelling case that Trump's own supporters were ready and willing to accept mandatory mask wearing in public because, as the *Times* explained, voters "were more concerned about getting sick than about the virus's effects on their personal financial situation." He also pointed out that "the president's approval rating on handling the pandemic had hit new lows and a little more than half the country did not think he was taking the situation seriously." Issuing a mask mandate, the pollster explained, would be politically wise, as 70 percent of likely voters in the battleground states Trump needed to win in the fall favored the requirement. The mandate was popular with Democrats, independents and, strikingly, a majority of Republicans.

Kushner had a strategy for using a mask mandate to renew Trump's political fortunes. He wanted to frame it as the way back to freedom and economic renewal, arguing that this simple public health measure was a "no-brainer," according to the *Times*, which reported that:

> Mr. Kushner had some reason for optimism. Mr. Trump had agreed to wear one not long before for a visit to Walter Reed National Military Medical Center, after finding one he believed he looked good in: dark blue, with a presidential seal.
>
> But Mark Meadows, the White House chief of staff—backed up by other aides including Stephen Miller—said the politics for Mr. Trump would be devastating.
>
> "The base will revolt," Mr. Meadows said, adding that he was not sure Mr. Trump could legally make it happen in any case.
>
> That was all Mr. Trump needed to hear. "I'm not doing a mask mandate," he concluded.
>
> Aside from when he was sick, he was rarely seen in a mask again.

Meadows succeeded in his political appeal to Trump, to devastating effect. But why did Meadows fight this fight? Why didn't he work with those around the president, as previous chiefs of staff had, to nudge Trump in the right direction? The answer had everything to do with the new politics of the Republican Party. Like Trump, Meadows had been an "art of the deal" real estate developer before entering politics in 2012. And, like Trump, Meadows had developed a win-at-any-cost mentality that invariably chose profit over ethics. Retired University of North Carolina-Asheville history professor Milton Ready, who has made a study of Meadows, argued that as a congressman Meadows represented "the 'greed is good' credo of Gordon Gekko in the 1987 movie *Wall Street* and the dominance of business values in American society."

Along with many of the right-wing members of the House who swept into Congress with the Tea Party movement of the early 2010s, Meadows had no political or public policy experience. He presented himself as "a business person to make tough decisions and get our economy moving again." Those "tough decisions" would, necessarily, reject science, logic and the rule of law if such niceties got in the way of his own political and economic advancement. "Perhaps the most interesting detail about Mark Meadows's rise can be found in his opportunistic nexus with the takeover of North Carolina by hard-right Republicans in 2010," explained Ready. "At the heart of all the gerrymandering, voting suppression and outright fraud now prevalent in North Carolina lie the self-interest of people like Meadows and the self-deception of their supporters."

Meadows characterized himself as a conservative, as did his fellow members of the "Freedom Caucus," most of whom argued that Republican Party leaders were insufficiently committed to downsizing government and proposed to turn the GOP toward a politics of ever deeper tax cuts for the rich and ever greater austerity for working Americans. This was not the conservatism of Barry Goldwater or Ronald Reagan, political figures who enjoyed the battle of ideas but still, at least occasionally, deferred to facts and logic. John Boehner, the former House speaker, who had one of the most conservative voting records in the chamber before he quit out of frustration in 2015, said of Meadows: "He's an idiot. I can't tell you what makes him tick." It was a somewhat kinder description than that of conservative lawyer George Conway, who described the developer-turned-politician as "a moron and a disgrace." Of the Freedom Caucus in which

Meadows emerged as the chief bomb thrower in the unlucky 113th Congress, Boehner said: "They can't tell you what they're for. They can tell you everything they're against. They're anarchists. They want total chaos. Tear it all down and start over. That's where their mindset is."

In practice, Meadows was less of an anarchist and more of a blowhard whose "ideology" was a stew of perceived grievances, conspiracy theories and misreads of public sentiment. During his seven years in Congress, and eventually as White House chief of staff, Meadows followed the same conveniently self-serving ideological course that proved popular with most of the wealthy businessmen who surfed the Tea Party–generated wave of resentment over the election of Barack Obama as president in 2008 into congressional election victories in 2010 and 2012. Former White House counsel John Dean identified these politicians, many of whom became Trump's most loyal lieutenants, as conservatives without conscience.

Raised as a proud "Goldwater Republican," Dean had deep roots in the "conscience of a conservative" politics that the 1964 Republican presidential nominee brought to American politics in the 1950s and nurtured into the 1990s. Long before Trump arrived on the scene, however, Dean recognized that the conservative ideology was being hijacked by Republicans who were inclined toward precisely the sort of reckless authoritarianism that would define the forty-fifth presidency. Dean began warning during the co-presidency of George W. Bush and Dick Cheney that the party of Goldwater and Reagan was being overtaken by charlatans who were threatening not just the Grand Old Party but the country. "Tough, coldblooded, ruthless authoritarians had 'co-opted' conservatism," Dean explained in his groundbreaking book, *Conservatives Without Conscience*, and were turning the GOP into a vehicle for enriching and empowering themselves at the expense of the common good—and, often, common decency. These "right-wing authoritarians" cloaked themselves in the garments of old-school conservatism; they spoke of religious morality and their fealty to the Constitution while practicing what Dean described as a "strident and intolerant politics" that invariably sacrificed the public on the altar of their own self-serving ambition.

Dean published his scathing critique of "right-wing authoritarians" in 2006, at a point when Mark Meadows was still pulling together land deals in Tampa, Florida. But Dean, who in 1973 as White House counsel recognized the cancer on Richard Nixon's presidency, anticipated Donald Trump's final chief of staff with the precision of someone who has seen a lot of bad players do a lot of bad things.

Of the "very self-righteous," "nasty and mean-spirited" and "prejudiced" conservatives without conscience who were becoming the face of the Republican Party, Dean observed: "They are typically men whose desire in life is to dominate others and to be in charge. They are very aggressive when they do so. They are highly manipulative. They are also people who have absolutely no appreciation of equality of others. They see themselves as superior, and they are amoral in their thinking." So amoral that, for reasons of political convenience, they might even reject public health mandates during a pandemic.

Meadows entered the Trump White House as a crude tactician who rejected moderation in favor of a narrow-gauge focus on satisfying talk-radio hucksters, Fox News bookers and the angriest elements of the Republican Party's base. Firm in his faith that tough-guy branding was more important than making popular appeals, Meadows refused to let science, or even practical politics, get in the way of playing to Trump's worst instincts. As such, in the late spring and summer of 2020, Meadows was the wrong person in the wrong room at the wrong time.

Not only didn't the country get a mask mandate when it needed one, refusing to wear a mask became a hallmark of Trump's re-election campaign. Republican loyalists, not just in the crowds at rallies but in state legislatures and governors' offices around the country, resisted mandates. Republican-led states rejected necessary interventions even as infection rates and death tolls spiked in places such as South Dakota, where Governor Kristi Noem proudly posted social-media photos of herself without a mask.

Meadows and a small circle of extremists kept promoting the do-nothing approach through the fall of 2020, even as President Trump, First Lady Melania Trump and scores of White House aides and visitors were diagnosed with the virus. When Meadows himself was diagnosed with Covid-19, according to the *Washington Post*, he attempted to hide his condition and "threatened to fire doctors from the White House Medical Unit if they reported information about growing numbers of coronavirus cases."

Trump, Meadows and those around them received the best of care. Despite their own inaction, they survived. But hundreds of thousands of Americans did not.

Around the same time that Meadows was talking Trump out of accepting a mask mandate, professors from the Massachusetts Institute of Technology and the University of British Columbia released a study based on data compiled by the Covid-19 Tracking Project. It determined that, of the almost 100,000 deaths that had been reported as of June 1, 2020, roughly 40,000 could have been prevented if workers who interacted with members of the public had been required to wear masks at the start of the pandemic. In the fall, another study, published in the journal *Nature Medicine*, projected 510,000 lives lost to Covid-19 by the end of February 2021, of which almost 130,000 lives could be saved with a strictly enforced universal mask mandate.

The statistics vary marginally. But study after study suggested that roughly 40 percent of coronavirus deaths could have been prevented with a universal mask requirement. Thus, of the roughly 400,000 coronavirus deaths in the United States reported by the end of the Trump presidency, approximately 160,000 were preventable. Mark Meadows can't be blamed for all of those deaths; after all, he didn't take over as Trump's chief of staff until late March of 2020. But if we simply look at the death toll since the late July Oval Office meeting when Meadows led the charge against a mandate, the number of fatalities that might have been avoided by the close of 2020 numbered well over 100,000.

On January 20, 2021, Mark Meadows left the White House as a sixty-one-year-old former presidential chief of staff. The infamously ambitious Meadows had ruled out a 2022 US Senate bid in his home state of North Carolina because Lara Trump, the president's daughter-in-law, was considering a run. But no one doubted that he would seek to leverage his connections to land a high-profile gig that would keep him in the political spotlight. In the closing days of Trump's presidency, *Politico* reported, "Aides inside the White House are well aware of that reputation and are now gossiping about what other role he might be trying to position himself for while serving as Trump's 24/7 aide." There was talk of a run for another office, or even a high-profile TV gig.

No matter how he winds up seeking to cash in on his record as Trump's closest adviser, there should never be a reference to Meadows that fails to recall the tens of thousands of dead Americans who might have lived if a dangerous anti-mask slacker had not been counseling the forty-fifth president of the United States to choose political calculation over public safety.

Mike Pompeo's Cold War against Science and Solidarity

Policy sits above conscience.
—William Shakespeare, *Timon of Athens*

Secretary of State Mike Pompeo was beside himself. The former congressman who had taken charge of the State Department after serving initially as the Trump administration's director of the Central Intelligence Agency rarely evidenced much passion, or even much interest, in Covid-19 during the initial stages of the crisis. Instead of embracing the work of mounting a global response to a global pandemic, Pompeo was more inclined toward arranging "emergency" arms sales to Saudi Arabia and scheming to overthrow the government of Venezuela. But on April 30, 2020, Pompeo had something to say to the leaders of countries that were being overwhelmed in the fight to contain the crisis: refuse medical reinforcements. Or, at the very least, make it harder for those who could lend a helping hand to provide life-saving care.

Several days earlier, on April 26, 216 doctors and nurses had flown into Johannesburg, South Africa, to provide critical support for that country's efforts to combat what was already one of the highest rates of confirmed Covid-19 infections in Africa. The doctors were specialists in combating infectious diseases and in providing care using a community health service model that was especially well suited to South Africa's urgent needs. The nation's health minister, Zweli Mkhize, hailed their expertise as medical missionaries who had toiled "in the frontline of fighting other outbreaks in the world, such as cholera in Haiti in 2010, and Ebola in West Africa in 2013."

But Mike Pompeo had a problem with these particular specialists. Why? They were from Cuba, a socialist country he had been demonizing since Donald Trump had invited the unreconstructed cold warrior to join his administration. "We've noticed how the regime in Havana has taken advantage of the Covid-19 pandemic to continue its exploitation of Cuban medical workers," Pompeo announced in a press briefing. Praising the right-wing government of Brazil for making it difficult for Cuban medical personnel to fight the pandemic in that Covid-ravaged country, Pompeo pressured the South African government to be similarly resistant to essential aid.

Though South Africa was a US ally, it refused the secretary of state's counsel. The South Africans pointed out that they had requested medical aid from Cuba, which over the previous six decades earned international acclaim for its health care system, its training of doctors and its record of dispatching "armies in white robes" to medical hot spots around the world. As recently as 2016, President Barack Obama had on a trip to Cuba declared that "no one should deny the service that thousands of Cuban doctors have delivered for the poor and suffering. Last year, American health care workers—and the US military—worked side by side with Cubans to save lives and stamp out Ebola in West Africa."

As part of his effort to "bury the last remnant of the Cold War in the Americas" and "extend the hand of friendship to the Cuban people," Obama had gone out of his way to celebrate the international humanitarian work of Cuban doctors. He recalled historic examples of cooperation, recounting how the Cuban physician Dr. Carlos Finlay's epidemiology research in the late 1800s "paved the way for generations of doctors, including Walter Reed, who drew on Dr. Finlay's work to help combat yellow fever," and he celebrated the renewal of that cooperation in the struggle to eradicate Elola during the 2013–16 global health emergency that was especially acute in Liberia, Guinea and Sierra Leone. "I believe that we should continue that kind of cooperation in other countries," Obama said.

But that was not how Pompeo saw it. The Trump administration had, since its inception in 2017, sought to undo the progress Obama made to ease tensions between the countries that had been so epic that they occasioned the Bay of Pigs invasion, the Cuba Missile Crisis and decades of embargoes, travel restrictions and proxy conflicts across Latin America and Africa. Now, instead of focusing on the threat posed by the pandemic, Pompeo employed old-fashioned "red scare" language wherever Cuban doctors showed up to fight the deadly disease and its spread to new regions of the world. Cuban media pointedly reported that President Miguel Díaz-Canel "noted on his Twitter account that while the US loses track of the deaths due to Covid-19, Secretary of State Mike Pompeo holds Cuba accountable."

Despite Pompeo's bluster, however, Cuban doctors were warmly welcomed by most of the rest of the world—as they had been for decades. Before the pandemic, more than 28,000 Cubans were providing medical care in sixty-seven countries across the planet. Some of those countries paid for the services with exchanges of funds or products that boosted Cuba's economy; others simply extended goodwill. When the pandemic hit, an urgent cry for humanitarian aid arose and Cuba responded by dispatching another 4,000 medics to more than forty countries around the world—including wealthy European nations that requested Cuban specialists skilled in combating infectious diseases.

"When the number of patients mounts but the number of healers does not, whom do you call?" reported the *Economist*. "That was the question for Giulio Gallera, the health minister in Lombardy, the Italian region worst hit by Covid-19. The army was erecting a field hospital with thirty-two beds in a car park in Crema, 50km (thirty miles) southeast of Milan. But what about doctors to attend them? 'Someone said to me: "Write to the Cuban ministry of health,"' recalls Mr. Gallera. 'Barely a week later, on March 22nd, fifty-two medics arrived from Havana, waving Cuban and Italian flags.'"

The doctors reached Italy at a point when international news agencies were reporting on overwhelmed hospitals and morgues that could no longer keep ahead of the death toll. Yet the Cubans were undaunted. "We are going to fulfill an honorable task, based on the principle of solidarity," Graciliano Díaz Bartolo, a sixty-four-year-old Cuban, told a Reuters news service reporter. Dr. Leonardo Fernández, a sixty-eight-year-old intensive care specialist, pulled aside a white mask and said: "We are all afraid but we have a revolutionary duty to fulfill, so we take our fear and put it to one side . . . He who says he is not afraid is a superhero. But we are not superheroes, we are revolutionary doctors."

The health care providers were treated as heroes. "They are lifesavers," declared Ralph Gonsalves, the prime minister of Saint Vincent and the Grenadines, who served as chairman of the Caricom alliance of Caribbean states. "In some Caribbean countries, they constitute the backbone of the response to the pandemic." In Jamaica, where almost 140 Cuban doctors and nurses landed at Kingston's airport in mid-March to help the country fight the rapid spread of the virus, Health Minister Christopher Tufton greeted them warmly: "In a time of crisis, the Cuban government, the Cuban people [have] risen to the occasion. They have heard our appeal and they have responded." Some of the highest praise came from hard-hit African countries like Togo, where foreign ministry aide Charles Azilan said, "As scientific and medical circles groped in the dark, Cuban medicine, strong from past experiences, brought appropriate answers."

Pompeo was furious with these responses. He didn't like it that countries around the world were welcoming medical personnel who identified as "revolutionary doctors" from an island nation the Trump administration had promised to isolate. He was enraged by news reports that burnished the image of Cuba with headlines like "Cuba Sends 'White Coat Army' of Doctors to Fight Coronavirus" (NBC News). So it was that, instead of focusing on fighting the disease, the Trump administration's chief diplomat spent an inordinate amount of time trying to get countries in Latin America to reject Cuban doctors or place restrictions on their ability to provide care. This had been Pompeo's focus from the time he took charge of the Department of State, and he was not about to make adjustments on account of a pandemic. In the name of the United States, he announced, "We applaud Brazil and Ecuador and Bolivia and other countries which have refused to turn a blind eye to these abuses by the Cuban regime and ask all countries to do the same, including places like South Africa and Qatar." In addition to muscling individual countries to distance themselves from Cuba, the secretary of state pressured the Pan American Health Organization (PAHO), the Americas office of the World Health Organization, to politicize its response to health crises. Trump's attacks on the

WHO drew a good deal of attention internationally. But the assaults on PAHO were not merely rhetorical. Enraged by PAHO's cooperation with Cuba, the Trump administration threatened further funding cuts, creating a financial crisis for the organization.

On July 7, 2020, the US formally withdrew from the WHO, which made things even worse for PAHO, and for the global fight to contain the pandemic. "The uncertainty about PAHO's future is worrying and happens exactly when the Americas, at the time of writing, records more than 10.1 million cases and 376,000 deaths from Covid-19, making it the world's most affected region," wrote Miguel González Palacios in the summer of 2020. Around the same time, the distinguished journalist Albor Ruiz complained of Pompeo's "sick obsession with Cuba's medical international cooperation, totally disregarding the coronavirus pandemic" in an article in *Al Día News*.

"With typical arrogance and contempt for human lives, Pompeo has criticized Qatar, South Africa and other nations for requesting doctors from Cuba to battle the coronavirus," noted Ruiz. "Not that the richest and most powerful country in the world is offering to send its own doctors to take the place of the ones from Cuba, the small, poor Caribbean island that has suffered a sixty-year blockade from the US, and has saved thousands of lives around the world through its international medical cooperation."

Before his tenure ended in January 2021, Pompeo's "sick obsession" would extend to returning Cuba to the US's list of "state sponsors of terrorism," in what he described as a countermove to the Cuban government's "malign interference" in the Western Hemisphere and around the world. That act was performed with nine days left in the Trump presidency. Pompeo's move was so over-the-top that the senior member of the Senate, the Vermont Democrat Patrick Leahy, labeled it "a blatantly politicized designation" that "makes a mockery of what had been a credible, objective measure of a foreign government's active support for terrorism."

Pompeo's decision to slap the "terrorism" label on Cuba was about much more than wrangling over Cuban doctors caring for Covid-19 patients in Milan or Johannesburg. A fierce partisan who defended Trump even after the outgoing president incited an insurrectionist mob to attack the Capitol in an attempt to overturn the results of the 2020 election, Pompeo was, in the words of military writer Sébastien Roblin, "throwing diplomatic banana peels in the path of his successors by formally, but oh so very spuriously, designating foreign actors he doesn't like as terrorists." The soon-to-be-former secretary of state was positioning himself for a potential Republican presidential bid in 2024 by playing "the red card," with an eye toward gaining the favor of Cuban-American voters in Florida and right-wing primary voters in the states that would choose the next GOP nominee.

Pompeo's ambition consumed him in the final days of the Trump presidency, overwhelming any sense of duty to his country, or to the millions of human beings who were struggling to survive a pandemic.

With "fancy dinners in the State Department diplomatic reception rooms to cultivate favor with Republican luminaries who could bankroll his future political ambitions," Elise Labott noted in *Foreign Policy*, and with "his use of government planes to go politicking around the country under the guise of giving foreign-policy speeches," Pompeo engaged in a last-minute reordering of US policies that represented "a cynical attempt to neutralize the incoming Biden administration's foreign policy while chumming the water for his political future." Labott observed that Pompeo "trampled on the one tenet of US foreign policy that each of his predecessors respected, however hard it was for them at the time: Politics stops at the water's edge. Pompeo spit on this notion, turning foreign policy into just another battleground for partisan bloodsport. His belief that he could one day become president turned every move he made as America's top diplomat into an opportunity to suck up to Donald Trump and inherit his political dynasty."

What made Pompeo's abuses all the more galling was the fact that he knew exactly what he was doing when he politicized US diplomacy in general, and the response to Covid-19 in particular.

Pompeo wasn't a stupid man. A graduate of West Point and Harvard Law School, he spent years going over intelligence reports as a member of the House Permanent Select Committee on Intelligence, as director of the CIA and as secretary of state. He knew Cuba was not the threat he made it out to be. He also knew that the Biden administration would almost certainly reverse Cuba's "terrorism" designation. Indeed, as Sébastien Roblin noted, that suited Pompeo and Trump just fine, as it created "new opportunities to gin up outrage against Biden and gum up the works of his foreign policy agenda."

Roblin and others referred to Pompeo's approach as "diplomatic vandalism" against American policy. It was that. Yet, in the context of the battle against Covid-19, it was something else: deadly.

Pompeo rose to prominence as a political protégé of billionaire conservative campaign donors Charles and David Koch—so it came as no great surprise that the only thing he took seriously about the pandemic was the opportunity for political positioning. In November 2020, when coronavirus cases were surging once more in the US and abroad, the State Department ordered that any events not deemed mission-critical should be organized as "virtual events as opposed to in-person gatherings." But an exception was made for a particular set of events, reported the *Washington Post*: "large indoor holiday parties hosted by Secretary of State Mike Pompeo and his wife, Susan, on the eighth floor of the State Department involving hundreds of guests, food and drinks." The *Post* cited an invitation to one such event, on December 15, titled "Diplomacy at Home for the Holidays," to be staged in the Benjamin Franklin Room, the department's top reception space, with its cut-glass chandeliers and tall Corinthian columns. "Invitations have already gone out to 900 people, said two US officials familiar with the planning," the *Post* reported, "raising concerns about a potential superspreader event." Ian Lipkin, the director of the Center for Infection and Immunity at Columbia University, said: "I'm flabbergasted. An indoor event of this kind is dangerous on so many levels. This has all the makings of a repeat of what we saw in the White House Rose Garden following the confirmation of Amy Coney Barrett."

Lipkin was referring to the September 26, 2020, outdoor reception at which more than 150 Trump administration allies and aides gathered—many without masks, most failing to practice social distancing—for a ceremony to announce the president's selection of Coney Barrett to replace Justice Ruth Bader Ginsburg on the Supreme Court. Within days, Trump and First Lady Melania Trump had tested positive for Covid-19. So, too, had others who attended the event, including two Republican senators, Mike Lee of Utah and Thom Tillis of North Carolina; University of Notre Dame President John Jenkins; former White House aide and Trump confidante Kellyanne Conway; and former New Jersey governor Chris Christie. "We had a superspreader event in the White House and it was in a situation where people were crowded together and were not wearing masks," Dr. Anthony Fauci said. "So the data speak for themselves."

But that data did not speak to Pompeo, who was determined to go ahead with tightly packed events in mid-December, some of which had the feel of "command performances" that would be difficult for diplomats and their families to turn down. The same went for catering workers who, their union explained, "often do not receive health insurance from their employers and must staff these events in order to keep their jobs." Noting those worries about vulnerable guests and workers, Lipkin said, "It's unfair, it's unethical and it flies in the face of what we need to do to protect each other."

Senator Robert Menendez of New Jersey agreed. Menendez, the ranking Democrat on the Senate Foreign Relations Committee, dispatched a letter calling on Pompeo to cancel the parties. "I am concerned that these parties pose a significant health risk, not only to attendees, but to the employees and workers who must staff these events, as well as to State Department employees who may feel pressured to attend," Menendez warned. "It is one thing for individuals to engage in behavior that flies in the face of CDC and public health guidelines. But it is another to put employees and workers at risk, some of whom include contractors, such as catering and wait staff, who do not receive the full benefits of federal employment and may not have health insurance."

As the dates of Pompeo's potential superspreader events approached, a hapless State Department spokesperson promised that "we plan to fully enforce social distancing measures at this reception, and face coverings are mandatory for admittance." Yet when the *Post* inquired as to how social distancing would be enforced or whether attendees could keep masks on at a reception that included food and drinks, the spokesperson did not offer a response.

On December 15, the largest of Pompeo's planned parties was held, yet barely 5 percent of those who had been invited showed up. The secretary of state skipped his planned speech at that night's event, and the next day, as the *Post* reported:

> Secretary of State Mike Pompeo canceled his final major holiday party of the year Wednesday after his exposure to a person who tested positive for the coronavirus forced him into quarantine, according to two officials familiar with the situation. The decision caps a run of indoor holiday parties hosted by Pompeo, his wife, Susan, and his top aides that health experts and US lawmakers warned could turn into superspreader events at a time when the novel coronavirus has killed more than 300,000 Americans.

Yet the cancellation came a bit late in the game for attendees and catering workers. "The State Department has hosted hundreds of diplomats and dignitaries since last week for indoor gatherings with holiday music, drinks and photo lines that resulted in the type of close congregation and unmasking that facilitates the airborne transmission of the virus through respiratory droplets," the *Post* noted.

There's no telling how many Americans were endangered by Pompeo's organization of superspreader events at the State Department. Yet, the figure was infinitesimal compared to the number of people around the world who were put at risk by the crude politicization of the pandemic response by the secretary of state throughout 2020.

This was especially true when it came to the race to identify vaccines.

As researchers around the world rushed to develop vaccines, international cooperation became critical, and initiatives aimed at worldwide distribution, like Covid-19 Vaccines Global Access (Covax), sprang up. Savvy world leaders understood that this cooperation needed to continue through the production and distribution of the vaccines. "Equal access to a Covid-19 vaccine is the key to beating the virus and paving the way for recovery from the pandemic," argued Prime Minister Stefan Löfven of Sweden. "This cannot be a race with a few winners, and the Covax Facility is an important part of the solution—making sure all countries can benefit from access to the world's largest portfolio of candidates and fair and equitable distribution of vaccine doses."

The notion of making vaccines available as a "global public good" to combat a global pandemic wasn't just a moral imperative. It was smart from a public health standpoint. And it was smart economics. A survey commissioned by the International Chamber of Commerce (ICC) determined that the monopolizing of vaccine supplies by wealthy countries did not insulate them from economic turbulence. "No economy, however big, will be immune to the effects of the virus until the pandemic is brought to an end everywhere," explained John Denton, the ICC secretary general. "Purchasing vaccines for the developing world isn't an act of generosity by the world's richest nations. It's an essential investment for governments to make if they want to revive their domestic economies." A *New York Times* review of the ICC study concluded: "If people in developing countries remain out of work because of lockdowns required to choke off the spread of the virus, they will have less money to spend, reducing sales for exporters in North America, Europe and East Asia. Multinational companies in advanced nations will also struggle to secure required parts, components and commodities."

Yet, true to form, Trump and Pompeo adopted a hyper-nationalistic approach that attacked the nations working to care for the sick in hard-hit regions of the world—as the Cuban doctors were—and that rejected pleas for an equitable distribution of vaccines that might beat Covid-19 and secure significant goodwill for the United States. Trump and Pompeo could have put the US on the right side of the fight against the pandemic, and of history. Instead, ABC News reported in September 2020 that the US had declined to join a 172-country effort to develop, manufacture and equitably distribute a vaccine. Why? Because the World Health Organization, which Pompeo was now constantly attacking for working with the Chinese government, had been encouraging countries to join Covax and the global vaccine alliance called Gavi in order to assure that developing countries were not abandoned. There were plenty of credible criticisms to be made regarding China's lack of transparency and its exploitation of the crisis to crack down on human rights. But the refusal to work with the WHO and other agencies that were seeking to develop a united front when it came to developing and distributing vaccines did nothing to hold China to account. It simply isolated the United States. "The decision undermines the global effort to collaborate on a vaccine by encouraging others to fend for themselves first," ABC's report explained. "Secretary of State Mike Pompeo said US opposition stems from the involvement of the World Health Organization, which President Donald Trump and other US officials have blamed for the novel coronavirus pandemic, although a senior official from the Department of Health and Human Services said later the decision was to keep vaccine resources in the US."

In the first weeks of 2021, as vaccines began to be distributed, alarming news circulated about the neglect of the poorest countries in the world, especially those in southern Asia and Africa. "As countries around the world start to inoculate their populations from the coronavirus, Africa is being left behind," Bloomberg reported in January. A map illustrating the level of vaccine distribution around the world had the US, Canada and most European countries shaded green to show relatively high levels. Africa was blank, with a notation that there was "no data." Scientists warned that many African countries would not see mass vaccinations until 2022, 2023 or even 2024.

"In Africa, we don't have the resources. It's as simple as that," explained Ellen Johnson Sirleaf, the former Liberian president and Nobel Peace Prize recipient who co-chaired a review of the global response to the pandemic. This lack of resources created a nightmarish circumstance for the poorest African nations, but it was also a threat for the US and other developed nations. Sirleaf warned that the pandemic threat would not be beaten "unless vaccine is seen as a free good on the basis that until everyone is safe no one is safe."

She was right, of course. Russ Feingold, the former senator from Wisconsin who chaired the Africa subcommittee of the Senate Foreign Relations Committee and who later served as the US special envoy for the African Great Lakes Region, has for decades warned about the folly of neglecting Africa in efforts to control the spread of infectious diseases. The calculus is not complicated. Diseases that go unchecked in Africa are "only one or two plane flights away" from London, Paris or New York. After the global struggles to contain the spread of HIV-AIDS, the HIN1 virus in 2009 and the Ebola virus in 2014 and 2015, leaders of countries around the world had come to understand this reality by the time Covid-19 hit. Countries were banding together to provide a global response to a global pandemic.

Yet, in the United States, Donald Trump and Mike Pompeo resisted cooperation, especially where it involved the most vulnerable regions of the planet. Trump's famous reference to "shithole countries" targeted African states, and his disdain for the continent, its fifty-four countries and its 1.4 billion people was on display throughout his presidency. "He opposed international trade agreements, including with African nations, that he viewed as unfair to the United States," explained John Campbell, the Ralph Bunche Senior Fellow for Africa Policy Studies at the Council on Foreign Relations. "He sought to reduce US funding for international organizations upon which Africa depends heavily for aid. And as a part of his administration's shift away from countering violent extremism and toward great-power competition with China and Russia, he proposed reducing the small US military presence in Africa." Campbell said Trump seemed "contemptuous" of Africa, and unlike his two immediate predecessors, he neither traveled to the continent nor engaged personally on policy issues of particular importance to Africa.

Pompeo amplified Trump's infamy, for purposes of partisan loyalty and his own advancement as a potential successor to Trump. Ultimately, a consensus emerged regarding Pompeo's tenure. The headline on Thomas Friedman's column in the *New York Times* read, "Mike Pompeo Is the Worst Secretary of State Ever." The headline on Jackson Diehl's column in the *Washington Post* announced, "Mike Pompeo is the worst secretary of state in history." *Slate* declared, "Worst Secretary of State Ever."

The reviews of Pompeo's tenure at the State Department generally concluded that he finished without a single diplomatic achievement to his name. The case was made for consigning Pompeo to the dustbin of history. Yet we dare not write him off as a bumbler or an unthinking Trump loyalist. Mike Pompeo knew what he was doing. His approach was deliberate and determined. He got the reports. He had access to the best intelligence in the world. He knew that that people were suffering and dying. He saw that a pandemic was spreading across the planet. He could have acted to save thousands of lives, hundreds of thousands of lives, millions of lives, yet he chose instead to wage a

Cold War against the cooperation that was required to beat the pandemic.

This is Mike Pompeo's legacy. At a time when the world was literally crying out for science and solidarity, America's secretary of state chose deadly lies and nationalistic division.

How Betsy DeVos Tried to Leverage a Pandemic to Privatize Public Education

. . . to rush into the secret house of death.
—William Shakespeare, *Antony and Cleopatra*

There could be no debating that Florida had become a pandemic hot spot by early July 2020. The total number of coronavirus cases in the state had surpassed 300,000, while the number of deaths topped 4,500. Things were getting worse at such a rapid rate that the local media could barely keep up with the bad news. "Florida Sets Single-Day Record for Coronavirus Deaths With 132, Adds 9,100 New Cases," announced the NBC affiliate in Miami on July 15. Twenty-four hours later, the *Miami Herald* was reporting, "Florida sees another coronavirus fatality record of 156 as nearly 14,000 new cases added."

But what was especially unsettling to public schoolteachers was the news of what might come next. Echoing messages from the Trump White House, the Republican governor of Florida, Ron DeSantis, began pushing for the reopening of schools across the state with this casual declaration: "We spent months saying that there were certain things that were essential—that included fast food restaurants, it included Walmart, it included Home Depot. If all that is essential, then educating our kids is absolutely essential." This was a typical rhetorical gambit from DeSantis, a career politician who had grabbed the governorship in 2018 with a campaign that dealt in enough racist tropes and crude innuendo to secure him a narrow win. Like Trump, DeSantis never allowed the facts, or concern for public health and safety, to get in the way of exploiting an opening to advance himself politically. And the governor knew that parents were anxious about the coming school year. If he could make himself look like an advocate for getting kids back into the state's classrooms, it might ease concerns about the ways in which his budgets and policies undermined public education.

DeSantis had no plan for getting the return to the classroom right, however. He merely brandished an executive order from Florida Education Commissioner Richard Corcoran, which required schools to reopen and to "provide the full array of services that are required by law so that families who wish to educate their children in a brick-and-mortar school full time have the opportunity to do so."

On July 14, four weeks before the first day of school, Florida Education Association president Fedrick Ingram reported that teachers were terrified. "You know what they're doing right now?" he asked. "With their lesson plans, they're preparing living wills. They're preparing wills to make sure that if anything happens to them, their families are taken care of. That's what's happening right now in the state of Florida with teachers and educational support professionals and cafeteria workers and bus drivers who don't do this for money."

Ingram was not engaging in hyperbole. A law firm in the Tampa Bay region was actually offering free living wills for "teachers involuntarily forced to return to the classroom." Inspired by news reports of three Arizona elementary school teachers who returned to work in June and contracted Covid-19—resulting in the death of sixty-one-year-old educator Kimberley Chavez Lopez Byrd—Gallagher & Associates Law Firm announced, "While we agree with medical experts that it is premature to reopen schools in this Tampa Bay hot zone, we want to do our part to help teachers that are forced to return." Attorney Charles Gallagher explained, "It's not physically possible, with the room they have logistically, to distance and it's not physically possible for them to be apart from other teachers, other kids."

Things were bad in Florida. But this wasn't just a Florida problem. Health care experts were raising alarms nationally. "While children are at less risk for serious illness from coronavirus than adults and often have mild or no symptoms when infected, the teachers and other adult staff in schools face higher risk," reported the Kaiser Family Foundation. "We used a similar approach to look at teachers and other instructors, and we find that one in four teachers (24 percent, or about 1.47 million people), have a condition that puts them at higher risk of serious illness from coronavirus."

Decisions about opening schools are generally made at the state and local level. But in the brave new world of the coronavirus pandemic, the danger of an uneven and ill-thought-out reopening of schools pointed to the need for clear standards and guidance. If ever there was a time when the country needed an experienced and engaged secretary of education to bring not just clarity but an appropriate sense of concern to a dangerous moment, this was it.

In other words, there could not have been a worse time in history for Betsy DeVos to be heading the US Department of

Education. A billionaire campaign donor who had spent decades seeking to subvert public education, DeVos was openly hostile to public school teachers and the unions that represented them—leading the National Education Association to note that as Donald Trump's appointee to the nation's top education post, she had "promoted the privatization of public schools through vouchers, called for deep cuts to federal funding, rolled back protections for vulnerable children and shilled for the for-profit college industry that has defrauded countless students." Not even a pandemic could cause DeVos to show concern for educators whose lives might be endangered. Trump's secretary of education wasn't about to say "no" to Republican governors like DeSantis. To do so would have put her at odds with her political bene-factor's cruel scheme to enhance his own re-election prospects by pressuring schools to reopen at a point when the country was experiencing a Covid-19 surge.

DeVos remained absolutely loyal to the president because he had empowered her to advance the privatization schemes that were her longtime passion. When he no longer empowered her after his defeat in the 2020 election and the January 6 storming of the Capitol by his supporters, she would quit the adminis-tration with a blunt rebuke to Trump on January 8. But while even the slightest prospect of a second Trump term remained, DeVos was more than ready to amplify the president's threats and build upon them, as part of a crudely cynical campaign strategy.

Trump had grown increasingly obsessed during the summer of 2020 with reopening schools—just as he had been obsessed with opening businesses in the spring of the year. The president imagined that doing so would create a sense of normalcy in the midst of the health care crisis he had so thoroughly mismanaged and an economic meltdown that extended from it. Trailing in the polls, Trump was determined to rush children back to school and get workers back to their offices, warehouses and factories in order to foster the fantasy that he had led the country out of the mess he made and now merited a second term. "SCHOOLS MUST OPEN IN THE FALL!!!" screamed Trump's Twitter feed on July 7. "The Dems think it would be bad for them politically if US schools open before the November Election, but is important for the children & families," the president tweeted on July 8. "May cut off funding if not open!"

As usual with Trump's digital pronouncements, his reopen-the-schools ranting was a muddle of misplaced urgency, factual distortions and nonsense. By the time Trump and DeVos came to the debate about reopening schools, Democrats and rational Republicans had for months been struggling to figure out when and how it might be safe to get students and teachers back in their classrooms. So, too, had the unions that represent teachers and advocate for public education. The American Federation of Teachers started developing plans in April 2020 with a recognition, as AFT president Randi Weingarten explained, that reopening schools had to be done safely and thoughtfully. "The fight against the coronavirus is far from over, and the second wave of the 1918 flu was worse than the first," she said. "Absent a vaccine, no one knows what the future will bring. Adhering to public health safeguards is critical."

For the most part, teachers, parents and students were not resistant to reopening. What they were saying was that any reopening had to be done right. What Trump and DeVos were saying was that they did not care if it was done wrong—even if that meant teachers, staffers and students were more likely to be infected, even if they and people they came in contact with might die. When Trump finally turned his attention to education concerns, at a point when schools had been closed for months, the president began by attacking Centers for Disease Control and Prevention guidelines that were essential to a safe and functional reopening of the schools. Then he threatened to withhold resources that are desperately needed to maintain public education—be it in-person or virtual.

Trump and DeVos turned a debate that should have been grounded in science into a political food fight. "Their goal isn't safety, it's politics," an exasperated Weingarten said in mid-July. Weingarten, a former social studies teacher at Clara Barton High School in Crown Heights, Brooklyn, urged students, parents and teachers to listen carefully to what Trump and his education secretary were saying about reopening. "Are they putting the safety of kids or educators first? No," she said. "Do they have a plan to actually reopen schools or resources for it? No."

President Trump's response was to retweet game show host Chuck Woolery's paranoid rants on how "the most outrageous lies are the ones about Covid-19. Everyone is lying. The CDC, Media, Democrats, our Doctors, not all but most, that we are told to trust. I think it's all about the election and keeping the economy from coming back, which is about the election. I'm sick of it."

There was plenty of political sickness in the Trump administration in the summer of 2020, and Betsy DeVos was spreading it. The broken-record critic of public education headed an agency that claimed its mission was to "play a leadership role in the ongoing national dialogue over how to improve the results of our education system for all students." Instead of leading an honest dialogue, however, DeVos was amplifying the anti-scientific claptrap that underpinned Trump's strategy for reopening schools.

CDC guidelines were clear about safe policies for schools: "Lowest Risk: Faculty and students engage in virtual-only learning options, activities, and events. . . . Highest Risk: Full-sized in-person classes, activities, and events. Students are not spaced apart, share classroom materials or supplies, and mix between classes and activities." Yet DeVos disregarded and dismissed these guidelines. "There is nothing in the data that would suggest that kids being back in school is dangerous to them," she claimed. Educators and public health experts who said different, she griped, were just "fearmongering and making excuses."

When confronted with the details of actual outbreaks, DeVos casually suggested that any "little flare-ups or hot spots can be dealt with on a school-by-school or a case-by-case basis." In a July interview with far-right Fox News host Tucker Carlson, DeVos echoed Trump's threats about withholding funds from schools that might fail to start full-time, in-person instruction in September. "We are looking at this very seriously," she said. "This is a very serious issue across the country." She was even more outspoken in another appearance on Fox, when she told Chris Wallace: "American investment and education is a promise to students and their families. If schools aren't going to reopen and not fulfill that promise, they shouldn't get the funds. Then give it to the families to decide to go to a school that is going to meet that promise."

This was DeVos returning to one of her favorite themes: taking money intended for public education and redirecting it to fund private schools. "It's the move toward privatization," said Jamaal Bowman, a public school principal who had recently won a Democratic primary for a US House seat representing the Bronx. "It's driven by market-based ideology and the so-called, quote-unquote 'choice movement.' So when we talk about vouchers and money moving with kids at the whim of the parents, that's what we're talking about. And it's an example of disaster capitalism within the public education sector."

Former secretary of labor Robert Reich was blunt. "Don't let DeVos use the pandemic to privatize education," he said. Representative Ayanna Pressley was even blunter. "You have no plan," the Massachusetts Democrat told DeVos on social media. Pressley spoke to the secretary of education in language that parents across the country well understood: "Teachers, kids and parents are fearing for their lives. You point to a private sector that has put profits over people and claimed the lives of thousands of essential workers. I wouldn't trust you to care for a house plant let alone my child."

Elaine Chao Let Them Die

You murd'ring ministers,
Wherever in your sightless substances
You wait on nature's mischief. Come, thick night,
And pall thee in the dunnest smoke of hell,
That my keen knife see not the wound it makes,
Nor heaven peep through the blanket of the dark,
To cry "Hold, hold!"

—William Shakespeare, *Macbeth*

Scott Ryan identified Covid-19 as a deadly threat when most Americans were still learning how to pronounce "coronavirus." A bus driver in Snohomish County, Washington, north of Seattle, he was worried even before the area was named one of the initial hot spots as the coronavirus pandemic began to sweep across the United States in the late winter of 2020. On February 28, Ryan jumped on an Amalgamated Transit Union Facebook site—he was a union steward—and spelled out the concerns his fellow Community Transit workers had for themselves and for the thousands of passengers they transported each day. "Our buses under 'normal' circumstances are germ tubes on wheels. Now we introduce a disease that zero people have been vaccinated for and has an incubation date of up to fourteen days without showing symptoms," Ryan wrote. "My personal thought? We are high-risk ticking time bombs for being exposed to someone with it."

The next day, Washington state officials reported what at the time was thought to be the first coronavirus-related death in the United States. The Washington governor, Jay Inslee, declared a state of emergency after a patient succumbed to the virus at the EvergreenHealth Medical Center in Kirkland, a community twenty-four miles down Interstate 5 from Everett, where Scott Ryan lived and worked. Fears were rising, but the Community Transit buses kept rolling. Drivers took precautions. "People are bringing their own supplies from home," ATU Local 1576 president Kathleen Custer said. "They're bringing their rubber kitchen gloves." The *Everett Herald* reported that "the union threatened to direct employees to disobey company policy by not collecting fare and only allowing passengers to board through the back door." As worries mounted, one of the drivers in Scott Ryan's unit said, "The only reason people are still going to work is they have to do what they have to do to get food on the table." Ryan, a forty-one-year-old father of three who coached his kids in baseball, wrestling and whatever other sports excited them, was in good health. But his wife, Heather, said, "He was worried about going into work every day."

One morning, in mid-March, Scott Ryan did something that was rare for him. He called in sick. His wife told the *Seattle Times* that within a day, he had a high fever and was experiencing tightness in his chest. Around the same time that President Trump was telling a press conference that the virus was "something we have tremendous control of," Ryan tested positive for Covid-19. The virus was sweeping through the ranks of

Community Transit drivers, as ten reported positive tests and close to a dozen more quarantined at home.

Scott Ryan was struggling to breathe. He started using inhalers. Then he was hospitalized. Several days later, one of his fellow bus drivers, Kyle Moore, was taking Heather Ryan and the couple's daughter to the hospital for a visit with Scott. A call came from the hospital. The message was a jarring one; there was almost no time left. Moore listened as the Ryan family said goodbye, a memory he would never forget. "That's the biggest thing that plays through my mind: Scott and the suffering he went through by himself—alone," he later told *Governing* magazine. "I would just like people to consider that."

Unfortunately, despite pleas from Scott Ryan's union and from unions representing train conductors, flight attendants, pilots and workers employed in the nation's transportation industries, Elaine Chao didn't consider that. As the secretary of transportation, Chao had immense power to respond to the pandemic by establishing rules to protect hundreds of thousands of bus drivers, airline workers and Amtrak employees who desperately needed federal intervention in a time of crisis.

Chao sat in the Cabinet post as the most politically connected of politically connected conservatives; her husband, Mitch McConnell, was the Senate majority leader when she was nominated by Trump for the DOT post and approved by the Senate. Before joining Team Trump, she had served as chair of the Federal Maritime Commission under President Ronald Reagan, deputy secretary of transportation under President George H. W. Bush and secretary of labor under President George W. Bush. She knew her way around transportation policy and worker safety issues as well as anyone in the Trump administration.

Chao well understood that the Department of Transportation had the authority to act to regulate interstate travel and—because it provided so much federal funding and oversight—to force local transit systems to implement public health mandates. Yet she refused throughout 2020 to act with the sense of foresight and urgency that was required to address the danger Scott Ryan identified before Covid-19 ended his life.

Chao failed to anticipate the threat, as Ryan had in February of 2020, and she failed to respond when she was alerted to it during the period in which the pandemic metastasized into a crisis of enormous proportions for public transportation in America.

Transit workers were among the first to recognize the threat. Amalgamated Transit Union members across the United States paused at 7:10 p.m. Eastern time on Friday, March 27, for a moment of silence to honor the memory of Scott Ryan, who was the first ATU member to die. Even as they planned that memorial for Ryan, however, reports were circulating of more deaths. Members of Transport Workers Union of America (TWU) Local 100 in New York City were mourning the passing of conductor Peter Petrassi and bus operator Oliver Cyrus, the first of their union brothers and sisters to succumb to Covid-19.

"In twenty-four hours, we lost two TWU brothers in New York City and an ATU brother in Washington State," ATU president John Costa said. "Transit workers from coast to coast are continuing to get exposed and infected from Covid-19, and agencies and governments need to act now to protect them. You shouldn't send troops into battle without protective armor, and you shouldn't send nurses and bus operators to work without proper personal protective equipment."

Frustrated by the failure of too many cities and too many transit systems to protect workers, the Transport Workers Union and the Amalgamated Transit Union entered into a historic agreement to take "whatever aggressive action is necessary" to "put maximum pressure on transit agencies that are failing to take protective measures to safeguard transit workers, including the provision of masks and gloves." They were mounting a defense not just of their own members but also of passengers who had become increasingly reliant on public transportation in a time of crisis. In a joint statement released in early April, the unions noted: "Hundreds of transit workers in more than twenty states have tested positive for the virus. New York City, where ten transit workers have died, is the national epicenter today, but the virus continues to rapidly spread across the country. Line of duty fatalities among transit workers have also been confirmed in Detroit; New Orleans; Philadelphia; Boston; Washington, DC; Rocky Hill, Connecticut; and Everett, Washington."

"It's just too much," Costa told me on April 3. He recounted the deaths of at least eight members of his own union over the previous week. "We are working in, and [passengers are] being brought to work in, forty-foot Petri dishes with absolutely no protective equipment," he said. Costa was furious at the uneven response from transit agencies to the threat posed by Covid-19. "Some of them are doing the right thing, and some are not," he said. I asked Costa what he meant by "aggressive action." He paused and replied: "We didn't sign up to die on these jobs. My operators are tired; they are scared; some of them are sleeping in their cars because they don't want to get their families sick." Costa said that if transit agencies wouldn't protect the workers, "we can't keep working."

That was a major concern not just for his industry but for the country. The ATU and the TWU represented more than 330,000 bus operators, train operators, conductors, track workers, car cleaners, mechanics and other transit workers in Atlanta, Boston, Chicago, Columbus, Dallas, Detroit, Houston, Miami, Phil-adelphia, San Francisco, the District of Columbia and dozens of other communities. Their members were the frontline workers who kept cities moving in times of crisis, getting doctors and nurses to work and patients to clinics and hospitals, and making it possible for delivery drivers, grocery store clerks and other essential workers to do their jobs. TWU president John Samuelsen declared, "We will not sit back and let transit workers be treated like cannon fodder in this war against the coronavirus."

The unions were sounding the alarm, crying out for action to save lives, telling anyone who would listen that dying is no way to make a living. They needed local and state officials to step up, and some did. In May, the *Washington Post* reported, "The Metropolitan Atlanta Rapid Transit Authority, relying on the money it received as part of the $2 trillion federal bailout package, distributed a one-time $500 'hero' bonus to more than 3,500 of its workers." The authority passed out surgical masks, gloves and sanitizing wipes, gave drivers seventy-five-dollar stipends to spend on supplies, provided an extra eighty hours of sick leave for employees infected by Covid-19, and arranged for free testing and counseling to deal with stress.

But for every encouraging story from Atlanta, Detroit or Washington, DC, there was bad news from another city. "In Florida's Miami–Dade County," noted the *Post*, "frustrated and angry transit workers have sued over a lack of protective equipment and challenged Transit Director Alice Bravo to ride the bus so she can see firsthand the lack of social distancing, sanitizer and adequate face masks for drivers. Their battle cry on social media: #RideNotDie."

What transportation workers needed most of all was a coherent and coordinated response that came from the top. On April 16, 2020, a group of leading scientists and medical professionals— including Jeremy Howard, a distinguished research scientist at the University of San Francisco, who had emerged as one of the leading experts on "flattening the curve" of the pandemic, and Dr. Anne W. Rimoin, a professor of epidemiology at the UCLA Fielding School of Public Health and Infectious Disease Division of the Geffen School of Medicine—joined the TWU's John Samuelsen in dispatching an emergency letter urging Chao to "require masks for all passengers and workers using the airline, public transit and passenger rail systems" in the United States. "The science is clear," they wrote. "People with Covid-19 are most infectious in the early part of the malady. During that time, many of them have no or few symptoms. Infected individuals are using public transit and passenger rail to go to work; they fly on airplanes; and they travel in their community to buy essentials. They spread the virus without even knowing it. As a result, transportation passengers and workers are at very high risk of contracting this dangerous illness. Our team of scientists and medical experts are willing to brief you on why it is essential to change policies immediately to stop the spread. The medical team is widely respected in their fields of expertise. . . . We must work together to save lives," Samuelsen and the scientists concluded. "We urge you to act now."

Less than ten days later, Sara Nelson, the president of the Association of Flight Attendants CWA, a union with 50,000 members flying for twenty major airlines, sent an equally urgent letter to Chao and Health and Human Services Secretary Alex Azar. "Since the initial outbreak of Covid-19 in China, flight attendants have been on the front lines of the growing global pandemic that has now infected more than 2.5M persons worldwide and contributed to over 175K hospital deaths, according to the Johns Hopkins University Coronavirus Resource Center," wrote the union leader. "Flight attendants have been hard hit by the virus. At airlines employing AFA member flight attendants, at least 250 have tested positive for the coronavirus that causes

Covid-19, and flight attendants have died as a result of the virus, too. The scars run deep; recent media reports document the guilt felt by those who question if we are helping to spread the virus, feelings of fear and grief as co-workers die, and wonder about when this will all be over."

Nelson explained what Chao should have already recognized. "Flight attendants are aviation's first responders, required by federal regulations to help ensure the safety, health and security of our globally interconnected aviation system," she wrote. "While this global system is integral to our modern economy, its essential interconnectedness also provides a convenient pathway for opportunistic pathogens to hitch rides on unsuspecting crewmembers and travelers and spread all over the world. As some of the most frequent travelers, flight attendants feel a deep responsibility to ensure that our workplace risks of acquiring and spreading communicable diseases are minimized as much as possible." To that end, Nelson urged the Department of Transportation, in coordination with the Department of Health and Human Services and other oversight agencies, "to use its authority to mandate masks in aviation for crew, employees and passengers; require personal protective equipment; and end all leisure travel until the virus is contained."

When she did not get a response, Nelson took to social media, posting images of crowded planes and maskless passengers. "ENOUGH!" she declared in a typical message. "This was TODAY on a four-hour flight. This is not okay. Masks must be mandated by DOT/HHS in airports and on airplanes. Essential travel only, with proper PPE. #Covid19#StopTheSpread." A few weeks later, her message was reduced to just five words: "We are dying for leadership."

Chao failed to provide that leadership, even as she heard from members of Congress. Peter DeFazio, Oregon Democrat and chair of the House Committee on Transportation and Infrastructure, began sending urgent warnings to Chao in late February 2020. His messages noted that the secretary and her aides had not implemented a 2015 recommendation from the Government Accountability Office for development of an aviation industry pandemic preparedness plan. "The Ebola outbreak of 2014 should have been a wakeup call for the Department of Transportation, in collaboration with airline and airport partners and other Federal departments and agencies, to develop a plan to limit the spread of pandemics through aviation system," wrote DeFazio and Representative Rick Larsen, the Washington Democrat who chaired the subcommittee on aviation, in a February 26 letter to Chao. "According to the GAO, the Department has not implemented this recommendation, and the Department's failure to do so is a reflection of a broader lack of preparedness for the arrival of a pandemic on our shores. We must not let a laissez-faire attitude toward public health endanger the welfare of people across the country."

Months later, on June 23, Heather Krause, the director of physical infrastructure issues for the GAO, testified before the House Subcommittee on Space and Aeronautics about the Department of Transportation's lack of a pandemic preparedness plan—yet Chao still refused to act. Several days later, the GAO recommended that "in the absence of efforts to develop a plan, we urge Congress to take legislative action to require the Secretary of Transportation to work with relevant agencies and stakeholders, such as the Departments of Health and Human Services and Homeland Security, and members of the aviation and public health sectors, to develop a national aviation-preparedness plan to ensure safeguards are in place to limit the spread of communicable disease threats."

There was no question that Chao had the authority to implement the plan, and to do much more than that to protect workers and passengers. The GAO's Krause told members of Congress at the June subcommittee session, "We continue to believe that DOT would be in the best position to lead . . . such a broad effort [involving] airlines, airports and other aviation stakeholders." Noting this assessment, Larry Willis, president of the AFL-CIO's Transportation Trades Department, sent an urgent letter to the Department of Transportation in July in support of "the Government Accountability Office's statement, and [we] believe that DOT is the appropriate body to implement a passenger mask mandate."

Nor was there any question that action was needed. Writing as the national death toll was surpassing 150,000, Willis, the head of a coalition of thirty-three unions ranging from the Air Line Pilots Association to the Brotherhood of Railroad Signalmen to the Marine Engineers Beneficial Association to the National Air Traffic Controllers Association to the Sailors Union of the Pacific to the Amalgamated Transit Union and the Transport Workers Union of America, noted that despite the DOT's inaction

thousands of workers in the passenger transportation industry have continued to go to work on planes, buses, ferries and trains in increasingly dangerous conditions. Regrettably, these employees have not been spared the effects of the disease, and each TTD union involved in passenger transportation has reported infections and deaths among their frontline workers. While these bus drivers, pilots, flight attendants, train crews, ferry operators and others are faced with an impossible choice every day between risking their health and losing their livelihood, we acknowledge that the irreplaceable services they provide must continue to keep the US economy running. Unfortunately, efforts to protect these employees from inherently hazardous workplaces and the threat of deadly communicable disease have been limited to a patchwork of state or local mandates, and a deeply inadequate federal response consisting of non-mandatory guidance.

Despite prodding from oversight agencies and members of Congress, despite the pleas from unions and their members, Chao maintained the laissez-faire attitude that so vexed DeFazio and Larsen. Chao was more than ready to engage in self-promotion, making a big deal about the fact that the DOT was distributing masks that could be used by workers and passengers on planes, trains and buses. But when it came to actually taking action, Chao recycled Reagan–era complaints about government being the problem. "When the federal government gets involved, we tend to be much more heavy-handed," she told *Politico*. The best that anyone could get out of her was the classic bureaucrat's dodge: a promise to "monitor" the crisis.

The union leaders I kept checking in with said the crisis had moved far beyond the monitoring stage. It was time to act. Yet Chao never shared their sense of urgency, or dread. While broadcast and cable television reports in the first months of the pandemic focused on the news from hospitals, where doctors and nurses and other frontline workers were risking their lives to fight Covid-19, there was only sporadic attention to the condition of transportation workers. Their unions kept track of the rates of infection and deaths. Facebook groups and hotlines were overwhelmed with reports of an emerging crisis. Clippings from daily and weekly newspapers across the country provided a grim reminder that transit systems were burying their own at a heartbreaking rate.

If Elaine Chao really was monitoring the crisis, she would have seen the pattern in the headlines from local papers and news sites:

DETROIT: "Bus Driver Dies of Covid-19 After Calling Out Coughing Rider"

CHICAGO: "Bus driver becomes 2nd CTA employee to die of coronavirus"

SAN ANTONIO: "VIA bus driver of nearly 30 years tragically passes away from Covid-19"

HONOLULU: "Driver for TheBus Dies Due to Covid-19"

LONG ISLAND: "Family speaks out after loss of MTA bus driver to Covid-19"

PHILADELPHIA: "SEPTA Bus Driver Dies From Coronavirus"

LOS ANGELES: "A second L.A. Metro bus driver has died of complications from Covid-19"

MIAMI: "Miami–Dade Bus Driver Dies From Coronavirus"

TEXAS: "CapMetro Bus Driver Dies of Coronavirus in Austin"

SOUTH CAROLINA: "Horry County Schools bus driver dies from the coronavirus"

MISSOURI: "Family says Francis Howell school bus driver who died from Covid-19 was told he had sinus infection"

NEW JERSEY: "Beloved Fair Lawn Bus Driver Dies of Coronavirus"

NEW YORK: "MTA workers dying from coronavirus at triple the rate of agencies that employ NYC first responders"

New York's Metropolitan Transit Authority was the hottest of the hot spots. The *Times* reported: "On March 24, MTA officials said fifty-two transit workers had been infected. A week later, the number jumped to 333, with seven workers dead. The true number of sick workers was most likely higher than official counts, but the authority was having trouble keeping track. The MTA had set up a hotline for workers to report positive test results and to receive guidance on whether they should self-quarantine. But it was so overwhelmed—with 7,000 to

8,000 calls per day—that it took some workers days to get through."

The Covid-19 death toll in New York City was mounting so rapidly that one bus driver, Danny Cruz, began to worry that people would lose sight of the human beings whose lives were being lost day after day, week after week, month after month. In early April, after the death of Oliver Cyrus, a fellow driver at his depot, Cruz tested positive. He survived, returned to work and started maintaining a Facebook list of the New York City transit workers who had died. "Every morning I wake up and one of the hardest things I have to do is to try to keep this updated," he wrote on his Facebook page on April 7. "Every time I have to add a name, my heart loses a beat." He asked: "Why is this happening? Why were we not better prepared? How many more members will we have to lose?"

At that point, there were forty-one names on the list. By mid-May, that number would reach 129.

In early May, Sujatha Gidla, an MTA conductor and author, wrote an article for the *New York Times*. "We work at the epicenter of the epicenter, with a mortality rate substantially higher than that of first responders," she noted. "Common sense tells you that subway trains and platforms are giant vectors of this virus. We breathe it in along with steel dust. As a conductor, when I stick my head out of the car to perform the required platform observation, passengers in many stations are standing ten inches from my face. At other times, they lean into the cab to ask questions. Bus drivers, whose passengers enter right in front of them, are even worse off."

Gidla's piece read like a horror story: "When I heard that a co-worker had died from Covid-19—the first in the Metropolitan Transportation Authority—on March 27, I thought, 'It's starting.' More deaths followed in quick succession, frequently more than once a day. Some of those people I used to see every day and fist bump . . . On Facebook, when bad news comes, my co-workers and I express grief and offer condolences to the families. But our spontaneous response is the numb curiosity of an onlooker. We knew this was coming. We knew many among us wouldn't make it through the pandemic."

The article also read as an indictment: "The conditions created by the pandemic drive home the fact that we essential workers—workers in general—are the ones who keep the social order from sinking into chaos. Yet we are treated with the utmost disrespect, as though we're expendable . . . Since March 27, at least ninety-eight New York transit workers have died of Covid-19. My co-workers say bitterly: 'We are not essential. We are sacrificial.'"

Throughout 2020, cries for action mounted. Yet, Chao remained aloof. "Secretary Chao's department—and every other federal agency—is not mandating masks as other countries have done," *Forbes* reported in June. "A passenger was fined €300 for not wearing a mask on a flight to Amsterdam. Masks have to be worn on a subway, bus, taxi or aircraft in South Korea under a law introduced last month. China advises on a route-by-route basis if flight crew should wear a standard surgical mask or N95, and after how many hours they should put on a new covering."

Forbes explained on June 17 that "Secretary Chao is openly wiping her hands of a mask requirement." That got the attention of Chao's publicity-conscious office. The next day, the magazine attached a notice that a Department of Transportation spokesperson had called to "dispute" that characterization. Yet, Chao's own words were damning. "It was originally suggested that the federal government mandate the use of masks," she said. "I think it is better to be resolved between parties of mutual concern." In other words, she would do nothing.

Chao's apologists said she did not want to ruffle Trump's feathers. But she was one of the most experienced and politically connected members of his administration. If anyone could have acted, it was her. And if she really was barred from acting, she could have resigned—as she eventually would in response to Trump's incitement of the January 6 attack on the Capitol—and used her exit statement to highlight the need for action. Unfortunately, when the lives of bus drivers and train conductors and flight attendants were at stake, the transportation secretary refused to use her authority or her bully pulpit to provide the protection that workers and their unions were demanding.

Spring gave way to summer, summer to fall. The death toll passed 100,000, then 200,000, then 300,000. Bus drivers and subway conductors and flight attendants kept getting sick, kept dying. The unions pleaded with employers for action to protect workers and passengers. Sometimes it came, sometimes it did not. So they kept pleading with Chao to put an end to the confusion with national orders. The unions formally petitioned the DOT early in the summer, asking that the agency "promulgate a regulation mandating that passengers traveling with DOT–regulated commercial transportation providers wear masks or face coverings." Months passed; the reply finally came in October. The petition was rejected. Chao's agency declared that "the concerns identified in the petition" were being adequately addressed "without the intention of a rule-making process."

Repeating the deregulatory dogma Chao had been spouting since her days in the Reagan administration, the letter reminded the petitioners that "the Department also embraces the notion that there should be no more regulations than necessary. We emphasize consideration of or regulatory solutions and have rigorous processes in place for optimal reassessment of existing regulations to ensure they remain cost justified and narrowly tailored to address an identified market failure."

The bureaucratic language was shocking at a point when countries around the world were tightening their regulations, and when the United States was experiencing a pandemic surge so severe that the virus was ravaging the White House itself. "On Friday evening—the same day that President Trump, the First Lady, and at least three US senators all tested positive for the novel Coronavirus—the US Department of Transportation (DOT) rejected a petition by the Transportation Trades Department, AFL-CIO (TTD) and our thirty-three member unions, for an emergency order requiring masks on all forms of commercial public transportation," read a statement from the labor coalition.

TTD president Larry Willis made no effort to hide his frustration. "Already, tens of thousands of frontline transportation workers—our members—have become ill or perished due to Covid-19 exposure," he said. "A federal commercial passenger and public transportation mask mandate would have offered an additional layer of protection not only for these workers, but the passengers they serve. In too many cases, those passengers are other essential workers just trying to get to their jobs on the front lines of the pandemic, or working families on their way to get groceries, medical appointments or check in with loved ones."

Willis's ire mounted: "It is unfathomable that in the midst of a global pandemic which has killed more than 209,000 Americans and left millions more sick and potentially facing lifelong side effects—including the president of the United States—that the US Department of Transportation would outright reject such a simple, science-backed, life-saving measure. The DOT's decision is heartbreaking, and in light of yesterday's news, frankly, shocking . . . Since Covid-19 first touched American shores, the president and his administration have shown callous disregard for human life in response to this virus. Failure by this DOT to issue a commonsense federal mask mandate for all modes of commercial passenger transportation is only a continuation of that failed response. Sadly, it is working people who will suffer because of this decision."

More workers got sick, and more died. In late November, the flight attendants union reported that it was seeing an average of fifty positive tests for Covid-19 tests each week—a five-fold increase from the rate during the summer surge. In December, the week before Christmas, the Amalgamated Transit Union mourned the death of its 100th member from the virus.

When Elaine Chao took charge of the Department of Transportation at the beginning of Donald Trump's presidency, she embraced a mission statement that said the agency was determined "to ensure America has the safest, most efficient and modern transportation system in the world, which boosts our economic productivity and global competitiveness and enhances the quality of life in communities both rural and urban." Safety came first in that statement. Yet Chao never put safety first. She put her Republican partisanship, her conservative ideology and her deregulatory dogma ahead of bus drivers and conductors like Scott Ryan, Peter Petrassi and Oliver Cyrus, and the hundreds of others who died on her watch.

Chao quit her post a few days before Trump's tenure ended, scrambling off the sinking ship after the January 6 attack on the Capitol, where her husband served, had been incited by the president she served. Chao was undoubtedly hoping to preserve her viability for a place in the next Republican administration. While elected officials are sometimes punished for their failures, Chao knew that for presidential appointees, accountability is rare. Indeed, her own experience told her that even a record of missteps and misdeeds was not necessarily disqualifying in the eyes of Republican presidents seeking to fill Cabinet posts.

But the speed with which a Democratic president moved to clean up the mess Chao had made of things served as an indictment of her inaction. On the day after he was sworn in as president, Joe Biden used an executive order to issue a sweeping mask mandate that applied to buses, ferries, trains, airports and planes. Federal agencies leapt into action even before the nomination of Chao's replacement, former South Bend, Indiana, mayor and 2020 presidential candidate Pete Buttigieg, was confirmed by the Senate. All the parts of the Department of Transportation began to move: the Transportation Security Administration, the Federal Aviation Administration, the Federal Railroad Administration, the Federal Motor Carrier Safety Administration, and the Federal Transit Administration went to work. Over the course of Biden's first week, the Department of Homeland Security announced that Transportation Security Administration workers would enforce mask mandates "at TSA screening checkpoints and throughout the commercial and public transportation system."

"What a difference leadership makes!" rejoiced Sara Nelson, of the flight attendants union. "The Biden Administration is demonstrating in their first days that combatting Covid-19 is the priority and essential to our health and economic stability. We look forward to working with the President and his administration on a fulsome plan to address Covid health and safety in aviation including masks, testing, contact tracing, limit contact in onboard service, robust cleaning procedures and more." At the end of her statement, Nelson attached a copy of the letter she had written nine months earlier to Elaine Chao.

The failure of Chao's Department of Transportation remained a life-and-death concern to the very end of her tenure. John

Samuelsen, the president of the Transport Workers Union, was not about to forgive and forget. "It's about damn time our government lived up to its obligations to public health," he said after Biden issued the mask-mandate order. "This action, taken on day one of President Biden's leadership, is a stark contrast to the failures of the past administration . . . There has never been any doubt that masks save lives. Throughout the pandemic, the TWU has seen this up close. Our members have risked their lives for the past year to keep America moving—often without appropriate personal protective equipment to keep them safe while doing this essential work. As a result, over 10 percent of our membership has died, tested positive for or quarantined after exposure to Covid-19."

That was just one measure of the grim legacy of Elaine Chao's deliberate refusal to protect the workers in the industries she was charged with regulating. It is easy for those in power to forget the men and women who died on the front lines, and easier still to neglect the reality that many of those deaths might have been prevented. But in New York City, a few days after Chao departed her latest sinecure in a Republican administration, subway riders got a reminder of the cost of official inaction.

On a cold morning in January, at 107 of the city's 472 subway stops, an eight-minute memorial video began showing. It featured the names, photos and job titles of 130 subway, bus and paratransit workers who had died from the coronavirus: train operators like Stanley Fong, station agents like Rhonda Garvin, conductors like Peter Petrassi, dispatchers like Lalu Pratap Jose, coach cleaners like Cathiea Thornton-Pope. Somber piano music played as Bengali, Chinese, Haitian Creole, Korean, Russian and Spanish translations of a poem by former US poet laureate Tracy K. Smith, "Travels Far," flashed on screens in the stations:

What you gave—
brief tokens of regard,
soft words uttered
barely heard,
the smile glimpsed
from a passing car.

Through stations
and years, through
the veined chambers
of a stranger's heart—
what you gave
travels far.

8

Mitch McConnell's Fatal Bargain

When extraordinary power and extraordinary pay are allotted
to any individual in a government, he becomes the center, round
which every kind of corruption generates and forms.
—Thomas Paine, *Rights of Man, Part I*, 1791

On May 15, 2020, two months into a pandemic that had destabilized the United States medically and economically, the House
of Representatives approved the Health and Economic Recovery
Omnibus Emergency Solutions (Heroes) Act. The US death toll,
which had just surpassed 86,000, was being described in media
reports as "appalling," horrifying," "overwhelming." It was clear
that action had to be taken. Since the enactment in late March of
the bipartisan Coronavirus Aid, Relief and Economic Security
(Cares) Act, new vulnerabilities had been exposed, new needs
had been revealed. The Heroes Act filled the void created by the
chaotic and unfocused initial response of legislators to a crisis they
were scrambling to keep up with. With its comprehensive approach,
this legislation was developed to address urgent demands for more
health care for those who had fallen ill and would be sickened by

the virus, for research into vaccines and for a social safety net to catch the millions of Americans who were falling through the cracks as factories ground to a halt, small businesses shut their doors and farmers struggled to stay on the land.

The Heroes Act was costly, with a $3 trillion price tag. But the Congress had already accepted that a lot of money was going to have to be spent to keep the country functioning—the House and Senate had approved the $2.2 trillion Cares Act with almost no debate—and serious members of the House acknowledged the urgency of new action. With its "strategic plan for testing, tracing, treating and isolating," House Speaker Nancy Pelosi said, "It's what this country needs to defeat the Covid-19 virus." Peter King, a New York Republican congressman who represented Long Island, voted with Democrats to pass the measure. "I can be as much a red state person as anyone," he said. "But now we're talking about survival. And this is no place for politics."

King didn't agree with everything in the Heroes Act, but he figured the Republican-controlled Senate would sort things out in negotiations between the two chambers. Pelosi was thinking the same way. "We're putting our offer on the table, we're open to negotiation," she said. "It is important to note that more than 80 percent of the priorities in the Heroes Act have been supported by the Republicans in the four previous Covid-19 acts of Congress." Senate Minority Leader Chuck Schumer said, "I am optimistic we can get something done." After all, the Heroes Act included $915 billion in vital funding for state and local governments that had been stretched to the breaking point in regions hard hit by the virus—including Senate Majority Leader Mitch McConnell's home state of Kentucky, where the Louisville *Courier-Journal* reported in mid-May that "Louisville alone faces a $115 million shortfall, and city leaders have warned of horrific cuts in services if further assistance isn't provided."

Louisville had been experiencing an economic boom, but the virus stamped it out, noted Representative John Yarmuth, the Kentucky Democrat who chaired the House Budget Committee. Indeed, not just Louisville but the whole state of Kentucky was hurting. "We have 700,000-plus unemployed right now; the state treasury is being destroyed," Yarmuth said. "Every community can make the same case."

Surely McConnell, the grand old man of Kentucky politics, who had begun his electoral career decades earlier as the top official in the Louisville region's Jefferson County, would want to find a way to get that money to the front lines. Right? Wrong. The message from McConnell and his closest Senate allies was that the Heroes Act was "dead on arrival." Even as the virus was still spreading, even as frontline workers were risking their lives on a daily basis, even as unemployment was spiking and families were fretting about hunger and homelessness, even as McConnell acknowledged with regard to the crisis that "clearly it is not over," the majority leader announced that it was time for a "pause" in congressional action. He refused to cooperate, refused to negotiate, refused to even consider the plan to fund the fight against the pandemic. "This is a totally unserious effort," McConnell proclaimed when asked about the House measure. He went to the Senate floor and aimed a shot explicitly at Pelosi. "This week," he said, "the Speaker published an 1,800-page seasonal catalog of left-wing oddities and called it a coronavirus relief bill."

But what about that word "pause"? Didn't it suggest McConnell was open to negotiation? Indeed it did. It quickly emerged that the majority leader was blocking debate on the Heroes Act as a bargaining strategy. Mitch had a very specific demand. Hospitals, states and cities would not receive needed aid, essential workers would not get any more protection, small businesses would not get a boost, unemployed workers would not get a hand until Congress approved and the states implemented liability shields for multinational corporations that allowed workers and consumers to get sick and die. "Let me make it perfectly clear," McConnell announced, "the Senate is not interested in passing a bill that does not have liability protection."

Schumer said he was shocked. "What alternative universe is he in?" the Democrat asked. The universe McConnell lived in during the pandemic crisis, it turned out, was the same one in which he had always lived: that of the "donor class" of billionaire campaign contributors and corporate CEO's who funded his campaigns and those of the Republican senators who empowered him. A classic PolitiFact assessment of an opponent's charge that McConnell was the top recipient of special-interest campaign contributions from lobbyists determined that the Kentuckian

isn't just the top congressional recipient of donations from lobbyists. According to his Open Secrets profile, he has received more money than any other lawmaker since 2013 from a number of industries. He's number one in campaign donations from people who work in the fields of—deep breath here—agriculture services, air transportation, auto dealers and manufacturers, building materials, business associations, coal mining, commercial banks, commercial TV and radio stations, electric utilities, food and beverage, food stores, general contractors, health services, home builders, insurance, medical devices and supplies, mining, mortgage bankers and brokers, pharmaceutical and health products, railroads, retirees, steel production and trucking.

In the fall of 2020, as he was bidding for his seventh term, Market Watch reported that "Senate Majority Leader Mitch

McConnell ranks as a favorite among the CEO's of S&P 500 companies, as the bosses have combined to give more money to the powerful Republican lawmaker's campaign than to any other candidate engaged in a competitive 2020 Senate race." Slathered in tens of millions of dollars in direct donations from CEO's and industry-tied political action committee contributions for his own campaigns and for those of the Republican Senate candidates whose victories were necessary to retain his majority leadership, McConnell wasn't about to reject demands for corporate liability shields. Faced with a choice between the health and safety of Americans and the bottom lines of the very industries that made him the most powerful man in Congress, McConnell chose his side.

From the beginning of the pandemic, the cunning majority leader was always on the watch for ways in which to exploit the crisis to the benefit of his donors. Even as he allowed relief packages to be voted on in March of 2020, he made demands that emergency legislation be crafted with an eye toward benefiting the economic elites that formed his real constituency. Now, it was time to go big. What the billionaires and the CEO's were demanding at the time the Heroes Act came up for consideration was protection against legal accountability for corporations that failed to protect workers and consumers, failures that literally let them get sick and die during the pandemic. "My red line going forward on this bill is we need to provide protection, litigation protection, for those who have been on the front lines," McConnell trumpeted in an April 27 Fox News interview. "We can't pass another bill unless we have liability protection."

McConnell had his marching orders from the US Chamber of Commerce and the industry lobbying shops on K Street. They wanted liability shields. This was nothing new. Big businesses always wanted a liability shield. What was different was that, with the arrival of the pandemic, they wanted to employ a "disaster capitalism" strategy to get what in less urgent times would have been deemed entirely unacceptable.

It is important to recognize that a liability shield was what the corporations *wanted*, not what they *needed*. While advocacy by McConnell and others for a liability shield was often framed around arguments that it was necessary to provide health care in a pandemic moment, veteran consumer activist Ralph Nader and a group of lawyers, law professors and activists noted in an April letter to President Trump and members of Congress that this was not the case. Warning of "the pernicious effort by corporate lobbyists, insurance companies and other special interest groups to put our fellow citizens at risk, and press for legislative immunity to escape liability for preventable harms causing injury or death," they explained that the push for liability shields was a transparent attempt to exploit the crisis. "There has still been a widespread effort to immunize harmful conduct by institutions and personnel from liability for casualties caused in 'good faith,'" wrote the experts. "This is bad law, and bad precedent, with risks far beyond the current pandemic . . . Immunity from liability is a legal contagion. Special interest groups often raise pleas for immunity from liability for injuring, even killing people. And more often than not, those pleas are a pretext to obscure or conceal serious wrongdoing; and to escape liability for harming, maiming, even killing people."

This was the truth, but Mitch McConnell rejected it. His campaign donors provided him with enough money to spin his own "truth." So he followed the marching orders from those donors through the remainder of the spring, summer and fall, all the way into the long dark winter of 2020. Month after month, as the pandemic took more and more lives, as the economic crisis devastated more and more families, McConnell kept saying that he could not respond to the needs of 330 million Americans until the demands of a few corporate CEOs were met.

By the summer of 2020, as coronavirus death tolls were hitting new daily records, Donald Trump signaled that he was prepared to sign a relief package that did not include a provision for liability shields. It had become painfully clear, even to the crisis-denying president, that the United States desperately needed a multitrillion-dollar intervention to provide the resources to fight a surging pandemic, provide for the unemployed and underemployed, keep small businesses and small farms afloat, fund state and local governments and schools and organize and implement the distribution of the vaccines vital to ending the crisis.

Trump wasn't being humane, of course—he was being tactical. Faced with a re-election fight that was looking increasingly difficult, he was not about to risk everything in order to secure a massive corporate bailout that allowed the wealthiest and most powerful businesses in the country to avoid liability for actions that sickened and killed Americans. When reporters asked White House spokeswoman Kayleigh McEnany on July 31 about the liability shield fight, she replied: "That's a question for Mitch McConnell . . . that's his priority. This president is very keenly focused on unemployment insurance."

Even after McEnany signaled that Trump was throwing McConnell under the bus, however, the majority leader refused to move. "We're not negotiating over liability protection," McConnell told CNBC. "We're not negotiating with Democrats over that."

McConnell became a broken record on the issue.

> No liability shield, no relief.
> No liability shield, no relief.
> No liability shield, no relief.

"The way you make a law is it has to pass the House and the Senate," he grumbled. "What I'm saying is we have a red line on liability. It won't pass the Senate without it." As McConnell dug in, he got more specific. He wasn't just talking about a federal shield. He was demanding that any federal relief for cities and states that had spent down their treasuries to keep ahead of the pandemic be conditioned upon the adopting of statutes letting corporations off the hook. "You have to carefully craft the liability protection to deal with the money that would be supplied to state and local governments," he specified, "conditioned upon them enacting at the state level the kind of legislation that would provide liability protection for those that are seeking to go forward and get the economy back to work."

In July, Senate Republicans codified McConnell's demands, proposing the Safeguarding America's Frontline Employees To Offer Work Opportunities Required to Kickstart the Economy Act, or "Safe to Work" Act, which sought to create immunity from personal injury lawsuits and federal enforcement actions for Covid-19–related exposures. Leaving nothing to chance, the measure proposed to shield corporations retroactively—back to December 2019—and to extend this protection against accountability five years into the future.

Unions and public interest groups had already warned that this was a very bad idea. "There are more than 50,000 dead Americans and counting and our economy is at a standstill, yet Leader McConnell and the US Chamber of Commerce want to give immunity to corporations that harm consumers and workers by not taking precautions against Covid-19," said Linda Lipsen, head of the American Association for Justice. Mary Kay Henry, president of the Service Employees International Union, fumed, "It's absolutely outrageous that employers and corporations are trying to shirk their legal responsibility at the same time they're refusing to provide protective equipment and paid sick days to their workers."

Advocates for taxpayers were just as concerned. "As much as Senator McConnell says otherwise, the immunity fight is a red herring," explained Steve Ellis, president of Taxpayers for Common Sense, a nonpartisan budget watchdog group. "Legal immunity will not heal the economy . . . The last thing millions of unemployed Americans need as they continue to recover from the devastating financial impacts of this pandemic is to pay the cost of businesses' mistakes."

Despite these warnings, and despite the stark evidence of irresponsibility on the part of US corporations since the pandemic hit, it took until December to get McConnell to move. By then, the wealthiest and most powerful nation in the world had the highest death rate in the world. Dr. Anthony Fauci told the American people, "When you're dealing with a baseline of 200,000 new cases a day and about 2,000 deaths per day, with the hospitalizations over 120,000, we are really at a very critical point."

But McConnell's move was on his own terms. Desperate to address the spiking caseloads and death tolls, some Democrats started to talk about going along with the grim reaper's ghoulish scheme for insulating irresponsible CEO's from accountability— a "Covid Emergency Relief Framework" scheme was proposed by corporate-aligned centrist Democrats and their Republican allies. It bowed to McConnell. A one-page outline of the plan circulated among members of Congress in early December, with approving nods from Democratic and Republican leaders, included among its proposals: "Provide short-term federal protection from coronavirus-related lawsuits with the purpose of giving states time to develop their own response."

That was precisely the sort of vague language that had been used in the past to take advantage of crisis moments to benefit the bottom lines of multinational corporations. Public interest groups fretted that if McConnell were given this opening, he would use it to write a big-business wish list into the Covid package that Congress was now rushing to approve before the holidays. Public Citizen warned that McConnell's agenda "to immunize businesses from liability" featured "provisions shielding employers from a range of workplace laws—including laws addressing discrimination, fair wages and occupational health and safety."

What seemed like a scene from Naomi Klein's *The Shock Doctrine* was playing out in plain sight, as corporations and their congressional benefactors exploited a pandemic to eliminate basic protections for workers and consumers. But if centrist Democrats were willing to compromise with McConnell, grass-roots activists and progressive groups were not. Public Citizen led the charge by asking and answering the questions that too many in the media neglected. "How would exempting employers from complying with the Occupational Safety and Health Act, the Fair Labor Standards Act, Title VII of the 1964 Civil Rights Act, the Americans with Disabilities Act, the Age Discrimination in Employment Act, the Worker Adjustment and Retraining Notification Act and the Genetic Information Nondiscrimination Act help to end the pandemic?" asked the group. "What does any of this have to do with restoring the economy? Nothing at all."

The awful truth of why corporations wanted the shield was summed up by the Reverend William J. Barber II, the North Carolina pastor and co-chair of the Poor People's Campaign. "This new proposal, if you go to the bottom," he said, "is pushing for a liability shield for businesses to protect themselves from lawsuits from poor/low-wealth workers if they get Covid because the business did not protect them. That's criminal."

The outcry gathered force. Members of Congress began to speak up and say they would not support a plan that included a liability shield. At a critical moment in the negotiations, Bernie Sanders, the Senate's leading progressive, announced that he would not support the relief package as proposed by its co-sponsors, Joe Manchin of West Virginia, the most conservative Senate Democrat, and Utah Republican Mitt Romney.

"Unfortunately, despite longtime Democratic opposition, this proposal provides 100 percent legal immunity to corporations whose irresponsibility has led to the deaths of hundreds of workers," thundered Sanders. "It would continue to provide a get-out-of-jail-free card to companies that put the lives of their workers and customers at risk. In fact, the Manchin–Romney proposal will, through this liability provision, encourage corporations to avoid implementing the commonsense safety standards needed to protect workers and consumers—and make a bad situation worse."

Sanders had other objections to the plan proposed by Manchin and Romney, noting in mid-December that "at a time when the Covid crisis is the worst that it has ever been in the US, with record-breaking levels of hospitalization and death, the Manchin–Romney proposal not only provides no direct payments to working families, it does nothing to address the health care crisis and has totally inadequate financial assistance for the most vulnerable."

McConnell, the wiliest and most relentless of legislators, rarely got caught out. This time, however, he had miscalculated. He let the ball get rolling on negotiations that he had delayed for the better part of a year. The Kentuckian imagined that he could manage the process. But he was outmaneuvered by Sanders, who joined an archconservative Republican, Senator Josh Hawley of Missouri, to propose adding $2,000 direct payments to the plan—an idea President Trump started tweeting enthusiastically about. In Georgia, where runoff elections were about to be held for a pair of seats that would determine control of the Senate, the demand for action was rising, as Democratic candidates Rev. Raphael Warnock and Jon Ossoff made an issue of the need for relief and, in particular, the direct-payment proposal. McConnell's grip on the negotiating process was slipping, and his ability to deliver the liability shield that he had "guaranteed" was slipping along with it.

On December 21, 2020, the Senate joined the House in approving a $900 billion aid package that did *not* include McConnell's protection for corporations. Public Citizen and their allies had succeeded in exposing a Shock Doctrine scheme and upending it.

So there's a happy ending, right?

Not exactly. It is true that McConnell and his benefactors got beaten in the liability-shield fight. But it is also true that, as House Majority Leader Steny Hoyer of Maryland explained, "We had a hiatus because the majority leader of the Senate said we should take a break, and see what happens . . . and, frankly, tens of thousands of people died, hundreds of thousands of people died."

On May 15, 2020, when the House approved the Heroes Act, 1,411,002 coronavirus cases had been identified in the United States. The death toll was 86,571.

Because of McConnell's stalling tactics, seven long months passed before the Senate approved a plan that was one-third the size of the Heroes Act. When the Senate finally acted, the Covid Tracking Project reported 17,828,084 positive cases in the United States. The death toll was 310,968.

How many lives could have been spared if Mitch McConnell had made serving the people a priority, rather than serving the corporate CEO's? How many illnesses might have been prevented? How many jobs might have been saved? How many suicides might have been averted?

Here's one way of looking at it. The United States accounts for 4.25 percent of the global population. Yet, at the time the Senate finally acted, the US accounted for roughly 20 percent of global coronavirus-related deaths.

One of the essential points of this book is that there is a lot of blame to go around for the way things went so badly in the United States. So, in fairness to Mitch McConnell, he can't be solely blamed for the excess deaths—roughly 170,000 by credible estimates—that were recorded during the period from May 15 to December 21. He has to share that blame with the president he empowered, Donald Trump, and with a few other bad actors.

But any calculus that does not assign McConnell that share is a fraud. And any politics that does not hold him to account for the deaths, the illnesses, the job losses, the suicides that could have been avoided, is a travesty.

How Rand Paul Got Covid-19 Wrong, Wrong and Wrong Again

Nothing can reach the heart that is steeled with prejudice.
—Thomas Paine, *The Crisis*, 1776

At the first peak of the coronavirus pandemic, in the spring of 2020, the one thing that Americans agreed on was that Dr. Anthony Fauci was doing a good job. A national survey in April by Quinnipiac University's well-regarded team of pollsters found that a remarkable 78 percent of voters approved of Fauci's response to the pandemic. There wasn't much of a partisan divide: 81 percent of Democrats thought that Fauci, the director of the National Institute of Allergy and Infectious Diseases, was getting it right, as did 77 percent of Republicans. Even as approval for President Trump and the Congress drifted downward, a *Newsweek* headline announced, "Americans Trust Fauci."

That rankled the president, who in mid-April retweeted a post from a failed Republican congressional candidate that featured a #FireFauci hashtag. But Trump never did fire Fauci, the octogenarian doctor, scientist and immunologist who had advised every president since Ronald Reagan on how to handle epidemics and pandemics. As frustrating as the circumstance was for Trump, there was no changing the fact that, across every demographic, across every region, overwhelming majorities of Americans expressed faith in Fauci, who calmly followed the science where it led him. They listened as he evolved his counsel based on what was learned about the virus—expanding from an initial urging that medical personnel wear face covering to a broader call for mask mandates, social distancing and a host of other precautions. The doctor did not get everything right every time. But he was diligent in his research, quick to admit missteps, and steady in his determination to see the crisis through. As such, the *Washington Post* explained, he became "the most prominent voice warning about how serious the novel coronavirus is."

That seriousness would bring him into conflict with the most prominent voice—aside from that of the president—among those who dismissed the seriousness of the novel coronavirus: Senator Rand Paul. When Fauci appeared before the Senate Committee on Health, Education, Labor and Pensions on May 12, 2020, the Kentucky Republican let rip. The only member of the Senate who had tested positive for Covid-19 to that point, Paul was furious with Fauci because the nation's most prominent expert on infectious diseases was not cheering on Trump's push to reopen businesses in order to get the economy back on track.

"I think we ought to have a little bit of humility in our belief that we know what's best for the economy," complained Paul. "And as much as I respect you, Dr. Fauci, I don't think you're the end-all. I don't think you're the one person that gets to make a decision. We can listen to your advice, but there are people on the other side saying there's not going to be a surge and that we can safely open the economy, and the facts will bear this out."

Fauci took all the hits, quietly listening as the senator—an eye doctor who had followed his physician father into libertarian-leaning Republican politics—mischaracterized his warnings about the virus and cast doubt on the data that the immunologist relied upon. Fauci, a man of science who was quick to admit when he was wrong but who was more often than not right, knew that his pronouncements were grounded in the rapidly evolving combination of data and common sense that made for the soundest available public health advice.

Finally, when Paul finished, Fauci replied. "I never made myself out to be the end-all," he said in his even, Brooklyn-accented rasp. "I'm a scientist, a physician and a public health official. I give advice according to the best scientific evidence." Turning Paul's inflammatory comments against the senator, Fauci said: "You used the word we should be 'humble' about what we don't know. I think that falls under the fact that we don't know everything about this virus, and we really had better be very careful."

None of this carried any weight with Paul, who had set out to discredit Fauci's warnings and would not back off. The senator, who was very good at telling others to be humble but not so good at remaining so himself, delivered an imperious warning to the scientists fretting about the danger of opening up the economy at a point when the virus was not contained.

"There have been more people wrong with modeling than right," Paul declared. "We're opening up a lot of economies around the US. And I hope that people who are predicting doom and gloom and saying, 'Oh, we can't do this, there is going to be a surge,' will admit that they were wrong if there isn't a surge, because I think that's what's going to happen in rural states."

Paul was not alone in his zeal for reopening. In many senses he was merely echoing the man who had beaten him in the race for the 2016 Republican presidential nomination. But of course, Paul, a graduate of the Duke University School of Medicine who had for decades traded on his medical degree as a mark of credibility, was a far more dangerous doubter than Donald Trump. As the headline of a *Los Angeles Times* column from May 2020 observed: "Rand Paul isn't a subliterate yawper like Trump. But he's spreading the same deadly coronavirus lies." The columnist, Virginia Heffernan, explained how "in measured professorial speech—a far cry from Trump's subliterate yawps—Paul, who has boasted that he likes spreading misinformation, was disseminating the kind of lies that get people killed. He took on Fauci with bothsides-ism, pretending there's a world of public health experts who disagree with Fauci's warning against recklessly reopening the economy. This just isn't true. No public health conflict exists."

What did exist, noted Heffernan, was the record of Rand Paul's wildly inconsistent sniping at Fauci and other public health experts. "In 2014, Dr. Paul performed a similar stunt with Ebola," she recalled. "In those days, he cautioned against the government underestimating the dangers of an outbreak in the US. Talking to far-right pundit Laura Ingraham, Paul intoned, 'This could get beyond our control' and blamed the Obama administration for 'political correctness' in showing concern for the people of West Africa. To Paul, carefully monitoring people in the US who'd been exposed while sending American health workers and military to help the afflicted in Africa meant that Obama's government was not making 'sound, rational, scientific decisions.'"

Paul's claims were unfounded. Heffernan pointed out that "Fauci, then as now the country's ranking infectious disease expert, studied the biology of Ebola. He and his White House bosses made the sound, rational, scientific decision that an emphatic effort to contain the virus where it originated would help make an outbreak in the US 'extremely unlikely.' Sure enough, there was no American outbreak—and now an Ebola vaccine exists." Heffernan noted that, "Fauci was right. Paul was wrong," and concluded, "If saving lives is the goal, baseline concern for the human species works better than partisanship and xenophobia."

That was good advice for Paul and for his media echo chamber.

Unfortunately, they weren't open to it.

Ingraham, who was using her evening program on Fox to describe the National Institute of Allergy and Infectious Diseases as an arm of "the medical Deep State," responded to Paul's clash with Fauci by rushing to Twitter, the president's favorite social media platform. "Rand Paul saves the day! Calls out the 'experts' and says you are not the 'end all' to make all decisions," she tweeted. "GAME, SET, MATCH."

This was never a game. This was reality. But for those who accepted the game metaphor and who were inclined to keep score, Rand Paul was about to lose the argument—in the worst of all possible ways. Fauci's May 12 visit to Capitol Hill came just before Republican efforts to reopen the economy ran up against the reality of a burgeoning pandemic.

Urged on by Trump, Republican governors across the country pressed for the reopening that the oft-derided experts—including Fauci—had warned against. As May gave way to June, people flocked to bars and beaches, especially in the Republican-controlled states of Texas and Florida, with nightmarishly predictable results. Efforts to flatten the curve with mask mandates, lockdowns and social distancing began to unravel. By mid-June, the *New York Times* was reporting that "thousands of Americans have been sickened by the virus in new and alarming outbreaks." Scientists predicted dire consequences. "You're going to see more infections and more mortality," warned Ali Mokdad, a professor at the Institute for Health Metrics and Evaluation at the University of Washington. While epidemiologists had long expressed fears of a resurgence in the fall—mirroring the seasonal outbreaks of flus—Bloomberg reported Mokdad's fear that the circumstance "could be worse because it will be starting from a higher base of infections."

Within weeks, it was clear that things had indeed gone from bad to worse. Texas, Florida and Arizona were reporting record levels of infections. Hospitals were filling to capacity. "People got complacent," explained Dr. Marc Boom, CEO of the Houston Methodist hospital system. "And it's coming back and biting us, quite frankly."

It kept biting. The US already had the highest Covid-19 death toll in the world—more than 120,000—on June 24. On June 30, Texas reported 6,975 new infections. That was not just a record for the Lone Star State; it was a higher single-day spike in cases than had been experienced by Italy on March 21, the most nightmarish day of the initial surge.

As Texas was reporting that hellish spike, Dr. Fauci returned to Capitol Hill to meet with the senators on the health committee. There was a sense of greater urgency in his voice when he appeared on June 30. "I am not satisfied with what's going on because we are going in the wrong direction if you look at the curves of the new cases, so we've really got to do something about that and we need to do it quickly," he said. "Clearly we are not in total control right now." Expressing frustration with the abandonment of guidelines for preventing the spread of the disease, Fauci warned, "We're going to continue to be in a lot of trouble, and there's going to be a lot of hurt if that does not stop."

Senator Elizabeth Warren pressed for details. What did he mean when he spoke of a lot of hurt? "We are now having 40-plus thousand new cases a day," Fauci said. "I would not be surprised if we go up to 100,000 a day if this does not turn around and so I am very concerned."

How many deaths? "It's going to be very disturbing, I will guarantee you that," he said.

It was a somber, sobering moment. Yet one member of the committee was as cavalier as ever. Rand Paul ridiculed Fauci for his seriousness. Hectoring the adviser to six presidents for delivering such a stark report, Paul chirped, "We just need more optimism."

Acting as if nothing important had changed, Paul continued: "I think government health experts during this pandemic need to show caution in their prognostications. It's important to realize that if society meekly submits to an expert, and that expert is wrong, a great deal of harm may occur when we allow one man's policy or one group of small men and women to be foisted on an entire nation."

The absurdity of Paul's pronouncement was recognized by the *Washington Post* in an assessment of the hearing headlined, "Rand Paul's crusade against Anthony Fauci takes a curious turn." The notion that Fauci has forced Americans to "submit" to him was "not at all borne out," the article concluded. In fact, the *Post* noted: "the resurgent coronavirus outbreak occurred after many states decided not to follow the federal guidelines during their reopenings. And those guidelines have been just that: guidelines. States have in many cases declined to follow them, and multitudes of Americans have declined to follow CDC guidelines on things like wearing a mask and avoiding crowded public places."

Why? In no small measure because politicians like Donald Trump and Rand Paul downplayed the seriousness of the threat posed by a deadly disease. Indeed, they had used their bully pulpits to cheerlead for a reopening that made no sense from a public health standpoint. That was to be expected from Trump, a subliterate yawper willing to sacrifice the lives of hundreds of thousands of Americans if it might benefit his re-election run. But Paul was a physician with a degree from a medical school that conducts a Hippocratic Oath ceremony for graduating students; Duke graduates pledge to serve with "uprightness and honor" and to hold themselves "aloof from wrong."

Now, as a United States senator serving in a time of great peril, Paul was wrong. Dangerously so. Indeed, as Virginia Heffernan noted in her assessment, "Paul is one of those figures in public life who is wrong, wrong and wrong again—and somehow is never called to account."

That lack of accountability only served to make Paul more persistent. And more dangerous.

Ten months after their initial Covid clash, Paul and Fauci met again at a Senate hearing on March 18, 2021. The surges that the senator from Kentucky claimed would not come had come—in the summer and again in the winter. The virus Paul had been so quick to dismiss had spread to every corner of the country. Almost 30 million Americans had tested positive for Covid-19, and 538,087 had died. Yet, Rand Paul was back at it, accusing the immunologist of "defying everything we know about immunity."

"You're telling everybody to wear a mask, whether they've had an infection or a vaccine," Paul told Fauci. "If people that have had the vaccine or have had the infection . . . if we're not spreading the infection, isn't it just theater?"

No, Fauci explained. People who have been infected could be re-infected, and people who have been vaccinated could still breathe in the virus and, though they might not be infected, could spread it to others through sneezes and coughs. That wasn't just Fauci's theory. That was a logical restatement of the science upon which the Centers for Disease Control and Prevention had relied when formulating guidances that urged Americans who have been vaccinated to wear masks when around people who are not vaccinated.

As particularly dangerous Covid-19 variants arrived in the United States, the urgency of masking up would remain until far more people were vaccinated, Fauci counseled. That was common sense. But Paul refused to accept it. Instead of absorbing the new information, with which he was obviously unfamiliar, the senator mocked Fauci for joining other public health experts in warning that Americans should wear two masks in order to protect against the more infectious variants.

"You've been vaccinated and you parade around in two masks for show," Paul grumbled. "You want people to get the vaccine, give them a reward instead of telling them that the nanny state is going to be there for three more years and you've got to wear a mask forever. People don't want to hear it."

Fauci, who earned a Presidential Medal of Freedom for telling people things they didn't want to hear, was clearly frustrated. "Here we go again with the theater," he said. "Let's get down to the facts. Let me just state for the record that masks are not theater. Masks are protective."

That was something a graduate of the Duke University School of Medicine should have been able to understand. And perhaps Dr. Paul did understand. After all, his wife bought $15,000 in stock in Gilead Sciences, a company that makes an antiviral drug used to treat Covid-19, in February 2020—a fact that the senator failed to disclose until sixteen months after the reporting deadline that was established to protect against trading based on insider information. But when the "Which Side Are You On?" moment came, Rand Paul rejected the side of science. Still entertaining presidential ambitions, Paul was playing to the conservative fringe that had made opposition to masking up a political fetish. And that's what worried Anthony Fauci most of all.

"If people hear what he says, and believe it, and you have an elderly person who has been infected, and they decide, well, Rand Paul says, 'Let's not wear a mask,' they won't," Fauci explained after the hearing. "They could get re-infected again and get into trouble."

The kind of trouble that occurs when an ophthalmologist puts politics ahead of an oath that demands he "abstain from all intentional wrongdoing and harm." Rand Paul has made it clear he will not hold himself to that high standard. But the voters of Kentucky, and the rest of the United States, might consider the conclusion of that oath. It translates from the Greek this way:

"Now if I carry out this oath, and break it not, may I gain for ever reputation among all men for my life and for my art; but if I break it and forswear myself, may the opposite befall me."

Have Another Shot of
Hydroxychloroquine, Ron Johnson

Where knowledge is a duty, ignorance is a crime.
                    —Thomas Paine, *Public Good*, 1780

Ron Johnson worked for a time as a caddy at a golf course. He took business and accounting courses in college. He went to work for a plastics firm set up by his wife's family. Then, as a Republican running in a fluky year when even the least-prepared Republicans were winning, he was elected to the US Senate. There he presented himself as something of an expert on viruses, pandemics, treatments and vaccines, even as the Associated Press took pains to explain that Johnson had "no medical expertise or background."

But nothing was going to prevent Ron Johnson from providing medical advice—even when it could get people killed.

The senior senator from Wisconsin did just that on April 22, 2021, when he went on a home-state radio show to complain about campaigns urging everyone to get vaccinated against Covid-19.

"The science tells us the vaccines are 95 percent effective, so if you have a vaccine quite honestly what do you care if your neighbor has one or not?" griped Johnson. "What is it to you? You've got a vaccine and science is telling you it's very, very effective. So why is there this big push to make sure everybody gets a vaccine?"

The solon, who by the spring of 2021 was widely recognized as the Senate's number-one conspiracy theorist, rolled on: "It's to the point where you're going to shame people, you're going to force them to carry a card to prove that they've been vaccinated so they can still stay in society. I'm getting highly suspicious of what's happening here."

The only thing to be suspicious about was why anyone was still giving this nutcase a microphone. Johnson had for years been spewing more BS than a Wisconsin manure spreader. With the arrival of Covid-19, he became a BS superspreader.

So it came as no surprise that, on a day when federal and state officials were fretting about the "vaccine hesitancy" among Trump-addled conservatives, here was Ron Johnson casting shade on the vaccination program that was essential to ending the pandemic and saving the lives of Americans who had barely survived a year of Covid hell. Yet, something about the senator's persistence was unsettling. He wasn't just prone to getting things wrong. He seemed to enjoy it.

For a man who refused to get a vaccine, Johnson had a lot to say about the jabs. He told right-wing radio host Vicki McKenna, "For the very young, I see no reason to be pushing vaccines on people." Johnson also announced that "I certainly am going to vigorously resist any kind of government use or imposing of vaccine passports . . . That could be a very freedom-robbing step and people need to understand these things."

Even for Ron Johnson, this was getting weird. His pontifications countered the counsel of public health officials who were trying to convince the vaccine-hesitant to get the shot so the nation could reach herd immunity, which, experts estimated, was achievable if 70 percent to 90 percent of the population bought into the project. But nearly half of Republican men said they did not plan to be vaccinated, according to several polls. That news spurred even Mitch McConnell and Donald Trump to—however grudgingly—encourage their supporters to get the vaccine.

Ron Johnson had a record of lining up wherever McConnell told him to stand, and Johnson was even more inclined to defer to Trump. But not this time. "The senior senator from Wisconsin," explained PolitiFact, "has taken a different approach."

"Different," in this case, was a nice way of saying "dangerously delusional." Johnson was spewing a tsunami of nonsense that forced media outlets to deploy thousands of words to correct all the misconceptions, mistakes and outright lies that flowed from the senator's perpetually open mouth. He was so very wrong, about everything. He complained that the vaccines were approved for emergency use only and could create unexpected risks. But the vaccines had been tested and retested. Manufacturers had been required to conduct clinical trials before their products received emergency use authorizations from the federal Food and Drug Administration. And the vaccination process continued to be monitored by local, state and federal authorities to assure that health and safety standards were maintained. There was zero evidence, PolitiFact noted, "to suggest that the manufacturers skipped important steps or blew safety standards, as those who seek to push vaccine misinformation typically claim."

Nor did it make any sense, as Johnson suggested, to vaccinate only the vulnerable—not if the goal was to beat back a pandemic. And the idea that those who had been vaccinated should not care if others got their shots was as ludicrous as it was blindly self-absorbed and thoughtless.

Even if Johnson didn't care whether his neighbors were immunized, observed Wisconsin health and science writer Madeline Heim, that wasn't the point. "Herd immunity is the motivation behind encouraging the majority of Americans to get the shot," explained Helm. "Reaching high levels of vaccination would mean new outbreaks of Covid-19 would die out quickly instead of growing and spreading. It would also help ward off new variants of the virus that pop up because it is able to replicate over and over again as infections spread. The sooner this happens, the sooner we can stop excess death and illness from the virus, roll back mask mandates and gathering limits, and resume normal life."

What was remarkable about Johnson's April 22 radio outburst was that it came after an incident a month earlier, when a Milwaukee TV reporter asked, "Did you get the vaccine or are you planning to get vaccinated?" Johnson replied, "No, I had Covid, so I don't believe, you know, I think that probably provides me the best immunity possible, actually having had the disease."

That earned Johnson, whom a Wisconsin website referred to as "our dumb senator," a rebuke from the *Washington Post*, which warned that his take on the coronavirus vaccine was dangerously unscientific. "Doctors, public health experts and the Centers for Disease Control and Prevention are clear: Get the coronavirus vaccine even if you had Covid-19," explained the *Post*, which described numerous instances of reinfections. "Yes, people who had the disease produce antibodies that provide immunity from the coronavirus. But that immunity fades over time, and the body's natural response may not be enough to prevent a repeat infection ninety days after the first one, the CDC says."

Then the paper opened up a can of fact-checker whoop-ass on Johnson. "Let's not mince words," declared the *Post*. "At a time when more than half a million people have died of Covid-19 in the United States, Johnson's comments are irresponsible and dismally uninformed. Many Americans who had the disease are wondering whether they should get the vaccine. They may look to their elected officials for guidance. Imagine what could happen if vulnerable viewers took Johnson's comments as advice and declined the shot. Senators have staffs. They have access to the latest research and data, and to leading experts. They go to good doctors. They shouldn't be making unscientific claims on television about coronavirus immunity."

Many of Johnson's Republican colleagues were accused of denying science as the pandemic swelled. But the senator from Wisconsin took denialism to levels unseen in Washington. Where Trump was erratic in his response to Covid-19, Johnson was jarringly consistent. He *always* got things wrong. Indeed, when he finished trumpeting his own falsehoods, he amplified the errors of others.

Johnson's career as a crackpot hit its pinnacle in the fall of 2020, when he was still serving as chair of the Senate Committee on Homeland Security and Governmental Affairs. In that capacity, Johnson organized a pair of hearings that were billed as featuring "medical professionals who advocate for alternative Covid-19 treatments and mitigation measures to those of the National Institutes of Health, Centers for Disease Control and Prevention, and World Health Organization." The headline of a *New York Times* op-ed piece gave a clearer sense of the hearings by labeling Johnson's cavalcade of fringe theorists and alternative healers "The Snake-Oil Salesmen of the Senate."

Scientists and medical experts were beside themselves. They asked why misinformation was suddenly shaping the Senate's agenda. The answer to that question had a name: Ron Johnson.

In mid-November 2020, when coronavirus infections were surging and the death toll was mounting, the senator opened the first of his hearings. "I believe international, federal and state medical agencies and institutions have let us down," he said. "I fear too many have been close-minded bureaucrats, potentially driven by conflicting interests and agendas." Johnson then proceeded to give a platform, in the Senate hearing room and nationwide via C-SPAN, to a trio of witnesses who promoted the use of hydroxychloroquine and other unproven "treatments" for the virus.

The witnesses added nothing new to a debate that was already settled. The United States Food and Drug Administration had, months earlier, revoked an emergency-use authorization for hydroxychloroquine, an anti-malarial drug touted in the spring of 2020 by President Trump as a Covid treatment that would be "one of the biggest game changers in the history of medicine." Under pressure from Trump, the FDA issued the emergency-use authorization "for certain hospitalized patients" in late March. But the scientists and regulators pulled the authorization in June. "We made this determination based on recent results from a large, randomized clinical trial in hospitalized patients that found these medicines showed no benefit for decreasing the likelihood of death or speeding recovery," the FDA said in a news release. "This outcome was consistent with other new data, including those showing the suggested dosing for these medicines are unlikely to kill or inhibit the virus that causes Covid-19." Two weeks later, the FDA updated its review of safety concerns regarding hydroxychloroquine to caution against its use outside of hospital settings and clinical trials, due to "reports of serious heart rhythm problems and other safety issues, including blood and lymph system disorders, kidney injuries and liver problems and failure."

Even Trump, who admitted that he championed the drug not on the basis of scientific studies but rather, "just a feeling," moved on to talking up other treatments. Indeed, after he came down with the virus in October, a *Vanity Fair* headline announced: "Quack Cures Lose Their Appeal Now That Trump Himself Is Sick with Covid-19."

Yet Johnson was still quacking about hydroxychloroquine and a host of other "alternatives" to what the doctor ordered. Scientists and physicians who recognized the danger of amplifying false narratives about Covid-19 were aghast when the senator organized a session that lent a veneer of legitimacy to modern-day patent medicine peddlers. "What he is doing is outrageous," Dr. Michael Carome, the director of Public Citizen's Health Research Group, said on the day of Johnson's hearing. "Facts don't matter. Evidence doesn't matter."

What mattered to Johnson was the opportunity to amplify conspiracy theories. "During the hearing," the *Milwaukee Journal Sentinel* reported, "Johnson pushed a baseless theory that the medical community was working to deny patients drugs such as hydroxychloroquine because they were cheaper than other treatments." Johnson, who was still struggling to pronounce the ailments he was proposing to cure, didn't come up with these theories on his own. He was channeling old claims by Trump, who at one point suggested that the media had failed to report on the "benefits" of hydroxychloroquine for political purposes, and from Trump operatives who claimed that pharmaceutical companies and physicians were disregarding alternative treatments because they wanted to peddle costlier drugs.

As he was wont to do, Johnson pulled all the conspiracy theories together. During his December 8 hearing he complained that "in today's biased media and social media, within academic journals, on campuses, in government agencies, in ivory towers, we are losing the freedom to obtain and distribute information." He derided National Institutes of Health guidelines. He whined about descriptions of his witnesses as "snake-oil salesmen." No, no, no, Johnson said, he wasn't extending invitations to quacks, he was inviting "the heroes that experts in the ivory towers of media have chosen to ignore and vilify." He demanded to know, "What could possibly be controversial about that?"

The answer came from physicians like Dr. Ashish Jha, a health policy researcher and the dean of the Brown University School of Public Health, who said Johnson's initial hearing in November "was a testament to how politicized science has become." Jha, who was invited by Democrats on the committee to offer a scientific perspective, found the experience baffling. "I shared evidence of studies that have failed to find the benefit of HCQ," explained Jha, using the acronym for hydroxychloroquine. "Three other witnesses shared personal experiences." But, he went on, Johnson and others "suggested my testimony was reckless because it would deny people access to lifesaving HCQ." A frustrated Jha found himself "defending evidence, doctors, and scientists." Finally, he declared, "There are key issues we need Congress to be airing right now. Hydroxychloroquine isn't one of them."

Johnson's response was to attack Dr. Jha's critique as "obnoxious." But Jha was not alone in his assessment. Doctors from across the country slammed Johnson over the hearings. They were joined by public health experts, researchers and scientists who rebuked the senator in excruciating detail.

Some of the criticism was specific. For instance, Jerry Avorn, a professor of medicine at Harvard Medical School, objected to the focus on hydroxychloroquine—and especially to Johnson's theorizing about the supposed suppression of information about the drug. "The idea that scientists are discouraging the use of [hydroxychloroquine] because it's cheap," Avorn said, "is about as crazy as the President's contention that the number of Covid-19 cases is being inflated because doctors make more money by doing so."

At a point when Johnson was also holding hearings where "experts" repeated Trump's lies about the 2020 presidential election, Avorn explained, "We need to base policy on reality rather than on crazy conspiracy theories, whether it's about the pandemic or elections." Dr. Robert Freedland, a Wisconsin physician, observed, "Instead of doing the hard work that will actually save lives, Senator Johnson is giving the platform to extremist views that go against evidence-based science."

Johnson carried on regardless. Two days after the second of his "alternative treatment" hearings, he joined a fellow Senate conspiracy theorist, Rand Paul, in formally requesting that US National Institutes of Health (NIH) director Francis Collins "expedite review of low-cost, widely available and potentially beneficial early-combination treatments including anti-infectives." Like? Hydroxychloroquine.

Johnson had turned his committee into "a forum for fringe doctors to push quack medicines that may actually harm you physically," the Wisconsin state treasurer, Sarah Godlewski, said after the December hearing. A few months later, when Johnson was casting shade on immunization campaigns, an exasperated Godlewski pointed out that the senator was "literally campaigning against widespread vaccines." She announced her candidacy for 2022 as a Democratic challenger to Johnson, whose "denial of science isn't just irresponsible," she said, "it's downright dangerous." Another Democratic challenger, Outagamie County Executive Thomas Nelson, told me the incumbent was "consumed" by conspiracy theories.

Warning that Johnson's "scientifically illiterate beliefs are deadly and will only prolong the Covid crisis," Nelson said what a lot of people were thinking: "Time for a new senator."

The Kristi Noem Nightmare

Virtue is chok'd with foul ambition, and charity chas'd hence by rancour's hand; foul subornation is predominant, and equity exil'd your highness' land.
— William Shakespeare, *Henry VI, Part Two*

South Dakota suffered more than most states during the coronavirus pandemic. As one of the least-crowded places in the nation—forty-sixth in population density, with just eleven people per square mile—it should have had an easy time social distancing. But one year into the crisis, South Dakota's Covid-19 per capita death rate was the eighth highest in the nation. South Dakota's per capita case rate was even worse: second in the United States, after neighboring North Dakota.

Only someone who was deliberately ignorant, ghoulishly dishonest, or perhaps both, would have suggested that South Dakota was a pandemic success story.

Meet Kristi Noem. She's the Republican governor of the Mount Rushmore state and a genuine contender for the 2024 Republican presidential nomination, if Donald Trump gets out of her way.

In February 2021, both Noem and Trump appeared at the Conservative Political Action Conference in Florida. The former president got the most attention for an aggressively combative and rigorously anti-factual address in which he did his best to rewrite recent history—claiming that he won the 2020 election when he actually lost by 7 million votes to Joe Biden, that he did nothing wrong on January 6 when he incited insurrectionists to launch a deadly attack on the Capitol, that Biden's $1.9 trillion coronavirus relief plan was a scheme to "bail out badly run Democrat cities" when it actually helped more Republican communities. Fact checkers had a field day with Trump's first major address since leaving the White House.

Yet it was Noem who delivered the most dangerously delusional speech of a conference where that commodity was in abundant supply. Switching her hubris to overdrive, she announced proudly that when Covid-19 swept across the Great Plains, "my administration resisted the call for virus control at the expense of everything else." To the people whom she hoped would see her as presidential (if not in 2024, then in 2028), Noem framed her appeal around a claim that, despite the death toll, she had responded correctly to the pandemic that devastated her state. The CPAC crowd ate it up. Fox News hailed Noem as a "breakout star" of the annual gathering, where she finished behind Trump and the Florida governor, Ron DeSantis, in straw polls but well ahead of the former secretary of state, Mike Pompeo, Senator Ted Cruz of Texas, Senator Josh Hawley of Missouri and other GOP prospects who had come to Orlando to audition.

Portraying herself as a champion of profits over people, Noem imagined Trump's America as a sort of economic nirvana before March 2020, when "a tragic nationwide shutdown" upended everything. Well, almost everything. Because, in Noem's retelling of the pandemic year, she came out as a hero, a little bit George Washington, a little bit Ronald Reagan, who stood among the graves of her fellow South Dakotans and defended business as usual.

"Now, most governors shut down their states," Noem said. "What followed was record unemployment, businesses closed, most schools were shuttered and communities suffered, and the US economy came to an immediate halt. Now let me be clear, Covid didn't crush the economy; government crushed the economy. And then just as quickly, government turned around and held itself out as the savior, and frankly, the Treasury Department can't print money fast enough to keep up with Congress's wish list. But not everyone has followed this path. For those of you who don't know, South Dakota is the only state in America that never ordered a single business or church to close. We never instituted a shelter-in-place order. We never mandated that people wear masks. We never even defined what an essential business is, because I don't believe that governors have the authority to tell you that your business isn't essential."

Noem's spin was surreal, considering the nightmare she had put South Dakota through. But like Donald Trump before her, Kristi Noem knew her audience. She recognized that the conservative campaign donors and activists who gathered for the annual conference, and who would determine the fate of presidential contenders like her, responded best to fiction. So she rewrote South Dakota's pandemic story as a Western starring a virtuous Kristi Noem as the vanquishing defender of the right to go maskless.

To pull it off, the governor just had to leave a few things out of her campaign hagiography. Like the fact that her state didn't actually go it alone. Trump approved a major disaster declaration for South Dakota so that federal emergency aid could be used to supplement the state's bumbling efforts to keep ahead of the burgeoning crisis. That declaration was fairly typical at the time, as states across the country were quickly overwhelmed by the demands placed on them by the pandemic. What was notable about the South Dakota declaration was that it came on April 5, 2020, just two days after Republican state representative Bob Glanzer lost an agonizing two-week battle with Covid. Glanzer was one of Noem's political allies, a former banker and manager of the South Dakota State Fair, and his death was big news in the state. The governor ordered flags lowered to honor the dead legislator, hailed him as a "true statesman" and declared, "No one was a better example of South Dakota values than Bob Glanzer."

Glanzer, however, didn't rate a mention in Noem's CPAC speech. Neither did the almost 2,000 other South Dakotans who died as the state endured a nightmare year in which it was repeatedly cited as a Covid-19 "crisis" zone, a "hot spot," the site of "superspreader events" and "ground zero" for one of the worst—if not the worst—coronavirus outbreaks in the country. Instead, the governor mocked social distancing and dismissed as tyrannical the counsel of doctors and public health experts who urged people to wear masks as protection against a contagious disease.

"We have to show people how arbitrary these restrictions are, and the coercion, the force, and the anti-liberty steps that governments take to enforce them," ranted Noem as the CPAC crowd cheered her on. "Often, the enforcement isn't based on facts. Justifying these mitigation efforts has been anything but scientific. Now, many in the media, they criticized South Dakota's approach. They labeled me as ill informed, that I was reckless, and even a denier. Some even claimed that South Dakota was as bad as it gets anywhere in the world when it comes to Covid-19. That is a lie."

In fact, Noem was lying. As early as mid-April 2020, when the virus was devastating the state's meatpacking plants and surrounding communities, the *Washington Post* made the connection between her inaction and the surge in infections: "South Dakota's governor resisted ordering people to stay home. Now it has one of the nation's largest coronavirus hot spots." Things got so bad that spring that the Oglala Sioux and Cheyenne River Sioux set up checkpoints on roads leading onto their South Dakota reservations in hopes of controlling the spread of the deadly virus. Noem's response was to threaten to sue the tribes. When hundreds of cases were recorded in Sioux Falls, the state's largest city, Mayor Paul TenHaken pleaded: "A shelter-in-place order is needed now. It is needed today." Noem refused.

In July, Noem welcomed President Trump to South Dakota for a campaign-season appearance at Mount Rushmore, the national monument honoring George Washington, Thomas Jefferson, Abraham Lincoln and Theodore Roosevelt. Trump had already signaled that he wanted his visage to join those of the revered presidents of the past. (When Noem told the story of her 2018 visit to the White House, she recalled that Trump said: "'Kristi, come on over here. Shake my hand.' And so I shook his hand, and I said: 'Mr. President, you should come to South Dakota sometime. We have Mount Rushmore.' And he goes, 'Do you know it's my dream to have my face on Mount Rushmore?' I started laughing. He wasn't laughing, so he was totally serious.")

Trump was obsessed with monuments in the summer of 2020. He used his July 3 event at Mount Rushmore to gripe about anti-racism campaigners who sought to remove statues honoring Confederate generals and slaveholders. "Our nation is witnessing a merciless campaign to wipe out our history, defame our heroes, erase our values and indoctrinate our children," the president told thousands of cheering, sign-waving supporters in South Dakota. "Angry mobs are trying to tear down statues of our founders, deface our most sacred memorials and unleash a wave of violent crime in our cities." He made no mention of the resurgence of the pandemic, or of the fact that health officials across the nation were urging Americans to scale back their plans for the July 4 weekend.

Nor did Noem. The governor talked up the event enthusiastically and welcomed plans to have the state chip in $350,000 for a fireworks show. Even as coronavirus infection rates were spiking nationally, Noem signaled that she had no problem issuing 7,500 tickets to Trump fans who would be packed into two seating areas and inviting another 3,000 people to crowd into an amphitheater and nearby viewing decks. Masks? Nope, no mandate. Noem told Fox News that the masses could decide for themselves. "Every one of them has the opportunity to make a decision that they're comfortable with," the governor announced. "But," she added pointedly, "we will not be social distancing."

Noem was saying what Donald Trump wanted to hear. At the time there was open speculation that Trump might dump the hapless Mike Pence as his vice president, and it was an open secret that Noem was positioning herself as a potential running mate for November—or, failing that, as a future contender in her own right. Either way, she went out of her way to let the president know she was on Team Trump.

On the big day itself, the governor greeted Trump with an $1,100 bust depicting his face on Mount Rushmore. The president was delighted. "I knew that that was something that he would find special," said the governor. After the event, a maskless Noem boarded Air Force One and flew back to Washington with Trump, and the two of them chatting up a storm. She made the trip even though she knew she had been exposed to the virus the day earlier while attending an event with Trump surrogate Kimberly Guilfoyle, the conservative media personality who was dating Donald Trump Jr. Noem hugged Guilfoyle on July 2. On July 3, the day of the Mount Rushmore rally, it was revealed that Guilfoyle had tested positive for Covid-19.

The Associated Press reported that Guilfoyle's infection prompted some Republicans "to take precautions against the spread of the coronavirus." That included Representative Greg Gianforte of Montana, who suspended in-person campaigning for his gubernatorial bid after both his wife and his running mate attended a fundraiser with Guilfoyle earlier in the week. The AP explained that "Noem doesn't plan anything similar or to get tested again for the virus" and that her press secretary "cast Noem's decision to fly on Air Force One as a demonstration of how to live with the virus."

Noem offered another demonstration of how to live with the virus in August, when she enthusiastically welcomed more than 400,000 bikers to the eightieth annual Sturgis Motorcycle Rally, Packing close to a quarter million mostly maskless people into a town of 6,796 didn't seem like a very good idea at a point in time when the country was experiencing a surge in coronavirus cases and deaths. Public health experts advised that this would be a very good year to press pause on the party. But the Sturgis City Council voted 8–1 to go ahead with the event that filled local bars and tattoo parlors, and Kristi Noem wasn't about to stop them. "We are not—and will not—be the subjects of an elite class of so-called experts," announced the governor.

Unfortunately for Noem and everyone who came to Sturgis, "the elite class of so-called experts" turned out to be right. Two weeks after the motorcycle rally ended on August 16, hundreds of attendees had tested positive, and Sturgis-tied cases had been identified in a dozen states. Deaths were already being reported.

Dr. Sadiya Khan, an epidemiologist at the Northwestern University Feinberg School of Medicine, told NBC News the timeline seemed to confirm fears that the rally had been a "superspreader event." Eventually, a study using genomic testing by the Centers for Disease Control and Prevention traced a serious Covid outbreak in Minnesota to Sturgis, as more than fifty Minnesotans who had attended the rally, and dozens of people who came into contact with them, came down with severe acute respiratory syndrome coronavirus 2 (SARS-CoV2). "The Sturgis Rally, which again wasn't even in Minnesota, had apparently spread the virus to at least 34 percent of Minnesota's eighty-seven counties," explained Bruce Y. Lee, a professor of Health Policy and Management at the City University of New York who examined the data. No surprise there. "Any time you have a mass gathering of hundreds of thousands of people and then they return to their home states, you're going to increase the likelihood of a 'superspreader' event,'" said University of South Dakota biomedical sciences professor Victor Huber.

The surge in coronavirus cases was especially pronounced in Noem's state. "We're really starting to see widespread community transmission in South Dakota," said Huber, who noted that an infection rate that had been "hovering at 8 to 10 percent" had spiked to over 15 percent.

The governor's response was to attack the messengers. Noem claimed researchers who were identifying alarming trends were simply doing "some back-of-the-napkin math and made up some numbers and published them." While some national reports had featured what appeared to be inflated numbers, the fact was that spikes in infections and deaths were being traced to the Sturgis rally. Instead of acknowledging that she had been wrong, however, the governor was the picture of Trumpian nonchalance. Appearing before the Sioux Falls Downtown Rotary Club as the case numbers surged in late August, Noem proclaimed: "I don't think any of this is a surprise because for the last several months I've told people that we will get more cases. We know for a fact we can't stop the virus."

What everyone else knew for a fact was that Kristi Noem *wouldn't* stop the virus. By the fall of 2020, South Dakota's death toll was spiking at a rate so alarming that the whole country took notice. Former Harvard Medical School professor William Haseltine, founder of the Virus Research Institute and author of *A Family Guide to Covid*, said the crisis in the Dakotas was "as bad as it gets anywhere in the world." Public health researcher Dr. Ali Mokdad told *USA Today* that South Dakota was experiencing per capita infection and death rates that experts would expect to see in a war-torn nation. "How could we allow this in the United States to happen?" Mokdad said. "This is unacceptable by any standards."

It wasn't really a case of "we"; it was a case of Noem repeatedly rejecting science and the pleas of doctors and public health professionals. As conditions in South Dakota and other states worsened, Dr. Anthony Fauci called for "intensifying the simple public health measures that we all talk about: mask wearing, staying distanced, avoiding congregate settings." South Dakota secretary of health Kim Malsam-Rysdon said the pandemic was making staffing shortages at hospitals worse. Dr. Robert Summerer of the South Dakota State Medical Association said, "We've really seen our numbers escalating—we're having challenges here finding beds for patients." The association called for a statewide mask mandate, but Noem refused. "Some have said that my refusal to mandate masks is a reason why our cases are rising here in South Dakota, and that is not true," she said, prompting the AP to report on November 16, 2020: "As Deaths Spiral, South Dakota Governor Opposes Mask Rules." Even as neighboring North Dakota adopted a mandate, Noem actually questioned whether wearing masks in public prevented infections.

Why was she rejecting science? The AP provided a clue: "The approach has given her significant influence within the Republican party. She spoke to incoming GOP members of Congress this weekend in Washington, DC, and posted photos of Monday meetings with members of President Donald Trump's Cabinet. She was not wearing a mask in any of the photos."

Nor was Noem wearing a mask when she appeared at CPAC on February 27, 2021, and cheerily announced: "We never focused on the case numbers. Instead, we kept our eye on hospital capacity." That was an odd thing to brag about, as South Dakota's largest newspaper, the Sioux Falls *Argus Leader*, had reported two months earlier that: "South Dakota's largest hospitals are at or above their capacity to care for critically ill Covid-19 patients, forcing some of the sickest patients to be flown out of state to receive care. . . . [It is] increasingly uncertain whether the sickest South Dakotans will be able to get treatment in the state, health providers say."

Nevertheless, Noem's big applause line in her CPAC speech was an attack on Fauci's warnings about pandemic surges: "Now, I don't know if you agree with me, but Dr. Fauci is wrong a lot." That gained the governor the raucous standing ovation that she was seeking. Fauci later responded with restraint, calling her remarks "unfortunate" and "not very helpful" at a time when coronavirus variants were spreading nationally and case counts were again rising in South Dakota.

Jonathan Reiner, a professor of medicine at the George Washington University Medical Center, was blunter. He called Noem's remarks "outrageous" and pointed to her refusal to institute a mask mandate as the virus burned across the Great Plains. "As a result, 10 percent of the people in South Dakota have been infected with the coronavirus," Reiner said. "Thousands of people have died. So her science denialism has resulted in the propagation of that disease unnecessarily throughout her state mercilessly."

Despite such grim assessments, Noem announced that she was speaking at the CPAC conference "to share some of the lessons from my state." One of the lessons she was most determined to deliver had to do with keeping schools open during the pandemic. "Now," she declared. "South Dakota schools are no different than schools everywhere else in America, but we approached the pandemic differently. From the earliest days of the pandemic our priority was the students, their well-being and their education. When it was time to go back to school in the fall, we put our kids in the classroom. Teachers, administrators, parents and the students themselves were of one mind to make things work for our children, and the best way to do that was in the classroom."

That was another big applause line, and Noem did not spoil it with facts. She neglected to mention the backlash she suffered after her campaign sent a fund-raising email that politicized the return to school with a promise that "Governor Kristi Noem will not issue a statewide mandate for distance learning, and is encouraging all families to send their children back to school—without masks." That drew a rebuke from the South Dakota Education Association for "turning school-opening decisions into a political football" in a way that "put lives at risk."

Nor did Noem mention the teachers and school aides who had died in her state, like Sharon Schuldt, a sixty-seven-year-old member of the nutrition team at Sonia Sotomayor Elementary in Sioux Falls, who fell ill in October and died after several weeks in a crowded hospital. It wasn't politically convenient for the governor to remember Ethel Rose Left Hand Bull, a fifty-five-year-old member of the Crow Creek Tribe who had served as a fifth-grade teacher on the Rosebud Reservation before she fell ill in June, spent two long months on a BiPAP machine and then shifted to a ventilator before dying in August—the same month she was supposed to receive her master's degree in education.

Noem's CPAC speech lasted the better part of a half hour, but there was no time to remember the workers lost in her state's several meatpacking facilities, like Blanca Margarita Ramirez Gonzalez, a twenty-three-year-old mother of three who worked at the Jack Links meatpacking plant in tiny Alpena. She loved her kids and music and playing basketball. But she died May 26, as the virus swept through the largest beef jerky plant in the world, infecting more than 100 workers and sickening dozens. Nor was there time for the governor to acknowledge the story of Agustín Rodriguez, a sixty-four-year-old immigrant from El Salvador who for two decades worked in the pork-cut department of the sprawling Smithfield Foods pork-processing plant in Sioux Falls, where 3,700 employees, a great many of them immigrants, spoke roughly forty languages. Smithfield announced the plant's first Covid-19 case on March 26, 2020. Instead of shutting down, according to the *Argus Leader* company officials "said they notified workers and cleaned the employees' workspace" and offered a $500 "responsibility bonus" to workers who showed up for all their shifts. Agustín Rodriguez kept showing up, even as he experienced a fever and a cough in early April. He finally called in sick and was hospitalized on April 4. He tested positive for Covid-19 and spent almost two weeks on a ventilator before becoming the first Smithfield worker to die on April 14. By then, hundreds of workers at the plant were infected, and Smithfield, under pressure from the United Food and Commercial Workers union, had temporarily halted operations at the facility.

By mid-April, media outlets across the country were identifying South Dakota's meatpacking plants as one of the most serious hot spots in the country. Yet Noem, who had only chosen to "recommend" that Smithfield "pause" operations, kept resisting pleas from local officials for her to issue the sort of "shelter in place" public health orders that businesses hated but that other governors, both Democrats and Republicans, were announcing. The governor claimed "a shelter in place would have had no impact on what happened at Smithfield."

That was a remarkable statement, considering the crisis that was unfolding in Noem's state, but more remarkable still was her agitation for Smithfield to reopen its Sioux Falls plant as quickly as possible. A day before Agustín Rodriguez died, the governor appeared on Fox News to announce that she was working at "getting them to full production so that they can do what they do best." A week later, she told a local radio that getting the plant up and running "shouldn't be too difficult." Noem's macabre rush to send workers back into the crowded plant led Sioux Falls AFL-CIO president Kooper Caraway to compare the governor, unfavorably, with the favorite author of right-wing advocates for "survival of the fittest" deregulation. "We are fighting a governor who makes Ayn Rand look like a liberal humanist," complained Caraway. "She has said she opposes shelter-in-place orders because people should be free to do whatever they want, regardless of how that might result in harm to others."

Rand, the Russian-American skeptic of altruism and author of *The Fountainhead* and *Atlas Shrugged*, was famous for such chilling epigrams as "The public good be damned, I will have no part of it!" But Noem was too smart a politician to speak so baldly. She framed her governing philosophy in more palatable terms, bragging to conservative campaign donors and activists that "my administration resisted the call for virus control at the expense of everything else." When a pandemic is infecting well over 100,000 of the people a governor has sworn to protect and killing more than 2,000 of them, however, it's only a matter of semantics.

For Kristi Noem, "resisting the call for virus control" was just another way of saying, "The public good be damned."

Ron DeSantis's Imperial Overreach

Let not light see my black and deep desires.
　　　　　　　　—William Shakespeare, *Macbeth*

Before Republicans were the "Party of Trump," they were the "Party of Reagan." The Great Communicator became the iconic figure in modern conservatism during more than two decades of political activism in which he redefined a once pluralistic party as an increasingly right-wing and dogmatic vehicle for an ideological agenda that extended from the pages of magazines such as *National Review* and from the arguments of economists such as Milton Friedman and Arthur Laffer. Unlike Trump, a damaged man whose erratic political philosophy began and ended with his own self-preservation, Reagan had actual ideas. Among the most foundational of those ideas was a faith that people were ill served by politicians in distant capitals and well served by the friends and neighbors they elected to town boards, city councils and county commissions.

Even Reagan's critics recognized a measure of logic in this stance. But Trump, with his big-government bent, did not approve of ceding power to the people. Nor did the most Trumpian of the nation's governors during Trump's tenure, Florida's Ron DeSantis, whose response to the coronavirus pandemic and its aftermath owed everything to the forty-fifth president's authoritarianism and nothing to the decentralizing instincts of the Great Communicator.

DeSantis was just two years old when, in one of the most compelling addresses of his many campaigns, Reagan outlined his views on the eve of the 1980 election that made him president. Putting an exclamation mark on the theme of his challenge to President Jimmy Carter, Reagan recalled the founding of the republic more than 200 years earlier and said, "many Americans today, just as they did 200 years ago, feel burdened, stifled and sometimes even oppressed by government that has grown too large, too bureaucratic, too wasteful, too unresponsive, too uncaring about people and their problems."

The problem, explained the former governor of California, was that too much of our governance was playing out in Washington, DC, a capital city bloated with politicians and lobbyists, as opposed to the town halls of communities across America. Reagan's promise was to "restore the health and vitality" of local government. The lives of the great mass of Americans could be improved, he said, by "returning to them control over programs best run at those levels of government closer to the people."

Reagan never really delivered, and his partisan successors failed even more miserably. But this message of "local is better" became a mantra for Republicans, who preached a gospel of municipalism that imagined a dramatically diminished federal government redistributing its largesse in the form of block grants to mayors, village presidents and town board chairs across the country.

Reagan's acolytes sang from the same hymnal. Members of Congress such as Jack Kemp, Vin Weber and a young Newt Gingrich, along with various and sundry Republican governors across the land, waxed poetic about the wonders of "devolution." All that was needed to solve the problems of America, we were promised, was to move the authority to make the big decisions out of Washington and back to Main Street. The emphasis on localism became so much a part of the Republican brand that, long after Reagan died, Americans kept telling themselves that the Grand Old Party was serious about returning power to the people. Even when Republican presidents and governors sought to pre-empt the ability of local governments to set policy, even when Republican congresses and legislatures used "shared revenue" schemes to dictate policies to local officials, voters still imagined that the Democrats were the party of big, "oppressive" government and that the Republicans were the defender of grass-roots democracy.

So when Florida voters narrowly elected DeSantis as their governor in 2018, the assumption was that he would show a generous measure of respect for the local officials who gathered in municipal buildings across the state to decide the destinies of villages, cities and counties.

It was a foolish assumption. DeSantis was a political career-ist who had served in Washington as a member of the House and tried to get himself elected to the Senate before settling for a gubernatorial bid in 2018. As soon as he was sworn in, it became clear that DeSantis was not interested in sharing power, let alone devolving it to others. In his first months in office, he suspended and replaced local and regional officials who displeased him. He signed legislation barring communities from declaring themselves to be "sanctuary cities" where immigrants would be protected from federal harassment and instead ordered cities and counties to cooperate with federal authorities. In the summer of 2020, when Black Lives Matter demonstrations filled the streets of Florida cities following the murders of George Floyd in Minneapolis and Breonna Taylor in Louisville, DeSantis announced that any municipality that moved to reduce law-enforcement spending would lose its state funding. While few if any Florida communities were seriously considering "Defund the Police" proposals, DeSantis amplified the threat at events that were always more like campaign rallies than policy discussions. "It's transparent and obvious that it's a political move to play into Trump's national message as if there is no law and order in this entire country," complained the state senate minority leader, Audrey Gibson, a Democrat from Jacksonville.

Frustrated mayors complained about the governor's micromanagement. Joseph Corradino, the mayor of Pinecrest, a Miami suburb with a population of 20,000, told the *Tampa Bay Times*, "There's no way the state can know what's better for the local government than the local government itself."

DeSantis disagreed, as he made abundantly clear during the months when the coronavirus pandemic went from surge to surge in Florida. DeSantis constantly steamrolled local officials, telling them what they could and could not do. If they tried to follow CDC guidelines, he overruled them. If they sought to add extra protections for the elderly, he rejected them. If they wanted to set up vaccination programs, he told them it was his way of the highway.

Like Trump, DeSantis was obsessed with opening up businesses and schools, even if that meant spreading the disease. And, like Trump, DeSantis was sure he knew more than the nurses, doctors, public health officers and scientists who were telling him to slow down the rush to reopen.

The governor spouted so much nonsense that YouTube pulled down a video of DeSantis trading quack theories with Trump-aligned "experts," culminating in a gubernatorial declaration that "wearing masks for the general public is not evidence-based." (Fact Check: It was.) YouTube monitors said the conversation violated the platform's ban on posting Covid-19 disinformation, which the video undoubtedly did. But DeSantis was furious. "What we're really witnessing is Orwellian," he sputtered. "It's a Big Tech, corporate media collusion."

You'd think that a governor who was so concerned about Orwellian pronouncements from on high would be wary of imposing the state's will on Florida communities. You'd be wrong.

At the start of May 2021, DeSantis formally ended the ability of local government officials to impose mask mandates, require social distancing and adopt rules regarding vaccinations—not just in response to the lingering coronavirus pandemic but in future public health crises. "This legislation ensures that legal safeguards are in place so that local governments cannot arbitrarily close our schools or businesses," proffered the governor in doublespeak worthy of Orwell's *1984*.

"I think folks that are saying they need to be policing people at this point—if you're saying that, you really are saying you don't believe in the vaccines," DeSantis claimed. "You don't believe in the data, you don't believe in the science. We've embraced the vaccines. We've embraced the science on it." Local governments weren't denying the data. They weren't saying they didn't believe in the vaccines. Local governments were striking the difficult balance that was necessary at a point when vaccination rates had yet to hit a level where it was safe to lift mandates. "I'm deeply concerned by this decision," said the Miami–Dade County mayor, Daniella Levine Cava, after DeSantis signed the bill. "We are still in a public health emergency and our economy has not fully rebounded from this crisis. Fewer than half of our residents have been vaccinated, and we still face a growing threat from new variants. . . . I urge the Governor to commit resources to helping to educate and persuade Floridians to get vaccinated, as we continue doing everything we can at the local level to make vaccines as accessible as possible and to motivate our community to take the shot."

But that wasn't going to happen. DeSantis refused to do the right thing. It wasn't that the governor was uninformed, or unable to assess the threats that would extend from his decisions; after all, he graduated magna cum laude from Yale in 2001, and Juris Doctor cum laude from Harvard Law School in 2005. The problem was that the governor was never going to put the health and safety of Floridians ahead of his epic ambition. "It feels like he's spiking the ball on the 10-yard line," complained Dan Gelber, the mayor of Miami Beach. "He's been following political ideology more than science during this whole pandemic."

Bingo!

DeSantis maintained a frenzied schedule as the first pandemic year gave way to the second. He was ordering schools to remain open even if health concerns arose, signing legislation protecting businesses from liability in cases where employees and customers were sickened, ranting and raving about how he would never allow vaccine passports and holding press conferences to talk about what a great job he was doing—despite the fact that, by the summer of 2021, Florida was experiencing a dramatic spike in positive tests and new fatalities. By August of 2021, as the Delta variant swept through the governor's insufficiently vaccinated state, hospitalization rates hit records. The number of confirmed Covid-19 cases pushed toward the 3 million mark, while the number of deaths surpassed 41,000.

Instead of changing course, DeSantis doubled down. He flew to Utah to tell members of the conservative American Legislative Exchange Council, "I think it's very important that we say, unequivocally, no to lockdowns, no to school closures, no to restrictions and no mandates." At home in Florida, he threatened to withhold the pay of school administrators who proposed mask mandates.

It was all very Trumpian. Or, perhaps it is more accurate to say, very DeSantisian. Because this governor was on a mission. If Trump decided to bid for the presidency again in 2024, the word was, DeSantis wanted to be his running mate. If Trump stood down, DeSantis was readying his own bid for the nation's highest office.

To advance that bid, he needed to be the governor who beat Covid-19. So, as Broward County mayor Steve Geller told a local TV reporter, the governor "simply declared that the crisis is over."

It wasn't the case that the crisis was over. But it was the case that Ron DeSantis, Geller noted, was demonstrating the extent to which he "cares more about politics than the public safety in the state of Florida."

13

Andrew Cuomo's Broken Halo

There is no man more dangerous, in a position of power, than he who refuses to accept as a working truth the idea that all a man does should make for rightness and soundness, that even the fixing of a tariff rate must be moral.

—Ida Tarbell, 1911

More than 15,000 people died in New York State's nursing homes, assisted living facilities and other adult care centers in the year that passed between those terrifying early days when the coronavirus pandemic hit New York with a vengeance and the time when mass vaccination programs finally began to provide a measure of protection. They were grandmothers and grandfathers, moms and dads, sisters and brothers with disabilities, human beings whose families had trusted in promises of care from institutions that were supposed to provide protection against disease and abandonment.

Many of those 15,000 New Yorkers who breathed their last breaths between the spring of 2020 and the spring of 2021 died unnecessarily—succumbing not just to the virus but because of the collapse of caregiving in a crisis moment so severe that healthy elders and people with disabilities were neglected. Their stories were part of a nightmare that, while especially terrifying in the Empire State, unfolded in states across the country. As the nationwide Covid death toll approached 100,000 in the fall of 2020, the Associated Press reported that "advocates for the elderly say a tandem wave of death separate from the virus has quietly claimed tens of thousands more, often because overburdened workers haven't been able to give them the care they need. Nursing home watchdogs are being flooded with reports of residents kept in soiled diapers so long their skin peeled off, left with bedsores that cut to the bone, and allowed to wither away in starvation or thirst."

A nursing home expert who analyzed data from the country's 15,000 facilities for the wire service's comprehensive study estimated that for every two Covid-19 victims in long-term care, a third died prematurely of other causes. Eight months into the pandemic, the AP reported that "those 'excess deaths' beyond the normal rate of fatalities in nursing homes could total more than 40,000 since March."

The victims in these care facilities often died alone. They were cut off from family members who might have prodded facility managers and regulators to do a better job of guarding against the spread of the disease, and who surely would have demanded more care once loved ones were infected. Even those who went out of their way to monitor the circumstances of elderly residents of nursing homes and care centers could not save them. Dawn Best regularly checked in on her eighty-three-year-old mother, who was living at the Gurwin Jewish Nursing Home, a well-regarded 460-bed facility on Long Island. Yet shortly after the nursing home locked down, Best noticed during a FaceTime call that her mother looked and sounded miserable. The daughter demanded that a doctor check on her mom and, within hours, she got an urgent call from a physician who told her: "The Covid is everywhere, It's in every unit. The doctors have it, the nurses have it and your mother may have it."

In the end, fifty-nine residents at Gurwin would be killed by the virus, according to media reports, which noted that "Best's mother never contracted it. She died instead of dehydration, her daughter said, because the staff was so consumed with caring for Covid-19 patients that no one made sure she was drinking."

How did things go so bad in that New York nursing home? How did the crisis turn so deadly, so quickly, in so many care centers across the state?

"There was a mandate weeks back that required us to take Covid-19–positive patients, and that was a very troublesome decision without planning," Gurwin CEO Stuart Almer told the investigative journalism project City Limits in May 2020. "It's just dangerous for any of us who are running nursing homes."

Prior to the March 25 mandate, Gurwin had just one person who tested positive. Then, according to Almer, they took on twenty-three Covid-positive patients from nearby hospitals, and by April 29, Gurwin had eighty confirmed Covid-positive residents—forty in a dedicated Covid-positive unit and the rest in other parts of the facility. By May 1, there were 150 documented cases at the facility, where nurses were overwhelmed by the caseload and the death toll—with one telling City Limits, "I can't even cry anymore."

Where did that mandate come from? From the man who was serving then as governor of New York, Andrew Cuomo, and from the state Health Department he oversaw. As Representative Elise Stefanik, a Watertown Republican who was no fan of Cuomo, put it: "The governor took executive action, forcing positive Covid cases back into nursing homes. There was zero transparency in terms of informing the seniors, the workers or the family members whether there were positive cases." Cuomo would eventually be forced to resign after an investigation by New York's attorney general found the governor had sexually harassed at least eleven women. His resignation upended an impeachment process that sought to address evidence of his abuses of office. But that was not the only scandal for which Cuomo merited impeachment.

The governor's wrongheaded decisions regarding nursing homes, his misdeeds, and his lies about the deaths in those facilities, demanded accountability when he was in office. The fact that he has resigned does not, in any way, lessen that demand.

Criticism of Cuomo at the time the mandate came down was dismissed by his political allies—and many in the media—as partisan bickering by Republicans, or ideological sniping from the progressives who often clashed with the centrist Democratic governor. Cuomo was the media darling of the early months of the pandemic. His detail-oriented daily press briefings were televised on national cable channels as a counterpoint to President Trump's weak and convoluted response to the crisis. *Entertainment Weekly* referred to the governor as "the hero that America never realized it needed until he was on our television screens every night." Cuomo seemed for a time to have mastered the Covid moment so completely that there was talk that he might be asked to replace Joe Biden as the Democratic nominee for president of the United States. And why not? While Biden was running better than Trump in many polls, Cuomo was a national superstar. And at home, he seemed untouchable. A Siena College poll conducted after the initial pandemic peak in March and early April found that 77 percent of New Yorkers had a favorable view of the governor. "Mired in middling poll numbers for the last two years, Cuomo is feeling the love from New Yorkers of all stripes in year three of his third term and his first global pandemic," Siena pollster Steven Greenberg said. "He is viewed favorably by 90 percent of Democrats, 73 percent of independents and 53 percent of Republicans, his first time favorable with Republicans in more than six years."

Cuomo didn't run for president. But he did cash in, signing a book deal for a reported $4 million and turning out a 320-page tome, *American Crisis: Leadership Lessons From the Covid-19 Pandemic*, between pandemic peaks. Even as his star shone, however, the nursing home mandate remained a persistent source of anger and frustration for New Yorkers who lost loved ones, and for legislators who represented them. State Representative Ron Kim, a Democrat who represented a district in Queens with a substantial immigrant population, recalled, "Constituents started reaching out to me, saying things like: 'My mom is stuck in a nursing home, and I know that Covid is transmitting in there and I can't get access. She's sleeping in a hallway, exposed, no PPE.'"

Family members of those who died were furious about the mandate. "It was the single dumbest decision anyone could make," Daniel Arbeeny said of the March 25 order. Arbeeny's eighty-nine-year-old father, Norman, died shortly after the family removed the elder Arbeeny from a Brooklyn nursing home where more than fifty deaths would eventually be recorded. "This isn't rocket science. We knew the most vulnerable—the elderly and compromised—are in nursing homes and rehab centers." At Cuomo's self-congratulatory press briefings throughout April 2020, the steady sour note involved conditions in these facilities. The governor kept getting pressed about breakdowns in communications, chaotic recordkeeping and very high death tolls. He admitted that reports from nursing homes around the state revealed "hellacious situations" and acknowledged that "the nursing home is the optimum feeding ground for this virus.

Vulnerable people in a congregate facility, in a congregate setting where it can just spread like fire through dry grass. We have had really disturbing situations in nursing homes, and we're still most concerned about the nursing homes." He even allowed, at an April 22 briefing, that "if somebody says to me, 'Should I put my mother in a nursing home now?' now is not the best time to put your mother in a nursing home. That is a fact."

Yet Cuomo, who seemed to be so on top of every other topic, was vague, contradictory and defensive when the discussion turned to why things had gone so awry in the nursing homes. The control-freak governor seemed to suggest that what was happening in care centers was beyond his control. "This happens to be a virus that happens to attack elderly people and nursing homes are the place of elderly people," he offered, exculpatorily. If blame shifting didn't work, Cuomo lied, as when he said on April 18, "I think we release probably more than any other state, in terms of nursing home data."

The constant questioning did, however, influence Cuomo. On May 10, he partially rescinded the mandate barring nursing homes from denying admission to patients on the basis of a positive Covid diagnosis. But even after he issued an executive order requiring hospital patients to test negative before being sent to nursing homes, CNN noted that "Cuomo shirked responsibility for the nursing home crisis." In response to questions at a May briefing during which the subject of nursing home deaths arose, Cuomo said, "We lost 139 people yesterday in hospitals. Who is accountable for those 139 deaths? Well, how do we get justice for those families who had 139 deaths? What is justice? Who can we prosecute for those deaths? Nobody. Nobody. Mother Nature? God?"

On May 21, several days after Cuomo tried to pin the blame on Mother Nature, the Associated Press reported that "more than

4,500 recovering coronavirus patients were sent to New York's already vulnerable nursing homes" under the Cuomo administration's order. Then in July, a New York State Department of Health report ("Factors Associated With Nursing Home Infections and Fatalities in New York State During the Covid-19 Global Health Crisis") upped the number to more than 6,000 Covid-positive patients admitted to long-term care facilities between March 25 and May 8 in 2020.

The news kept getting worse, and Cuomo kept obfuscating, dissembling and lying. In late September, during an interview with a radio station in New York's Finger Lakes region, the governor was asked about his administration's March 25 mandate. He claimed it was just an "anticipatory rule" that was circulated out of an abundance of caution to assure the state would not run out of hospital beds. "We never needed nursing home beds because we always had hospital beds," said Cuomo. "So it just never happened in New York where we needed to say to a nursing home, 'We need you to take this person even though they're Covid-positive.' It never happened."

CNN's Fact First site reviewed the governor's claim, and the assessment was not kind. "Cuomo's assertion that 'it never happened' is false," concluded the analysts. "According to a report from the New York State Department of Health, '6,326 Covid-positive residents were admitted to [nursing home] facilities' following Cuomo's mandate that nursing homes accept the readmission of Covid-positive patients from hospitals. Whether or not this was 'needed,' it did in fact happen."

Cuomo's office griped about the CNN review, claiming that in his radio interview the governor had only been referring to the anticipated hospital bed shortage when he said "it never happened." But what was at issue was not the hospital bed count. It was the readmissions of Covid-positive patients to nursing homes, the deaths of patients who were infected with the virus in those facilities and the complaints that patients who did not succumb to the virus had died amid the tumult that overwhelmed care centers.

Ron Kim, the legislator from Queens, kept talking about the nursing home deaths, and about Cuomo's failure to take responsibility for his actions. When I spoke with Kim, he explained to me, "This isn't anything personal, with Governor Cuomo. I mean, I actually stood with (the governor's administration) at the beginning of the pandemic when many progressive Democrats didn't want to give them extra powers, you know? Many of us acted in good faith. But he failed us, and there's evidence of his failures throughout this process." The legislator, whose district had been especially hard hit by the pandemic, was initially something of a voice in the wilderness. But as the months passed, Kim's colleagues, such as Assembly Health Committee Chairman Richard Gottfried, a Manhattan Democrat, began demanding details about nursing home deaths. Cuomo and his aides kept stonewalling, even as more Democratic legislators challenged the Democratic governor to share the data—and tell the truth. New York Attorney General Letitia James launched an investigation, the results of which were released on January 28, 2021. The report confirmed that a far larger number of nursing home residents had died from Covid-19 than had been acknowledged by Cuomo's Department of Health. Indeed, James concluded, the nursing home data may have been undercounted by as much as 50 percent.

The report exposed Cuomo. Ensuing revelations added even more compelling details to the case against the governor. The *New York Times* summed up that argument when it wrote:

> For most of the past year, Gov. Andrew M. Cuomo has tried to brush away a persistent criticism that undermined his

national image as the man who led New York through the pandemic: that his policies had allowed thousands of nursing home residents to die of the virus.

But Mr. Cuomo was dealt a blow when the New York State attorney general, Letitia James, reported on Thursday morning that Mr. Cuomo's administration had undercounted coronavirus-related deaths of state nursing home residents by the thousands.

Just hours later, Ms. James was proved correct, as Health Department officials made public new data that added more than 3,800 deaths to their tally, representing nursing home residents who had died in hospitals and had not previously been counted by the state as nursing home deaths.

Several days after James issued her January 28 report, a top Cuomo aide, Melissa DeRosa, quietly acknowledged to legislators that the state had withheld data out of fear that a transparent approach might inspire critical tweets from President Trump and an inquiry by the Trump administration's notoriously politicized Justice Department. "But instead of a mea culpa to the grieving family members of more than 13,000 dead seniors or the critics who say the Health Department spread Covid-19 in the care facilities," reported the *New York Post*, "DeRosa tried to make amends with the fellow Democrats for the political inconvenience it caused them. 'So we do apologize,' she said. 'I do understand the position that you were put in. I know that it is not fair. It was not our intention to put you in that political position with the Republicans.'"

Gottfried, the Democrat who chaired the Assembly Health Committee, was having none of it. "I don't have enough time today to explain all the reasons why I don't give that any credit at all," he reportedly told DeRosa.

Instead of easing pressure on the governor, the revelation that he and his aides withheld data created a crisis of confidence in an already embattled chief executive. Cuomo finally admitted that his administration's "lack of transparency" had created a circumstance "filled with skepticism, and cynicism, and conspiracy theories which furthered the confusion." Yet, as the *New York Times* noted, "He stopped short of a full apology for his handling of information about the death toll in the state's nursing homes."

After listening in on DeRosa's call with legislators, Ron Kim said it sounded "like they admitted that they were trying to dodge having any incriminating evidence that might put the administration or the [Health Department] in further trouble with the Department of Justice. That's how I understand their reasoning of why they were unable to share, in real time, the data."

Kim summarized why the Cuomo administration's apology fell flat. "It's not enough how contrite they are with us," he said. "They need to show that to the public and the families—and they haven't done that."

That comment, when it was published in the *New York Post*, triggered a late-night call from Cuomo to Kim's home. Kim recalled that in the call the governor "goes off about how I hadn't seen his wrath and anger, that he would destroy me and he would go out tomorrow and start telling how bad of a person I am and I would be finished and how he had bit his tongue about me for months. This was all yelling. It wasn't a pleasant tone."

But Kim was not intimidated. With a group of Democratic colleagues, he signed a letter that declared, "It is now unambiguously clear that this governor has engaged in an intentional obstruction of justice, as outlined in Title 18, Chapter 73 of the United States Code." In response to what they described as "criminal use of power," Kim and State Senator Alessandra Biaggi, a Bronx Democrat, announced that they were introducing legislation to repeal the amendments to the state Executive Law, which had been enacted in the early days of the pandemic to expand the governor's authority.

"This is a necessary first step in beginning to right the criminal wrongs of this governor and his administration," wrote Kim and his colleagues, who explained that, if legislators failed to hold Cuomo to account "then we too shall be complicit along with this administration in the obstruction of justice and conscious omission of nursing homes death data. We must absolutely consider above all the sanctity of the democratic institution that we call the Legislature of the State of New York, and resolutely pursue justice in the face of an executive who we can say without hesitation has engaged in intentional criminal wrongdoing."

Cuomo was furious. Not with himself, or with aides who had given him terrible advice, but with Kim. At a February 17, 2021, briefing, the embattled governor claimed that Kim was a racketeer who had engaged in behavior that the governor said he believed to be "unethical if not illegal."

In fact, it was the governor whose behavior had come under scrutiny—not just for covering up nursing home deaths but also, according to a number of women who stepped up to tell their stories, for sexual harassment. By mid-March 2021, senators Chuck Schumer and Kirsten Gillibrand had joined New York City mayor Bill de Blasio, state comptroller Thomas DiNapoli, twenty members of the state's congressional delegation and dozens of legislators in calling for the governor's resignation. Ron Kim was one of them.

The lurid allegations of harassment drew most of the headlines. Kim took them seriously. But he also kept pushing on the nursing home issue. With a growing cadre of legislative allies, he made progress on one of the most vital fronts: an effort to repeal a corporate immunity shield for hospitals and nursing homes that had been inserted into the state budget Cuomo crafted, shepherded to passage and signed into law at the height of the pandemic, in April 2020.

"Imagine fielding hundreds of calls from worried constituents at the peak of the first Covid-19 wave, trying to help scared families protect loved ones in nursing homes," Kim explained. "Imagine being stonewalled by those nursing homes and the department of health as you sought answers to life-and-death questions, knowing that Governor Andrew Cuomo's directive forced these unprepared facilities to take in thousands of Covid-positive patients. This was what I was going through as a New York state assemblyman when I received a call from a *New York Times* reporter about a corporate legal-immunity provision that gave for-profit nursing homes and hospitals get-out-of-jail-free cards."

Cuomo's shield was similar to the immunity shield that Mitch McConnell, then the Senate majority leader, had demanded at the federal level. Both removed one of the most powerful tools families and advocates for the elderly and the disabled could use to pressure nursing homes to maintain health and safety standards. Indeed, the shield's language specifically barred family members, guardians and patients from suing nursing homes over care "related to the diagnosis or treatment of Covid-19." And it was retroactive to before Cuomo issued his order requiring nursing homes to accept Covid-positive patients.

"They decided to protect the business interests of those who should have done everything possible, spent every dollar, to save people's lives," Kim, furious, told *Jacobin*. "But the moment they got the legal immunity, it was clear that they felt like they didn't have to invest anymore in PPE, or hire more staff members. They completely shut down. They had a license to kill. That's what the immunity was."

Cuomo aides claimed that the governor's decision to insert the immunity protection into the budget at the last minute before it was enacted was "intended to increase capacity and provide quality care, and any suggestion otherwise is simply outrageous." But the governor did not brag about his decision. Indeed, as Kim wrote in an essay for the *Guardian*: "Many of my colleagues had no idea the 2020 budget contained a legal shield that gave nursing home executives, trustees and board members blanket immunity. I voted against the budget bill, but if more members knew about the full implications of the legal immunity clause, there was no chance it would have passed."

Why was Cuomo so determined to add the immunity shield? One answer, outlined by investigative journalist David Sirota, had to do with campaign contributions that benefited the governor when he was seeking a third term in 2018. The immunity provision was inserted in Cuomo's budget eighteen months after the Greater New York Hospital Association steered $1.25 million into the coffers of the Cuomo-controlled New York State Democratic Committee, which was assisting his re-election run. As Sirota explained: "The GNYHA donations—which were a huge increase from prior years—made the group one of the New York Democratic Party's largest contributors during Cuomo's campaign. Three of the hospital association's top officials separately gave more than $150,000 to Cuomo's campaign between 2015 and 2018. In all, during the governor's second term, Cuomo's campaign and his state party committee raked in more than $2.3 million from hospital and nursing home industry donors and their lobbying firms, according to data compiled by the National Institute on Money in Politics."

Nor did Cuomo and his allies stop taking big money when the 2018 campaign was done. "Health care groups and lobbyists tied to nursing homes flooded Gov. Cuomo's campaign coffers with cash last year, as the state shielded hospitals and long-term care facilities from the threat of lawsuits stemming from the coronavirus outbreak," according to a New York *Daily News* article in February 2021. Pointing to evidence that Cuomo accepted more than $125,000 in donations from health care industry interests and lobbyists during the period when the 2021–2 budget was being crafted, Kim demanded that the governor release all details of interactions between the governor's administration and the lobbyists, return all the money given by the industry and repeal the immunity clause so that patients and family members could sue to hold the owners of hospitals or nursing homes to account.

"It's clear that that industry wrote the bill, and they're one of the only groups that had access at that time," said Kim. "You can't put a toxic bill like that in the budget without having full access to the executive office."

While parts of the immunity provision were repealed by the legislature in the summer of 2020, Kim, New York City Public Advocate Jumaane Williams and others pressed for a full repeal of the clause and a federal inquiry into all the issues raised by the nursing home deaths. There were also calls for Comptroller DiNapoli to formally refer the matter to Attorney General James so that she could launch a broader state probe of the nursing home toll.

Cuomo felt the heat. Despite his crude private and public attacks on Ron Kim, he agreed on April 6, 2021, to sign a bill sponsored by the legislator that fully repealed the broad liability protections granted to nursing homes and hospitals at a point when Cuomo could, supposedly, do no wrong.

That was a victory. But the legislator was not done with the governor. "Now," said Ron Kim, "we must hold Andrew Cuomo accountable for his abuse of power and deadly decisions that led to countless deaths."

Months later, after Cuomo announced on August 10 that he would resign rather than face a fight over whether he should remain in office, Democratic leaders in the New York legislature signaled that they would not pursue the impeachment process they had initiated. Kim disapproved. "I can comfortably say that many of our colleagues are still puzzled about how we arrived at this point where we failed to properly hold Andrew Cuomo to account," he explained. Then, with the clarity that had distinguished his long struggle with the governor, Kim declared, "We must reconvene to discuss our legal and constitutional duty as it pertains to impeachment."

While others blinked, Ron Kim maintained a clear vision of why accountability was needed, and of what had to be done to achieve it.

The Deadly Delusions of Wisconsin Supreme Court Justice Rebecca Bradley

It shall be so. Madness in great ones must not unwatched go.
—William Shakespeare, *Hamlet*

Wisconsin Supreme Court Justice Rebecca Bradley was not the only jurist who decided against public health as the coronavirus pandemic took hold. But she did so more absurdly and more dangerously than any other, staking out an awful four-corner intersection of intellectual dishonesty, historical revision, partisan gaslighting and willful indifference to a deadly virus.

Scant attention was paid during the course of 2020 and 2021 to the damage conservative judicial activists such as Bradley did to the fight against Covid-19. But it was real, and widespread. Across the country, jurists struck down mask mandates, social distancing rules and plans for shuttering restaurants, bars and schools, along with other measures meant to slow the spread of Covid-19. The US Supreme Court's conservative majority even stepped in to tell officials in New York, and later in California, that they could not block indoor church services where the virus might spread. The nation's highest court struck something of a balance, however, with a determination that states could bar the singing of hymns and the chanting of prayers in closed spaces. Chief Justice John Roberts even admitted, somewhat grudgingly, that "federal courts owe significant deference to politically accountable officials with the 'background, competence and expertise to assess public health.'"

At the state and local levels, however, reactionary jurists abandoned the chief justice's balancing of public safety with civil liberties and embraced a radical interpretation of the law that imagined public health mandates as "tyranny." The state court that did the most to politicize the fight against the virus and to undermine efforts to establish a united front on behalf of science and common sense was Wisconsin's. There, according to CNN, judicial interventions against public health orders created "coronavirus chaos." Public health officers and scientists warned that this chaos would lead to more confusion, more sickness and more death. Yet the conservative majority on the Wisconsin court kept stirring it up.

In April 2020, after states across the country had moved presidential primary election dates to avoid forcing people who could not obtain absentee ballots to go to polling places in the midst of a pandemic, Wisconsin's Supreme Court prevented the Democratic governor, Tony Evers, from implementing a plan for extended voting by mail. That decision created a circumstance that the Wisconsin health services secretary, Andrea Palm, said would "without question, accelerate the transmission of Covid-19 and increase the number of cases." This increase, warned Palm, a former chief of staff for the US Department of Health and Human Services, "would result in more deaths." In May 2020, after the court struck down the state's "Safer at Home" public health orders, Madison mayor Satya Rhodes-Conway noted, "The

Wisconsin Supreme Court is the only court in the nation to strike down a public health order that has been a major success in preventing death and illness in Wisconsin."

The court's decisions served to "deepen the tribal thinking that's already emerged around even basic facts," observed Dietram Scheufele, a University of Wisconsin–Madison professor who specialized in communication about scientific issues. They also made no sense. In an assessment of the state Supreme Court's interventions against public health orders, Ruth Conniff, a veteran commentator on Wisconsin politics, described "an unpleasant racial undertone" in the legal assault on public health orders that protected the most vulnerable in a state where "for a variety of reasons, the victims of Covid-19 have been disproportionately black and brown." She also noted the logical fallacy of imagining that the disease would not eventually spread far beyond the urban centers where it initially caused so much devastation. Yet that is the fallacy the court kept embracing, even as the virus did indeed spread to the suburbs and ultimately to rural communities.

"In addition to being heartless," Conniff wrote of the court's anti-scientific approach, "this kind of thinking is downright delusional." And it can safely be said that Rebecca Bradley was the most dangerously delusional justice.

That was no small matter on a shambolic court that drew national attention as a "Fight Club," after a 2013 incident in which a conservative male justice wrapped his hands around the neck of a liberal female jurist and attempted to put her in a chokehold. Plagued by controversy from the time in the early 2000s that out-of-state billionaires and their corporate allies began to flood Wisconsin with campaign dollars to secure a pro-business majority, the titularly nonpartisan state Supreme Court was widely understood as a redoubt of what the Brennan

Center for Justice referred to as "million-dollar justices." Despite its record of ethical lapses, rank partisanship and sexist violence, however, no one expected the court's conservative majority to prevent the state from responding to the coronavirus pandemic. Until it did.

Throughout 2020, the Wisconsin court operated as the judicial extension of Republican legislative leaders who made no secret of their determination to thwart the state's Democratic governor as he sought to combat Covid-19. Channeling the deliberate deceptions, delaying tactics and warped priorities of President Trump, the Republican who controlled the Wisconsin Assembly and Senate refused to cooperate with Evers, who in 2018 had narrowly defeated their long-time Republican ally, Scott Walker, to take charge of the politically divided state. A former high school science teacher who had spent his lifetime as an educator, Evers took the pandemic threat seriously from day one. As a cancer survivor, the almost seventy-year-old governor was well aware of the danger an insufficient response might pose to vulnerable Wisonsinites. He reached out immediately to Assembly Speaker Robin Vos, an ambitious conservative who was thought to be considering a gubernatorial run of his own, and Senate Majority Leader Scott Fitzgerald, a stalwart Trump backer who in the fall of 2020 would win a gerrymandered US House seat, fly to Washington and promptly vote to overturn the results of the presidential election that swept Trump from office. Instead of welcoming the chance to be a part of the solution, Vos and Fitzgerald mocked the governor for the rigor with which he approached the crisis. Evers tried everything: scientific and political arguments, cajoling and begging. But, after a brief flurry of activity in April 2020, the Republicans refused to call their chambers into session, making Wisconsin's the least active full-time state legislative body in the nation during the pandemic.

While states as distinct as Montana, Maryland and Vermont saw bipartisan cooperation between governors of one party and legislatures of the other, Wisconsin stalled out so completely that Tim Carpenter, a veteran Democratic state senator from Milwaukee, referred to the chamber in which he had served for decades as a "farce" where throughout the year GOP leaders failed "to convene session to debate and pass bills to help Wisconsinites during the Covid-19 pandemic and the resulting economic fallout" and refused "to accept any responsibility for their total mismanagement of the virus." Late in 2020, meanwhile, at a point when each day was bringing reports of spiking infection levels and record death tolls, Vos claimed that the legislature had done its part to combat Covid-19. The nonpartisan fact-checking service PolitiFact reviewed his statement and rated it "False," noting that "Wisconsin lagged behind many other states in passing Covid-19 legislation, to the point where lawmakers lost out on federal aid for unemployment." When a top Vos lieutenant, Assembly Majority Leader Jim Steineke, claimed that legislative Republicans had engaged in the "give and take that is needed to get things done" and that "Assembly Republicans have come to the table and made concessions," PolitiFact again attached the "False" label. "This characterization of the Assembly action is disingenuous at best," explained the fact checkers.

As the virus raged, another veteran Democratic state senator, Jon Erpenbach, complained: "Republican leadership refuses to take this seriously. They are dragging their feet." But there was one front on which Vos and Fitzgerald were quite active. When Governor Evers issued public health orders, the Republican legislative leaders sued to overturn them. The suits usually succeeded, as they ended up in the Supreme Court, where five conservative justices had turned the judicial branch into a third chamber of the Republican-controlled legislature. It got so bad that Mayor

Tom Barrett of Milwaukee observed at the pandemic's peak: "Right now our Supreme Court acts more like a jukebox for the Republican leadership in the Legislature. They put in a coin and the Wisconsin Supreme Court plays the song they want them to play."

Even as the court met virtually to protect the health and safety of the seven justices, the majority engaged in right-wing judicial activism so detrimental to the fight against Covid-19 that critics of the conservative justices referred to them as a "death cult." The most over-the-top judicial activist on a high court bench crowded with reactionaries was Rebecca Bradley. A controversial Scott Walker appointee, Bradley won a full ten-year term on the bench in a 2016 election in which, to secure her victory, almost $2 million was spent by the Wisconsin Alliance for Reform, a group organized by a former operative for the billionaire right-wing donors Charles and David Koch. She quickly earned a reputation as the most strikingly ill-informed and wrongheaded of the justices in a majority that was often referred to as a "clown car."

Bradley confirmed her status in an outrageously clumsy concurrence with the decision by the court's right-wing majority to overturn the Safer at Home emergency order that Evers had urged the state Department of Health Services to issue, and then extend, as the pandemic swept the state in the spring of 2020. In her critique of the public health measures (which simply sought to align Wisconsin with other states that were encouraging people to slow the spread of the virus by staying at home), Bradley devoted several pages to comparing public health mandates with the World War II–era removal of 120,000 Japanese Americans from their homes and communities and the forcible detention of these citizens in distant internment camps.

This was an astonishing extension of Bradley's line of questioning during oral arguments on the case, which had shocked

Japanese-American civil rights leaders. Bradley interrupted a lawyer for the state with an announcement that "I'll direct your attention to another time in history, in the *Korematsu* decision, where the [US Supreme Court] said the need for action was great and time was short, and that justified, and I'm quoting, 'assembling together and placing under guard all those of Japanese ancestry' in assembly centers during World War II."

The US Supreme Court's 1944 decision in the case of *Korematsu v. United States* approved the internment of Japanese Americans in the aftermath of Imperial Japan's surprise attack on Pearl Harbor on December 7, 1941. Along with the Dred Scott decision, it was one of the most shameful judicial assaults on civil rights and civil liberties in the nation's history. On February 19, 1942, President Franklin Roosevelt issued Executive Order 9066, which declared that "the successful prosecution of the war requires every possible protection against espionage and against sabotage to national defense material, national defense premises, and national defense utilities as defined." To that end, FDR directed the Secretary of War and the military commanders "to prescribe military areas . . . from which any or all persons may be excluded." While the order permitting the exclusion of US citizens from vast sections of the country threatened the rights of German-Americans and Italian-Americans during the course of World War II, it primarily targeted Japanese-Americans living on the West Coast, roughly 112,000 of whom were held in what were effectively American concentration camps through the duration of the war.

Fred Toyosaburo Korematsu, a welder who was born in 1919 to Japanese-American parents in Oakland, California, refused to obey the order. He was arrested and convicted under Public Law No. 503, a measure Roosevelt had signed to allow for criminal prosecution of violations of military orders issued pursuant to Executive Order 9066. Sent to a relocation center in Utah, Korematsu was forced to work for $12 a month and slept in a horse stall. Korematsu, whose loyalty to the United States was never in question, appealed his conviction and internment in a case that eventually made its way to the nation's high court. On December 18, 1944, a 6-3 majority upheld the conviction. In a groundbreaking dissent, Justice Frank Murphy wrote that the exclusion and internment of Japanese-Americans "falls into the ugly abyss of racism" and compared it to "the abhorrent and despicable treatment of minority groups by the dictatorial tyrannies which this nation is now pledged to destroy." While the position taken by Murphy did not prevail inside the US Supreme Court chambers in the fall of 1944, it won in the court of history. Today, the American Constitution Society identifies *Korematsu* as a "justifiably reviled Supreme Court decision, one long regarded as a leading case in the American constitutional anti-canon." Bruce Fein, a constitutional lawyer who served as associate deputy attorney general under President Ronald Reagan, wrote, "*Korematsu* has joined *Dred Scott* as an odious and discredited artifact of popular bigotry." And in 2018, US Supreme Court Chief Justice Roberts repudiated the *Korematsu* decision in his majority opinion in the case of *Trump v. Hawaii*, where he wrote, "*Korematsu* was gravely wrong the day it was decided, has been overruled in the court of history, and—to be clear—'has no place in law under the Constitution.'"

Given Roberts's relatively recent citation of the *Korematsu* decision, it was not surprising that a state Supreme Court justice might reference it. But Justice Bradley's choice to direct the attention of Wisconsin Supreme Court to "another time in history" and "the *Korematsu* decision" was a shocking twist in a deliberation about requirements for social distancing in order to stop the spread of a virus.

After she directed attention to the *Korematsu* decision, Bradley asked state Assistant Attorney General Colin Roth: "Could the secretary under this broad delegation of legislative power or legislative-like power order people out of their homes into centers where they are properly social distanced in order to combat the pandemic? The point of my question is what are the limits, constitutional or statutory? There have to be some, don't there, counsel?"

The justice was channeling a critique of public health orders promoted by some of the loonier followers of President Trump, who imagined that mask mandates and social-distancing orders were a form of oppression. At rallies opposing public-health orders, protesters declared, "We're here to fight tyranny" and carried signs that portrayed masks as "the new face of tyranny."

For his part, Roth calmly noted that the state's statutes permitted the secretary of the Department of Department of Health Services to "forbid public gatherings in schools, churches and other places to control outbreaks and epidemics." The lawyer directed the justice to legislative language that clearly established the DHS "may authorize and implement all emergency measures necessary to control communicable disease." He explained that, were the court to strike down the Safer at Home order: "The disease will spread like wildfire, and we will be back into a terrible situation with an out-of-control virus with no weapon to fight it. People will die if this order is enjoined with nothing to replace it. That is exactly what will happen."

Bradley registered no reaction. She just kept suggesting that asking people to wear masks to prevent the spread of a deadly virus could put Wisconsin on a slippery slope to round-ups of minorities, internment camps and tyranny.

The justice's line of questioning provoked a national outcry. *Esquire*'s Charles Pierce observed that Bradley was "boldly exploring the experimental side of Bad Historical Analogy Theater." The Japanese American Citizens League (JACL) rebuked Bradley, with the group's Wisconsin chapter president, Ron Kuramoto, saying: "I believe Wisconsin Supreme Court Justice Rebecca Bradley poses a false equivalency when she uses the Safer at Home policy as a comparison for Executive Order 9066, which forced my parents, extended family, and over 120,000 Japanese Americans out of their homes and into, in some cases, horse stalls at Santa Anita Racetrack in California, then transferred and imprisoned my own and other families for over three years in shoddily built tarpaper barracks in the desert or other desolate places. Bradley's hyperbole denigrates my parents' suffering and endurance."

That would have caused any reasonable jurist to pause. But Bradley was not serving as a reasonable jurist. She had positioned herself as a hyper-partisan, hyper-ideological judicial activist who played the same game of win-at-any-cost politics that her legislative allies, Vos and Fitzgerald, practiced with abandon.

So it was that in her concurrence with the high court's 4-3 decision to align itself with the extreme stance of Vos and Fitzgerald, Bradley amplified her internment analogy. Aware that her questions had caused offense and inspired a lively debate about her competence, the justice was desperate to cover for herself. Bradley claimed in her concurrence that "although headlines may sensationalize the invocation of cases such as *Korematsu*, the point of citing them is not to draw comparisons between the circumstances of people horrifically interned by their government during a war and those of people subjected to isolation orders during a pandemic." But, of course, that is precisely what she was doing. Indeed, the next line she wrote acknowledged that she was recalling legal wrangling over the internment of Japanese-Americans "to remind the state that urging courts to approve the exercise of extraordinary power during times of emergency may lead to extraordinary abuses of its citizens."

That was too much for one of the country's more prominent Japanese-Americans. On the morning after the Wisconsin Supreme Court ruling came down, actor George Takei objected. Takei, famous for his role as Hikaru Sulu, the helmsman of the USS *Enterprise* in the *Star Trek* television series and in a half dozen *Star Trek* films, recalled in a Twitter post his own family's internment:

"Justice Rebecca Bradley of the WI Supreme Ct compared WI's stay-at-home order to 'assembling together and placing under guard all those of Japanese ancestry in assembly centers during World War II.'

"I'm in my own home watching Netflix. It's not an internment camp. Trust me."

That Time Rahm Emanuel Offshored America's Ability to Fight a Pandemic

The marketplace, by itself, cannot resolve every problem, however much we are asked to believe this dogma of neoliberal faith. Whatever the challenge, this impoverished and repetitive school of thought always offers the same recipes. Neoliberalism simply reproduces itself by resorting to the magic theories of "spillover" or "trickle"—without using the name—as the only solution to societal problems.

—Pope Francis, October 5, 2020

When the coronavirus pandemic hit, one of the most asked questions in America was, Why were we so unprepared? There was plenty of blame to go around in a country with a long history of rejecting the sort of planning that other countries recognize as essential. Necessarily, a lot of the blame for the immediate catastrophe was placed at the doorstep of Donald Trump. A PBS *Frontline* documentary, produced as the pandemic was unfolding in the spring of 2020, detailed the president's "halting" response in the months before infections and death tolls surged. "I would equate it to something like seeing a hurricane offshore that has just taken out a couple of the Caribbean Islands and is strengthening to category five as it heads for Florida," said Jeremy Konyndyk, who had coordinated the Obama administration's response to the 2014 Ebola outbreak, "and not bothering to tell people to get off the beach and board their windows [and] only starting to do that when you see the storm start coming to shore, by which point it's, of course, far too late."

Trump's Democratic critics embraced that assessment with relish in a presidential election year, as they amplified *Frontline's* review of "the Trump administration's reorganization of an Obama–era National Security Council–level pandemic response office, and its early emphasis on simply closing borders to combat the virus rather than implementing comprehensive preparedness, social distancing and testing strategies." They also noted the struggles of the CDC to develop and mass distribute a working Covid-19 test in the critical early stages of the pandemic. In February, when testing should have been ramping up, Scott Becker, of the Association of Public Health Laboratories, said: "We were left without the biggest tool in our tool box at that point. We were flying blind."

All true. But the tendency to blame the sitting administration for a lack of preparedness missed the point that, in many senses, the crisis was decades in the making. While there had been positive steps along the way, like President Obama's work on creating the pandemic response office, the truth is that the missteps and misdeeds of Republican and Democratic administrations had left the United States vulnerable.

Partisans on all sides like to suggest that when problems have deep and intersecting roots, it is difficult to identify their sources. But that's just a dodge favored by a permanent political class that, even as it engages in the internecine conflicts of the moment, tends to coalesce to protect itself. There are, of course, instances when forensic political science may be required to identify the guilty men and women. But there are always some culprits who stand out, for what they did at specific times in the past, and for the consistency of their stances on the wrong side of history.

Which brings us to Rahm Emanuel. When the pandemic struck, Emanuel emerged as one of the most prominent Democratic commentators on the crisis in general and its economic consequences in particular. A top adviser to the most recent Democratic presidents, a former congressman and a former mayor of Chicago, Emanuel was all over television and in the newspaper op-ed columns, announcing with his typical bravado: "We need to use this crisis to fix our public health system, our medical infrastructure and our industrial capacity. Trump may be outmatched by the moment, but the rest of the United States can rise to meet this crisis."

What Emanuel didn't say was that one of the most coherent explanations for the lack of preparation on the part of the United States could be traced to his long tenure in positions of influence. And, more specifically, to his use of those positions to advance a free-trade agenda that led to the offshoring of basic industries that were vital to producing the tests, protective gear and medical equipment that was needed to combat a fast-approaching pandemic.

Much is made of the devastating impact that the free-trade policies of the past thirty years have had on American workers, and rightly so. As Policy Matters Ohio noted in its 2020 study, *Promises Unfulfilled: Manufacturing in the Midwest*, "Despite promises of creative destruction, where manufacturing jobs would be replaced by a new generation of well-paid service work in a knowledge economy, corporate offshoring and closures destroyed jobs that were never replaced with new ones of comparable quality." But the loss of jobs and wages was just part of the story. The United States also lost basic industries that produced essential goods.

"Production has shifted overseas so extensively that the United States is now dependent on other countries, particularly China, to supply many of our necessities, from medical supplies to 5G to the simplest of screws," political economist Dan Breznitz, co-director of the Innovation Policy Lab at the Munk School of the University of Toronto, and David Adler, a specialist on industrial policy, explained as the pandemic took hold. "Ninety-five percent of surgical masks and 70 percent of respirators used in the United States are produced abroad. The last domestic penicillin plant closed in 2004."

This was the harsh reality that Rahm Emanuel began forging when he served as Bill Clinton's neoliberal senior adviser—the "Rahmbo" of the 1990s—and that he extended as Barack Obama's foul-mouthed chief of staff in 2009 and 2010. It was the project he was prepared to continue when, after the election of Joe Biden to the presidency in November 2020, Emanuel indicated that he very much wanted to join the newest Democratic administration. This permanent fixture in Democratic administrations was initially touted as a potential cabinet member, perhaps as secretary of transportation, or even as the new US trade representative. But it didn't happen, after intense opposition to Emanuel's potential nomination surfaced among progressives nationally and particularly in Chicago, where he had served a scandal-plagued eight years as the city's chief executive. Emanuel started angling for a major diplomatic post, despite a well-documented record of distinctly undiplomatic behavior.

In the spring of 2021, there was talk of handing Emanuel a plum ambassadorship in Beijing or Tokyo. That talk did not sit well with those who knew his record on the international stage. At a point when unions, environmental groups and human rights organizations were stressing the need for international solidarity in the face of the overwhelming challenges posed by the pandemic and the economic downturn stemming from it, Emanuel remained an advocate for the failed free-trade policies that harmed workers and communities in the United States and countries around the world. Putting the Wall Street–aligned fixer whom Public Citizen Global Trade Watch director Lori Wallach described as a "corporate hack extraordinaire" in a position where he could again influence US trade policy with China, Japan and other countries, would, Wallach warned, be "catastrophic" for human rights, worker rights and environmental justice. Many concurred with her assessment. "We've said it before and we'll say it again—Rahm Emanuel is a ladder-climbing hack who is unfit to serve anywhere in the Biden administration," said People's Action deputy director Bree Carlson.

Opposition to any Emanuel nomination for any post in a Democratic administration focused primarily on his 2011-to-2019 track record in Chicago, where he earned the label "Mayor 1%." The details of his tenure were more than sufficient to disqualify him from consideration. "As the former mayor of Chicago, Rahm Emanuel has shown us that he is not a principled leader or person," National Association for the Advancement of Colored People president Derrick Johnson said. "His time in public service proved to be burdened with preventable scandal and abandonment of Chicago's most vulnerable community. How can we expect him to do better on a federal level? His actions and approach to governing are detrimental to the Biden administration and, more importantly, the American people."

The NAACP had many allies when it came to warning against putting Emanuel in any position of public trust. More than two dozen groups—including People's Action, Progressive Democrats of America, the Working Families Party, Roots Action, and Black

Youth Project 100—issued a statement opposing an ambassadorial nomination for Emanuel. In it, they insisted that "Emanuel's disgraceful behavior as mayor of Chicago cannot be erased or ignored. At a time when the Democratic Party leadership has joined with most Americans in asserting that Black lives matter, it would be a travesty to elevate to an ambassadorship someone who has epitomized the attitude that Black lives do not matter. After being elected mayor of Chicago in 2011, Emanuel presided over a scandal-plagued administration that included the closing of forty-nine public schools, many in Black neighborhoods. As he faced a reelection campaign, for thirteen months Emanuel's administration suppressed a horrific dashcam video showing the death of Laquan McDonald, an African-American teenager who had been shot sixteen times by a Chicago police officer as he walked away from the officer. Soon after a judge ordered the city to release the video, polling found that only 17 percent of Chicagoans believed Emanuel when he said he'd never seen the video; most city residents wanted him to resign as mayor." President Biden disregarded the warnings and in August tapped Emanuel for the post in Tokyo.

The decision to offer Emanuel an ambassadorial post, especially one with a major trading partner, stirred unique concerns stemming from the record of Emanuel's tenures in the Clinton and Obama administrations, when he was an ardent advocate for Wall Street–friendly free trade policies. Those concerns were heightened by scorching realities that the pandemic brought to light. Critics of Emanuel recognized that dispatching an architect of the corporate globalization agendas that had already devastated American manufacturing to Beijing or Tokyo at a point when the global economy of the post-pandemic era was being organized, made no sense—for beleaguered workers in the United States, China, Japan or the rest of the world. And for the mission of planning to avert future pandemics.

As a senior adviser to Clinton, Emanuel stamped a cruel brand on the administration, creating a pro-corporate image that would haunt the Democratic Party for decades. After the Clinton presidential library's release of Emanuel's memos from the 1990s, Chicago's WMAQ-TV reported that they revealed the aide had been "urging the president to crack down on undocumented immigrants and take a stronger stand on combating crime as part of a strategy to appropriate GOP platforms for political gain." Emanuel proposed that Clinton adopt a hard-line stance in favor of roundups, detentions and deportations so that the president could "claim a number of industries free of illegal immigrants."

At the same time that Emanuel wanted to punish immigrants who were working for subsistence wages in meatpacking plants and warehouses in the United States, he wanted to go easy on multinational corporations that had rigged trade policies in order to maximize not just their profits but their ability to move high-paying manufacturing jobs out of American cities and towns. It was Emanuel who was the strategist in the Clinton administration's bitter fights for the North American Free Trade Agreement, approval of the General Agreement on Tariffs and Trade, US entry into the World Trade Organization and the initiation of a trade regimen with China that human rights advocates denounced.

In every instance, Emanuel battled unions, environmentalists, democracy activists and advocates for planned industrial policies who warned about the danger of offshoring basic industries. Those fights divided the Democratic coalition against itself and left party leaders—including presidential nominees such as Al Gore in 2000 and Hillary Clinton in 2016—vulnerable to attacks from crudely cynical Republicans like Trump for "selling out" working-class Americans. Later, as chief of staff for the Obama administration, Emanuel continued to promote neoliberal policies. Famously, he spewed obscenities at progressives who wanted to include a public option for purchasing health care coverage in the Affordable Care Act. When union members sought more protections for American workers and domestic manufacturing at a critical stage in negotiations to prop up the auto industry, Emanuel reportedly shouted, "Fuck the UAW!"

After Emanuel left the Obama White House and returned to Chicago, Politico reported on how he served as an "unabashedly pro-trade" mayor in an article headlined: "Chi-town opens arms to China." He was especially outspoken in support of the Obama administration's push for the proposed Trans-Pacific Partnership, and for the Transatlantic Trade and Investment Partnership with member countries of the European Union. Emanuel organized mayors to support what he said would "amount to the biggest free-trade push in US history." He did so even as Chicago fair-trade activists warned of the threat those agreements posed for US manufacturing and international human rights.

"Trade can't be free when workers in one country are denied their basic human rights," explained Carson Starkey, who during Emanuel's mayoralty served as director of the Illinois Fair Trade Coalition. "We've seen this in US–China trade relations, with big corporations racing to relocate jobs to wherever labor is the most exploited and environmental regulations are the weakest, profiting off of brutal sweatshop working conditions. Now, amazingly, the administration is proposing an even worse Trans-Pacific Partnership trade agreement with countries like Vietnam, where the average minimum wage is just a third of that in China's manufacturing sectors."

Emanuel did not always succeed in promoting free trade deals. But, even as objections to the TPP and the TTIP schemes were being raised by prominent Democrats, he defended them with his usual combination of certainty and belligerence. As mayor, he traveled to Asia as an advocate for trade deals that big investors loved but unions despised. In 2018, when he visited Tokyo, he was described as a "pro-globalization" campaigner who declared, "I do believe in open trade, especially with our friends across the globe."

The problem with that belief, which was shared by Wall Street–aligned Democrats and Republicans, was that it severely undermined the diversity of US manufacturing. Whole industries shut down as production was offshored, according to a 2020 Economic Policy Institute report, which detailed how the United States lost more than 91,000 manufacturing plants and nearly 5 million manufacturing jobs since 1997.

Offshoring at that level did not have to happen. Yes, of course, in an increasingly globalized economy, countries would trade with one another and some manufacturing facilities, and jobs would be moved. But, as Lori Wallach noted in 2008, "The wide-scale export of US jobs is not inevitable, but rather is a result of our current failed trade agreements, which provide expansive new protections for US firms to ship investment and jobs offshore."

Even as the factory closings mounted, Emanuel kept promoting free trade dogma in the Clinton administration, in the private sector, as a member of Congress, as a member of the Obama administration, as a mayor and after he left City Hall as a political commentator. He wasn't alone, but he was always the loudest—and, often, most listened to—Democratic advocate for the billionaire-approved line on trade policy.

When the coronavirus pandemic hit, Americans began to recognize the full impact of decades of free trade absolutism. "The scale of the plague is surprising, indeed shocking, but not its appearance," said Noam Chomsky in April 2020. "Nor the fact that the US has the worst record in responding to the crisis. Scientists have been warning of a pandemic for years. Scientific understanding is not enough. There has to be someone to pick up the ball and run with it. That option was barred by the pathology of the contemporary socioeconomic order. Market signals were clear: There's no profit in preventing a future catastrophe. The government could have stepped in, but that's barred by reigning doctrine. 'Government is the problem,' Reagan told us with his sunny smile, meaning that decision-making has to be handed over even more fully to the business world, which is devoted to private profit and is free from influence by those who might be concerned with the common good. The years that followed injected a dose of neoliberal brutality to the unconstrained capitalist order and the twisted form of markets it constructs."

Scholars of industrial policy—or, in the case of the United States, the lack of industrial policy—recognized in the crisis a measure of the country's decline as a manufacturing power. Describing "the panic in the United States over the lack of masks and ventilators for Covid-19" in the darkest days of the pandemic, Dan Breznitz and David Adler delivered an urgent message for Americans: "Please, don't let those scary few weeks fade too quickly. The scramble for medical equipment was a telling moment for the American economy because it revealed something alarming: The United States can no longer produce what it needs in a time of crisis, even if those things were invented here."

This was Emanuel's legacy, and it haunted America when the pandemic hit. Instead of taking steps to assure that critical personal protective equipment and other medical supplies would continue to be manufactured in the United States, the country had for decades embraced trade policies that, as Senator Sherrod Brown of Ohio told me when we talked about the shortages, actually encouraged firms to move production overseas. "That's why we didn't have the protective equipment we needed," Brown explained in the spring of 2020.

With Senator Tammy Baldwin of Wisconsin, a fellow Democrat who shared his concern about the loss of basic industries, Brown wrote early in 2021 to the Biden administration about how the pandemic had "demonstrated the risks of long foreign supply chains." That, they explained, triggered "shortages for crucial items like Personal Protective Equipment (PPE), ventilators and chemical inputs for pharmaceuticals due to lack of domestic industries in those products."

This wasn't hard to anticipate. During the trade debates of the 1990s, 2000s and 2010s, Brown, Baldwin and dozens of other principled Democrats had warned of concerns about free trade policies that were dictated by investors rather than the public interest. Unfortunately, Rahm Emanuel was on the other side of those debates—the wrong side—and his neoliberal hectoring left America unprepared.

Pfizer's Vaccine Profiteering

The rugged face of society, chequered with the extremes of affluence and want, proves that some extraordinary violence has been committed upon it, and calls on justice for redress.
—Thomas Paine, *Agrarian Justice*, 1797

The Rev. Martin Luther King Jr. spoke the most fundamental truth of the coronavirus pandemic forty-four years before the crisis hit. "We are concerned about the constant use of federal funds to support this most notorious expression of segregation," King said on March 25, 1966, at the second convention of the Medical Committee for Human Rights. "Of all the forms of inequality, injustice in health is the most shocking and the most inhuman because it often results in physical death."

When Covid-19 struck, King's words were frequently recalled, because the passing decades had not addressed health inequality. The Rev. William Barber II saw the truth immediately, observing in March 2020:

This moral crisis is coming to a head as the coronavirus pandemic lays bare America's deep injustices. While the virus itself does not discriminate, it is the poor and disenfranchised who will experience the most suffering and death. They're the ones who are least likely to have health care or paid sick leave, and the most likely to lose work hours. And though children appear less vulnerable to the virus than adults, America's nearly forty million poor and low-income children are at serious risk of losing access to food, shelter, education, and housing in the economic fallout from the pandemic. The underlying disease, in other words, is poverty, which was killing nearly 700 of us every day in the world's wealthiest country, long before anyone had heard of Covid-19.

As the pandemic grew more severe, physicians and scientists filled in the details. The Centers for Disease Control acknowledged that "longstanding systemic health and social inequities have put many people from racial and ethnic minority groups at increased risk of getting sick and dying from Covid-19." The *Lancet* observed that the pandemic "has highlighted the equity gap in outcomes for marginalized communities, specifically the Black community, as starkly shown by the disparate morbidity and mortality from Covid-19 in individuals from these communities compared with the majority white population." An Economic Policy Institute study determined that "persistent racial disparities in health status, access to health care, wealth, employment, wages, housing, income and poverty all contribute to greater susceptibility to the virus—both economically and physically." A Brookings Institute review of the data explained: "The coronavirus does not discriminate, but our housing, economic and health care policies do. Environmental racism, unaffordable housing, a lack of job opportunities, poverty and inadequate health care are underlying social conditions, strongly influenced by policy, which place Black people and their neighborhoods at risk. To flatten the curve of Covid-19 and prevent future pandemics from wreaking the same havoc, these conditions must be addressed."

Surely, this was the time to address racial, social and economic injustices that had always existed but that were now fully exposed. Yet through 2020 and into 2021, injustices persisted—not merely because it was difficult to undo them in short order but because the structures that had been established for responding to health care challenges actually perpetuated inequalities. So it was that, a year into the pandemic, when the United States and countries around the world were racing to administer the vaccines that would save lives and restore a measure of economic and social stability, a new phrase entered the vocabulary to go along with "health inequality": "vaccine inequality."

The international picture was jarring. In February 2021 *Science* magazine pinpointed "a stark reality" in the global response to the coronavirus pandemic. "Countries in Europe, Asia and the Americas have administered more than 175 million shots to protect people against Covid-19 since December 2020, with most countries giving priority to medical workers," the magazine reported. "But not a single country in sub-Saharan Africa has started immunizations—South Africa will be the first, this week—leaving health care workers dying in places where they are scarce to begin with." But inequality was not just evident in studies that compared wealthy and impoverished nations; it was present within wealthy nations. "A racial gap has opened up in the nation's Covid-19 vaccination drive, with Black Americans in many places lagging behind whites in receiving shots," explained the Associated Press in January 2020. "An early look at the seventeen states and two cities that have released racial breakdowns through Jan. 25 found that Black people in all places are getting inoculated at levels below their share of the general population, in some cases significantly below. That is true even though they constitute an oversize percentage of the nation's health care workers, who were put at the front of the line for shots when the campaign began in mid-December."

There were lots of explanations for the inequities, including the failure of the deliberately neglectful Trump administration to take the basic steps that were required to develop a smart and fair program for vaccination distribution in the United States, let alone the world. Much was made of the reticence of particular communities to trust vaccination programs administered by a government with an ugly history of medical experimentation without transparency and medical neglect without compassion for racial and ethnic minorities.

But not much attention was given to another factor: the way the US economy is rigged to benefit multinational corporations at the expense of common sense and common decency. It's not just capitalism that is a problem, although the pandemic certainly revealed a great many flaws in the theory that the market can resolve societal challenges. It's the way in which capitalism works in a country like the United States: with its cronyism, corruption, racketeering, lack of oversight and open invitations to the sort of cozy deal-making that well serves corporations but ill serves humanity. Despite all the acknowledgments of inequality, the structures remained unchanged.

So it was that a year of pandemic profiteering gave way to the inevitable vaccine profiteering. While the early reporting on the rollout of vaccines tended to portray pharmaceutical corporations and their CEO's as heroic figures, that was always a fantasy. By and large, they were in it for the money. And one company, Pfizer, was in it for very big money. First out of the gate with a complex vaccine, Pfizer raced to cut deals with countries around the world that were desperate for doses.

They were very good deals for Pfizer, which made it clear from the start of the race to find a vaccine that it intended to cash in on the pandemic. In the summer of 2020, long before anyone had gotten a jab, Pfizer CEO Albert Bourla announced that "we do anticipate making a profit on the vaccine." To those who suggested that Big Pharma should forgo big paychecks in order to address a crisis that had already taken so many lives and destabilized so much of the world, Bourla said, "You need to be very fanatic and radical to say something like that right now."

In fact, several pharmaceutical companies recognized a duty to forgo the most egregious forms of profiteering, in order to assure that vaccines got to people that needed them in the smoothest and most efficient ways possible. "US drugmaker Johnson & Johnson, along with AstraZeneca, which is developing a coronavirus vaccine in partnership with Oxford University, have both pledged to make their vaccines available on a not-for-profit basis during this pandemic," reported the *Guardian* in November 2020. "AstraZeneca, which is charging governments $3 to $5 a dose, also said last week that low-income countries would receive its vaccine on a cost basis 'in perpetuity.'"

And here's the twist. The other vaccines, which came online shortly after Pfizer's, were easier to store and distribute. In other words, they were far better suited to a mass vaccination program that sought to get doses to people who lived in underserved urban neighborhoods and remote rural areas, and who might lack the resources and options to make multiple appointments for multiple shots. But Pfizer stuck to the plan to turn an outrageous profit. How outrageous? Company estimates acknowledged that the profit per dose could be as high as 30 percent. But in a July 2020 note to investors, SVB Leerink analyst Geoffrey Porges estimated that the company's profit margin for the vaccine could be as high as 80 percent.

Based on a deal reached in the summer of 2020 with the US government, Pfizer agreed to supply 100 million vaccination doses, with an option to deliver another 500 million doses. The price tag for the company's two-shot course of vaccinations would be $39, or $19.50 per dose. The company would maintain that price in negotiations with other countries, said Bourla, who told a July conference call, "All the countries that are developed right now will not receive a lower price for the same volume commitment than the US."

Pfizer's profit? According to the *Guardian*: "Pfizer and the German biotech firm BioNTech stand to bring in nearly $13 billion in global sales from their coronavirus vaccine next year, which will be evenly split between the two companies, according to analysts at the US investment bank Morgan Stanley. Pfizer's half would be more than the US pharmaceutical group's best-selling product, a pneumonia vaccine that generated $5.8 billion last year."

Of course, people in the United States and around the world welcomed the sense of urgency that Pfizer and other pharmaceutical companies brought to the race to develop vaccines. Speed was of the essence in so vital an undertaking. When vaccine breakthroughs were announced, they were widely celebrated. Most observers accepted that the drug companies would benefit financially. What they didn't count on was the fierce determination of a particular company to maximize its own benefits.

How did Pfizer take advantage of the pandemic? Let's turn to John A. Quelch, the dean of the University of Miami Patti and Allan Herbert Business School and a professor in the

Miller School of Medicine's Department of Public Health. "Pfizer's strategy is simple," he explained in December 2020. "Be first to market and make a boatload of money by 'skimming the cream,' supplying vaccines to those willing to pay. Pfizer has cut deals at high prices with about 20 developed countries. Their government agencies can't reject the Pfizer vaccine as too expensive because they can't ask their frontline healthcare workers to wait for a cheaper alternative. They have to act now."

For the *Tampa Bay Times*, Quelch wrote: "Pfizer set out to be first across the finish line and reap a public relations bonanza. That's why it pursued an mRNA vaccine, which can be developed and manufactured much faster than traditional vaccines. But Pfizer's vaccine has to be stored at minus-70 degrees Celsius to retain its efficacy. Developing countries do not have and cannot afford such a cold chain. That means Pfizer is off the hook to provide low- or no-cost doses to billions of people in poorer nations. The Moderna vaccine, also an mRNA vaccine, was designed to require normal vaccine refrigeration at around minus-20 degrees Celsius. Note, also, that Pfizer declined US government subsidies to fund its vaccine development. This preserved Pfizer's negotiating independence, avoided bureaucratic delays and helped Pfizer get to the finish line first. Taking no subsidies enabled Pfizer to deflect any government pressure to make its vaccine available at lower cost."

Savvy observers like Quelch may have been on to Pfizer, but the company kept cutting highly profitable deals. On December 23, 2020, the US Department of Health and Human Services and the Department of Defense announced plans to purchase an additional 100 million doses of Covid-19 vaccine from Pfizer. The deal included options for the purchase of an additional 400 million doses of the Pfizer vaccine.

Sweet for Pfizer, but tough for US taxpayers. The government would pay for the vaccines and distribute them free of charge to Americans at immense cost and immense inconvenience, because of the requirement that the Pfizer vaccine be refrigerated at exceptionally low temperatures and distributed in two doses. As Quelch noted in December, "Pfizer wanted to book a second big order now before the J&J results come in."

In other words, Pfizer's strategy was to play on the desperation of people and policy makers for a vaccine that might slow the spread of Covid-19 and save lives. This approach was guaranteed to benefit the bottom line of what was already one of the most profitable pharmaceutical giants in the history of the world. But it was bad practice for the United States and other countries that needed to use their resources to develop and implement comprehensive plans for getting vaccines to the people who needed them most.

Pfizer's strategy worked. In February 2021, the company announced that it expected to take in $15 billion from vaccine sales during the course of the year—making its product one of the highest revenue-generating drugs in the history of the world. Pfizer predicted that it expected to take in as much as $61 billion in 2021—almost $20 billion more than it had made in 2020. The Covid vaccine, an entirely new product developed as an emergency response to a crisis, would account for as much as 25 percent of Pfizer's profits, more than the company took in from its next three best-selling products combined.

By May of 2021, an industry monitor, *Pharmaceutical Technology*, reported, "Pfizer has vastly exceeded its Covid-19 vaccine sales forecast of $15bn, and now expects the jab to bring in $26bn of revenue in 2021—an increase of 73 percent on previously anticipated figures—with 1.6 billion doses set to be delivered under current contracts. It's possible that even this adjusted forecast will prove to be an underestimate, with Pfizer expected to secure further lucrative supply contracts throughout the year."

Pfizer CEO Bourla claimed the company's massive windfall was well deserved, bragging to interviewers that "the private sector found the solution for diagnostics, and the private sector found the solution . . . for therapeutics and vaccines."

But Pulitzer Prize–winning journalist Michael Hiltzik of the *Los Angeles Times* poked a great big hole in that assertion with a January 2021 assessment of how pharmaceutical companies were cashing in on the pandemic that labeled Pfizer's profits—and those of another pharmaceutical giant, Moderna—"a scandal."

"The notion that the 'private sector' achieved all this entirely on its own is the bedrock of the pharmaceutical industry's position that it deserves everything it can get," Hiltzik wrote. "But it's wrong. None of its diagnostics, therapeutics or vaccines would exist if the US and other developed countries hadn't funded research before the companies stepped in to exploit it. The role of public funding in drug development has been an open secret for decades. Its role in developing the Covid vaccines shouldn't escape scrutiny—and the private sector should be made to pay it back. Patent and IP (intellectual property) rights are worth billions, too, and the taxpayers should get their share."

Pfizer's profiteering did not surprise members of the AIDS Coalition to Unleash Power, better known as ACT UP, which got its start in the 1980s when playwright Larry Kramer and other activists formed the grassroots group to engage in direct action to demand that politicians and corporations respond to the AIDS crisis. ACT UP, which remained active in New York and other cities around the world, had long focused on the nefarious role played by pharmaceutical corporations in creating the health inequality that Dr. King called out decades earlier.

Years before the pandemic hit, ACT UP organized mass rallies outside the Pfizer headquarters in New York, where ACT UP activists aligned with campaigners from other health advocacy groups to deliver the message "Pfizer Greed Kills."

At a 2016 protest, activists warned that the pharmaceutical industry's "lies and continuous acts of financial greed" were limiting access to treatment and costing people their lives. ACT UP assembled this prescient set of complaints:

- Pfizer price gouges: In January 2016, Pfizer hiked the price of over 100 medicines, by up to 20 percent, including treatments for breast cancer, mental health, HIV, epilepsy, prostate cancer, pneumonia, skin and gut infections, acute myeloid leukemia, erectile dysfunction, menopause symptoms, diabetic peripheral neuropathy, fibromyalgia and heart disease. These price increases deviate from costs of inflation and regularly occur over the years.
- Pfizer lies: They claim that R&D for a medication costs over $1 billion. Their propaganda deceives the public to justify that they deserve billions of dollars in profit in order to recoup costs. Pfizer uses millions in public funds to develop drugs and needs to open its books to reveal the true R&D costs.
- Pfizer steals: Pfizer merged with Irish company Allergan in 2015 to permanently avoid paying up to $35 billion in US taxes. This is one of the largest tax dodges ever. Pfizer extorts money from patients who cannot afford its drugs while evading taxes.
- Pfizer kills children: Pfizer has refused to negotiate with Médecins Sans Frontières (MSF) to lower the price of the pneumonia vaccine to $5 per child. The vaccine can

save millions of children's lives, but is too expensive for many developing countries. In 2014 alone, Pfizer made $4.4 billion from vaccine sales. We support MSF and demand Pfizer to disclose the prices they charge all countries for this vaccine.

"The system is not fair; we effectively pay twice for medicines while Big Pharma profits," Mark Harrington, an activist with the Treatment Action Group, explained at the time. "We need a new approach for making drugs for serious and life threatening diseases—having the public invest in the research at the beginning and then pay again for the drugs at the end, while the profit is privatized in the middle—there is something very wrong with that model."

He was right, as became all the more evident when the coronavirus pandemic hit. One of the first groups to respond to the crisis was ACT UP New York, which renewed the message "Silence=Death." The group used virtual organizing to challenge the Trump administration's lies and the failure of policymakers in general to respond to a health care crisis that, once again, hit people of color, working-class communities and the vulnerable hardest. One activist created a graphic that recalled the famous jacket worn by the late artist David Wojnarowicz, with its message "If I die of AIDS—forget burial, just drop my body on the steps of the FDA."

The new image, overlaid on a surgical mask and sent out over Twitter, read: "If I die of Covid-19, forget burial. Drop my body on the steps of Mar-a-Lago."

"Yesterday, a friend posted that people he knew were losing people to Covid-19 and the government had blood on its hands," Jennifer Johnson Avril, the director of advocacy communications at New York's Housing Works and a former ACT UP member, told *Out* magazine as the pandemic ravaged the city in March 2020. "I immediately thought of David Wojnarowicz's jacket and posted the line. The federal government has already killed some of us, we just haven't seen the body count yet. I'm angry, we're angry, and we've just begun to fight." She said that the specific use of Mar-a-Lago, as opposed to a government building, was purposeful.

ACT UP New York activists well understood that Covid-19 wasn't AIDS, but they recognized that "the parallels are clear as day." They maintained that "vulnerable communities are taking the brunt of this pandemic due to overwhelming neglect" and that "all the barriers in place (healthcare, pharma greed, housing, stigma, etc.) that have kept HIV alive will keep this virus alive."

That reference to "pharma greed" drew on the group's experience and became a focus of its activism, and that of other health advocacy organizations that saw stark evidence of the inequality, the corruption and the greed that killed. "We've seen this same practice happen time and time again," announced ACT UP New York. "This virus will disproportionately affect people living with HIV and our long-term survivor community and we will give it our best fucking fight to eradicate it with direct action."

To that end, ACT UP New York activists conducted a "Free the Vaccine" campaign to demand an end to the profiteering that led to "vaccine apartheid." They demonstrated outside the Pfizer headquarters in New York, on March 11, 2021, alongside activists from Health Gap, Housing Works, the Center for Popular Democracy, People's Action and other groups.

"If we should have learned anything from the AIDS epidemic, it is that putting profits ahead of people continues to kill, and allows epidemics to spread globally," said ACT UP member Kate Barnhart. "We need to stop doing that. We need to realize that no CEO needs $17 million a year in compensation. We need to realize that these drugs that these companies like Pfizer are selling do not cost that much to manufacture. It's all profit. They will tell you that they need to make these profits for research, but a lot of the research is actually funded by our tax dollars. We paid to develop this vaccine; it's our tax dollars going to buy the vaccines. They are profiting off of Covid. They are profiting off people's suffering and off of people's deaths. They need to let the patents go. They need to let companies make this vaccine available globally and to those in need here in the US."

That was a necessarily militant message and it gained traction with honest policymakers, such as Senator Bernie Sanders. "It is unconscionable that amid a global public health crisis, huge multibillion-dollar pharmaceutical companies continue to prioritize profits by protecting their monopolies and driving up prices rather than prioritizing the lives of people everywhere, including in the Global South," Sanders said. "Our government has invested enormous sums of taxpayer dollars into the production of these technologies. All people should benefit. Not just a few already obscenely wealthy CEO's and shareholders in the wealthiest country on earth. We need a People's Vaccine, not a profit vaccine."

Dr. Roona Ray, a physician at one of New York City's hardest-hit hospitals echoed that call—and Dr. King's message from more than five decades earlier—at the rally outside Pfizer headquarters. Noting that the people she served in the New York borough of Queens were primarily people of color and immigrants who "got sicker and they died more frequently" from Covid-19 than other communities, she said, "Now, we're seeing with the vaccine, that the same communities that were worst affected by the disease are now getting access to the vaccine the least.

"In my ten years of working here," she concluded, "I've seen how the American health care system is disproportionally racist and classist, gives disproportionate access to health care to those who are healthy and wealthy, and often whiter communities. Now, we are here to say, as health care workers, that this kind of racism and inequality in health care—especially with Covid-19 and with Covid-19 vaccines—cannot continue in our name. Pfizer and pharmaceutical companies like Pfizer cannot make profits in our name at the expense of people's health and lives."

Drowning Grover Norquist's Anti-Government Delusion in the Bathtub of His Own Hypocrisy

I have heard of your paintings too, well enough. God has given you one face and you make yourselves another. You jig and amble, and you lisp, you nickname God's creatures and make your wantonness your ignorance.

—William Shakespeare, *Hamlet*

At the end of a long career in the service of economic inequality, Grover Norquist will be remembered for only one line: "I'm not in favor of abolishing the government. I just want to shrink it down to the size where we can drown it in the bathtub."

But that does a disservice to Norquist, whose incendiary rhetoric extended far beyond his murderous rumination. The Harvard-educated Republican operative, who founded the right-wing Americans for Tax Reform organization at the behest of former president Ronald Reagan, has said a lot of other interesting things. Like when Norquist was asked to look into his conservative crystal ball and identify the era he wanted to take

America back to and replied, "The McKinley era." Why? "You're looking at the history of the country for the first 120 years, up until Teddy Roosevelt, when the socialists took over." History will also record that the first 120 years of the American experiment featured, among other things, slavery; Jim Crow segregation; the rise of the KKK; genocidal massacres and dislocations of Native Americans; denial of the franchise to the overwhelming majority of citizens; and a general betrayal of the founding premise that "all men (and women) are created equal." Some of the worst abuses of robber-baron capitalism did begin to be addressed when Theodore Roosevelt, a relatively progressive Republican, assumed the presidency on 1901 after the assassination of the favorite president of the profiteers. But Roosevelt, who after all had been William McKinley's running mate, stopped far short of wholesale reform, let alone socialism.

What Roosevelt did do, as William Greider noted in his 2003 reporting on the course Norquist was setting for his Wayback machine, was to enact "the first federal regulations protecting public health and safety and a ban on corporate campaign contributions" and endorse "the concept of a progressive income tax." That was too much for Americans for Tax Reform because, as Norquist explained on behalf of Microsoft, Pfizer and his many corporate allies, "The issue that brings people to politics is what they want from government. All our people want to be left alone by government."

Except, of course, when the coronavirus pandemic hit and the government started bailing Americans who were having trouble pulling themselves up by their bootstraps. Suddenly, government was good. And Grover Norquist was first in line for a handout.

As the pandemic destabilized America in March 2020, Congress moved with rare speed to provide the resources to fight the virus but also to address the threat of mass unemployment.

The Coronavirus Aid, Relief and Economic Security Act, or
"Cares" Act, which allocated $2.2 trillion in response to a
burgeoning crisis, was approved unanimously by the Senate on
March 25, approved by a voice vote in the House of Representatives on March 26 and signed into law by President Trump on
March 27. This was big government the way Franklin Roosevelt
and Lyndon Johnson imagined it: moving fast, leveraging all of
its authority and getting things done.

In other words, it was precisely what fiscal conservatives had
been crusading against for decades, with Grover Norquist at the
head of the charge. The rush to act did not sit well with the
hardest-core conservatives in the House. Kentucky Republican
Thomas Massie drove to Washington to try and force a debate
but was shut down by House Speaker Nancy Pelosi and Minority
Leader Kevin McCarthy—a rare instance of the Democratic and
Republican leadership acting in concert. "Pelosi and McCarthy
are still working together to block a recorded vote just to insulate
members of Congress from ACCOUNTABILITY," griped
Massie on Twitter. "Biggest spending bill in the history of
mankind, and no recorded vote? #SWAMP."

Instead of generating a populist outcry, however, Massie's
lonely agitation made him "the least popular man in Washington." Former secretary of state John Kerry quipped: "Congressman
Massie has tested positive for being an asshole. He must be
quarantined to prevent the spread of his massive stupidity." That
line from a liberal Democrat so amused Trump that he retweeted
it. For added measure, the president urged his fellow partisans
to "throw Massie out of Republican Party!"

Massie's rebellion against big spending went nowhere because,
as Senator Bernie Sanders explained to me: "there are millions
of people who are unable to pay their rent, pay their mortgages,
pay their credit cards, pay their automobile loans, and they

are frightened about what happens to their credit ratings. They're frightened whether or not they're going to get evicted, whether they're going to lose their homes." Effectively, said Sanders, "what this crisis does is rip away the Band-Aid and say, 'Hey, this is the reality.'" And in March and April 2020, reality was hard to argue with, even for Republicans who had been raised on Ronald Reagan's dimwitted bromide, "Government is not the solution to our problem; government is the problem."

Sanders, the nation's most prominent democratic socialist, had his own complaints about the Cares Act. He believed it didn't go big enough when it came to guaranteeing health care, medical leave and longer-term assistance. But, he said, "the good part, you know, I think, is that we did manage to get a lot of money out in terms of expanding unemployment in a way that hadn't been done before. Not only will people be getting $600 more than the usual unemployment check, but we expanded it to many workers who were not eligible for unemployment. It's not enough money, but most of the adults in this country will get $1,200. Children will get $500. There's a lot of money to prop up small businesses, loans that can be forgiven if they hang on to their employees."

What the senator was talking about was the Paycheck Protection Program, which initially allocated $349 billion for small business loans and grants so that firms could avoid the mass layoffs that would destabilize the US economy. The program was quickly expanded, with the approval of the Paycheck Protection Program and Healthcare Enhancement Act, which authorized another $320 billion in funding. It's no wonder Sanders liked it. This was the sort of intervention that democratic socialist countries had long used to stabilize mixed economies and to preserve small businesses and farms. And the PPP proved to be very popular in the United States—especially among the people who complained the loudest about democratic socialism.

We know this because, in July 2020, when the Small Business Administration released the names of recipients of the government largesse it was distributing as part of the Paycheck Protection Program, Grover Norquist's Americans for Tax Reform Foundation was right there at the top of the list.

Norquist's group gobbled up small business relief funds from the very government that its leader had proposed to drown in a bathtub. "The nonprofit foundation—which advocates restraint in government spending and says it works to educate taxpayers on 'costly government programs'—took a loan between $150,000 and $350,000 from the Paycheck Protection Program," explained a Bloomberg report, which noted with barely contained amusement that it was a big government agency that was bailing out one of the loudest critics of big government.

Norquist had not volunteered the information that he was grabbing up government cash. (Hardly surprising, given that Norquist had once authored a book titled *Leave Us Alone: Getting the Government's Hands Off Our Money, Our Guns, Our Lives.*) But once it was revealed that he was accumulating taxpayer-funded benefits, he scrambled to make excuses. "Americans for Tax Reform (ATR) did not apply for or receive any grant or loan from the Paycheck Protection Program, designed to keep people employed during the pandemic," read a news release issued by the group. "Americans for Tax Reform Foundation (ATRF)—a legally and financially separate research and educational 501(c)3—was badly hurt by the government shutdown. It applied for and received a loan and has as a consequence been able to maintain its employees without laying anyone off."

Nice try. What Grover Norquist failed to highlight was the fact that, at the top of the list of the employees who didn't get laid off, was Grover Norquist. Instead of admitting his hypocrisy, Norquist sought to obscure it with inside-the-Beltway doubletalk. But no one who read the letterheads of the "legally and financially separate" organizations was buying the BS. The Americans for Tax Reform Foundation and Americans for Tax Reform posted identical statements trying to explain away the conservative hand that got caught in the federal cookie jar. "According to 2018 Internal Revenue Service filings accessed from nonprofit database Guidestar," noted the Capitol Hill newspaper *Roll Call*, "both the Foundation and ATR each listed Norquist as its president and each paid Norquist $125,000 annually."

Norquist wasn't the only anti-government humbug scrambling to come up with explanations for why they'd tapped into the public money stream. Taxpayers for Common Sense, a Washington-based group that endeavors to "cut unnecessary subsidies," posted a video featuring the head of the organization. "I'm Steve Ellis, president of Taxpayers for Common Sense—your friendly, nonpartisan budget watchdog," it began. "Loans from the Paycheck Protection Program, brought to you by the Cares Act, have been in the news. I want to give you some information about it. Especially since our organization received a loan of $173,800."

The head of the group that boasts on its website, "We don't take money from corporations, unions, the government or anyone with a financial stake in our work," tried to turn getting caught into a virtue. "If anything could underscore the exceptional times we're in, this is it," he chirped. "The first time in our twenty-five years that we received any government assistance."

Extraordinary times, indeed. So extraordinary that the "radicals for capitalism" who run a group that takes its name from viscerally anti-government author Ayn Rand signed up for a loan of between $350,000 and $1 million. That was such an unexpected revelation that the California-based Ayn Rand Institute didn't even bother to explain why an organization that champions the memory of a woman who argued that "the only proper purpose of a government is to protect man's rights" was living large on the government dime.

Rand's writing was always characterized by what the conservative intellectual William F. Buckley Jr. termed "ideological fabulism." Buckley acknowledged that "I had to flog myself to read it," but also acknowledged, "the influence she had, you wouldn't believe." Her devotees included former Federal Reserve chair Alan Greenspan, former House speaker Paul Ryan, sitting senators like Ron Johnson and Rand Paul and millions of others who found virtue in the "stiff and soulless" prose of Rand. How soulless? "Out of a lifetime of reading, I can recall no other book in which a tone of overriding arrogance was so implacably sustained," Whittaker Chambers wrote in his 1957 review of her most famous novel, *Atlas Shrugged*. "Its shrillness is without reprieve. Its dogmatism is without appeal." While Buckley and Chambers had tried to warn conservatives off Rand's toxic brew, Randian Republicans like Ryan shaped a partisanship—and, where they could, a governance—characterized by the author's "scorn for charity, for altruism."

That's why conservative and libertarian hypocrisy is so worthy of note. Decades of anti-government lies, beginning with Reagan's "government is the problem" demagoguery and amplified by Norquist's "drown it in the bathtub" dogma, have framed out a politics that normalizes neglect of the common good. Republicans may have pioneered this politics, but Democrats like Bill Clinton bought into it with their "era of big government is over" claptrap. The lies and the policies that extended from them undid much of the best work of the New Deal and the Fair Society and created a US government that was not just uncaring but dramatically ill prepared for crises. The constant diminishment of government by Republican and Democratic administrations turned America into a country that was uniquely vulnerable to the coronavirus pandemic.

Grover Norquist never actually succeeded in shrinking the size of government. It got bigger under successive administrations. But he did succeed in making it crueler and stupider. Constant prodding by Norquist and his allies made federal policymaking increasingly reactionary and dysfunctional. With his demand that Republicans abide by the so-called Taxpayer Protection Pledge, the Reagan acolyte earned the title Arianna Huffington accorded him: "the dark wizard of the Right's anti-tax cult." Political analyst Charlie Cook called Norquist "the single most influential conservative in Washington," while a *60 Minutes* profile portrayed Norquist as "responsible more than anyone else for rewriting the dogma of the Republican Party."

This dangerous dogma caught up with America in the early days of 2020. Anti-tax policies advocated by Norquist and his acolytes had starved state and local governments and killed off planning and preparation at the federal level. Worst of all, they had created cynicism about the capacity of government to tackle great challenges. That cynicism was carefully nurtured by political charlatans who were in the service of the billionaire campaign donors, by Republican strategists and by the Fox News commentators who peddled the lie that the private sector could do a better job than government . . . right up to the point when the pandemic hit and everyone turned to the government for relief.

This was the same lie that gave rise to the run-government-like-a-business mantra, which created the space for Donald Trump to run government into the ground. It is easy now to blame Trump for failing to respond in urgent and humane ways to the pandemic. But the truth is that Trump was merely a manifestation of the dogmatic politics that Grover Norquist and his kind inflicted upon us. While other countries responded effectively to the pandemic, and to the mass unemployment it fostered, the United States struggled—and, too frequently, failed. There is nothing wrong with heaping blame on Trump for his rejection of science and common decency; he did a miserable job. But there is something wrong with the narrow analysis that fails to recognize where Trump and today's Republicans came from.

When the death rate in the United States was soaring in early April 2020, the *New York Times* published a number of examinations of why the fight to contain the virus was so much more successful in other countries. One of the most exhaustive of them was headlined "A German Exception? Why the Country's Coronavirus Death Rate Is Low." It noted that "the pandemic has hit Germany hard, with more than 100,000 people infected," but also that "the percentage of fatal cases has been remarkably low compared to those in many neighboring countries." Germany's success was attributed to many factors, including the national health care system and the robust economic planning that corporate apologists like Norquist so rigorously opposed. But Professor Hans-Georg Kräusslich, the head of virology at Heidelberg's University Hospital, a prestigious research institution that stood in the thick of the fight, pointed to another factor altogether: acceptance of the social-distancing orders, mask requirements, testing protocols and all the other initiatives put in place by Chancellor Angela Merkel and government leaders across Germany.

The *Times* noted that the restrictions met with little opposition and were being broadly followed, and that this was crucial to blunting the impact of the pandemic. "Maybe our biggest strength in Germany is the rational decision-making at the highest level of government combined with the trust the government enjoys in the population," Professor Kräusslich observed.

That trust, essential in a pandemic moment, is what Grover Norquist and the dark wizards of the modern conservative movement stole from America. This is their true crime. And it has cost us exponentially more than the loan money that this guilty man collected when it was no longer possible to obscure his hypocrisy.

The Pandemic Profiteering
of Jeffrey Preston Bezos

*The Aristocracy are not the farmers who work the land . . . but
are the mere consumers of the rent.*
—Thomas Paine, *Rights of Man, Part II*, 1792

It is no secret that the coronavirus pandemic made the rich richer.
From the first days of the crisis, as unemployment rates soared
and small businesses locked their doors, there was furtive talk
about how the very wealthy didn't seem to be suffering as much
as everyone else. After the Federal Reserve in the United States
and central banks around the world raced in to shore up the
markets, the headlines told the story: "The super-wealthy won
big as Covid-19 spread," "Super-rich increase fortunes by more
than a quarter during market turmoil," "It's been a fabulous
pandemic for the super-rich." Nine months into the pandemic,
the watchdog groups Institute for Policy Studies and Americans
for Tax Fairness produced a comprehensive report that showed
"the collective wealth of America's 651 billionaires has jumped
by over $1 trillion since roughly the beginning of the Covid-19

pandemic to a total of $4 trillion at market close on Monday, December 7, 2020."

At a point when most Americans were reflecting on the hardest year in their experience—and preparing for what President-elect Joe Biden warned would be "a very dark winter" when "things are going to get much tougher before they get easier"—billionaires were adding up the receipts from the best year of their lives. The total wealth of the privileged 651 had spiked so rapidly, so exponentially, that it now rivaled that of the 165 million women, men and children who form what business commentators dismiss as "the bottom half" of the country's economic equation.

Based on an analysis of *Forbes* magazine research on billionaires, the study by the two watchdog groups determined that the total net worth of the nation's wealthiest few had increased by 36 percent since the rough start of pandemic shutdowns. Published at a point when members of Congress were wrangling over whether it was fiscally responsible to allocate another $908 billion in pandemic relief, the study noted that the nation's billionaires had made more than that much money since big business idled workers, small businesses collapsed and tens of millions of Americans started worrying about how they were going to feed their families and keep their homes. "Their pandemic profits are so immense that America's billionaires could pay for a major Covid relief bill and still not lose a dime of their pre-virus riches," said Frank Clemente, the executive director of Americans for Tax Fairness.

Indeed, according to the watchdog groups' analysis, the $1 trillion wealth gain by those 651 billionaires in the first nine months of the pandemic shutdown was:

- More than it would cost to send a stimulus check of $3,000 to every one of the roughly 330 million people in America. A family of four would receive over $12,000.

Republicans have blocked new stimulus checks from being included in the pandemic relief package.

- Double the two-year estimated budget gap of all state and local governments, which is forecast to be at least $500 billion. By June, state and local governments had already laid off 1.5 million workers and public services—especially education—faced steep budget cuts.
- Only slightly less than total federal spending on Medicare ($644 billion in 2019) and Medicaid ($389 billion in FY2019), which together serve 120 million Americans (69 million in Medicaid, 63 million in Medicare, less 12 million enrolled in both).
- Nearly four times the $267 billion total in stimulus payments made to 159 million people earlier this year.

What was it about the elites that made them immune to the economic turbulence of 2020? Bankers suggested that the very rich simply had very good instincts. In an interview with the *Guardian* for an October assessment of the global bloating of billionaire bank accounts, UBS's Josef Stadler speculated that "billionaires typically have 'significant risk appetite' and were confident to gamble some of their considerable fortunes" on the prospect that stock values would rebound after their collapse in March. It was a portrayal of the super-rich as swashbuckling adventurers who were willing to "ride the storm to the downside" in order to ride it "up on the upside." In other words, the billionaires had "the stomach" to buy low and sell high.

But perhaps there was more to the calculus of wealth accumulation than intestinal fortitude? Chuck Collins, the co-editor of the inequality.org website, suggested that the redistribution of wealth upward might have something to do with billionaires "extracting wealth at a time when essential workers are pushed into the viral line of fire."

Bull's-eye!

Meet Jeffrey Preston Bezos, the billionaire who had mastered the art of wealth extraction long before 2020 and then cashed in when the pandemic arrived.

It looked at the start of the year like 2020 might be a rough one for the richest man in the world. Bezos had lived his own "American Dream," parlaying a $250,000 investment from his parents into an epic fortune and his very own cult of personality in a country that treated billionaires like the royalty it had supposedly tossed aside in 1776. Yet Bezos's life had grown complicated. Instead of the usual profiles of the alchemist who turned everything he touched into gold, 2019 had produced lurid reports of marital infidelity and "a cache of lewd selfies." Suddenly, the media were reporting on what the fifty-five-year-old billionaire described as "a long period of loving exploration and trial separation," and detailing the $38 billion settlement that ended his twenty-five-year marriage with MacKenzie Scott Bezos. That sharing of the Amazon wealth made the former Mrs. Bezos the third-richest woman in the world, a title that became even more secure as her fortune grew to over $57 billion during the course of the pandemic. As for Mr. Bezos, he was feeling restless. Reorganizing the command structure of the online bookselling venture that had over a quarter century grown into the world's most valuable brand, he launched a series of moves that eventually changed his CEO title to that of executive chairman. So much turbulence. And yet, Jeff Bezos got by.

Bezos, the planet's first centi-billionaire, saw his personal net worth leap to $191 billion during the worst months of the pandemic. By early 2021, he was up $73 billion—a better than

70 percent improvement in his fortunes from the time the pandemic took hold and Amazon took off as the definitional corporation for a moment when almost everyone was shopping from home. The online retailer, which was just passing the $1 trillion valuation mark in January 2020, pushed past $1.7 trillion just twelve months later. Bezos was surfing a wave, and he wasn't anywhere near the crest. A "Trillion Dollar Club" report on wealth accumulation during the pandemic conducted by the business platform Comparisun speculated that despite "losing an estimated $38 billion as part of his recent divorce, Jeff Bezos is still by far the world's richest person and his net worth has grown by 34 percent on average over the last five years, which could potentially see him become the world's first trillionaire as early as 2026, at which point he'll be aged sixty-two."

Bezos was making so much money that he could do pretty much anything—even shoot himself into outer space, as he announced he would do in the summer of 2021.

How could Bezos help but be grateful? And yet he seemed nervous. It was almost as if Bezos, a keenly observant man, knew that his was an ill-gotten gain. In February 2021, as media reports recounted Bezos's reclaiming of the "wealthiest man in the world" title from fellow swashbuckler Elon Musk, Amazon's lawyers and PR operatives were maneuvering feverishly to prevent New York attorney general Letitia James from calling out the corporation's failure to protect workers from a pandemic that was making the company's very wealthy CEO very much wealthier. Even as Amazon was seeking to present itself as a benevolent behemoth with a new ad campaign and sly strategies for cozying up to the Biden administration, Bezos's lawyers set out to pre-empt the legal accountability that James was in a position to demand. They filed a lawsuit in Brooklyn federal court on February 12, 2020, claiming that the attorney general would be exceeding her authority if she went after the firm for failing to follow safety protocols and protect workers at its New York City warehouses. The company's complaint argued that "Amazon has been intensely focused on Covid-19 safety and has taken extraordinary, industry-leading measures grounded in science, above and beyond government guidance and requirements, to protect its associates from Covid-19."

James, a courageous Democratic prosecutor who had recently taken on the nation's top Republican, President Donald Trump, as well as New York State's top Democrat, Governor Andrew Cuomo, did not blink. "Throughout this pandemic, Amazon employees have been forced to work in unsafe conditions, all while the company and its CEO made billions off of their backs," she declared. "This action by Amazon is nothing more than a sad attempt to distract from the facts and shirk accountability for its failures to protect hard-working employees from a deadly virus. Let me be clear: We will not be intimidated by anyone, especially corporate bullies that put profits over the health and safety of working people. We remain undeterred in our efforts to protect workers from exploitation and will continue to review all of our legal options."

Then she sued the tech giant, which had been dogged by protests from workers in New York who were disciplined and fired for pointing out that Amazon had neglected employee health and safety from the start of the pandemic. Citing "flagrant disregard for health and safety requirements [that] threatened serious illness and grave harm" to workers at Amazon facilities in the New York City boroughs of Queens and Staten Island, the suit charged: "Amazon has cut corners in complying with the particular requirements that would most jeopardize its sales volume and productivity rates, thereby ensuring outsize profits at an unprecedented rate of growth for the company and its shareholders."

The lawsuit provided the details of an investigation that the attorney general's office explained had "uncovered evidence showing that Amazon's health and safety response violated state law with respect to cleaning and disinfection protocols, contact tracing and generally permitting employees to take necessary precautions to protect themselves from the risk of Covid-19 infection, among other things." For example, the suit continued, "Amazon was notified of at least 250 employees at the Staten Island facility who had positive Covid-19 tests or diagnoses, with more than ninety of those individuals present in the facility within seven days of notification to Amazon. However, in all but seven of these instances, Amazon failed to close any portion of the facility after learning of the positive cases." The suit also charged that "Amazon implemented an inadequate Covid-19 tracing program that failed to consistently identify workers who came into close contact with employees who tested positive for Covid-19," and that on occasions when a worker reported having close contact with a co-worker with a positive Covid-19 test, "Amazon dismissed the worker's concerns and did not investigate or follow up on the reports."

These weren't new complaints. In March 2020, Christian Smalls, a management assistant at the Staten Island warehouse, organized an employee walkout to protest Amazon's failure to protect workers as the first blast of Covid-19 paralyzed New York City. He highlighted the fact that the virus was spreading at Amazon's 4,000-worker JFK8 fulfillment center, where the first positive case was reported March 11. In a series of media interviews, Smalls detailed concerns that the company had not provided masks, disposable gloves and other forms of protective gear. At the same time, he said, workers who feared losing their paychecks at a point when layoffs were occurring throughout the city kept showing up to do their jobs. "I brought to the attention of the company that people were being sick in my department daily," said Smalls, who told CNBC the company was unresponsive when he and others called for shuttering the warehouse and sanitizing the facility. "I witnessed people who had various symptoms: dizziness, vomiting, people were fatigued." Smalls explained that every day he was sending someone home. "I felt like the building was getting sick, one by one—it's like a domino effect," he said. "The number one objective right now is to save my people. We need to close down," added Smalls, who with allies from groups such as Make the Road New York and New York Communities for Change called for a strike on March 30. "Since the building won't close by itself, we're going to have to force [Amazon's] hand," Smalls told CNBC. "We will not return until the building gets sanitized."

On March 30, in one of the first labor actions that put a spotlight on the exploitation of frontline workers, Amazon employees walked off their jobs at JFK8. Smalls showed up with a sign that read, "Our health is just as essential." The Staten Island protest drew national attention. "We weren't able to shut down the building per se, but people heard us," Smalls told Fox Business. In a *Guardian* opinion piece he wrote: "I am getting calls from Amazon workers across the country and they all want to stage walkouts, too. We are starting a revolution and people around the country support us."

Faced with a demand to do more to protect workers from a deadly pandemic, Amazon did what any multinational monopoly with a boss on his way to trillionaire status would do. It fired Chris Smalls. The company claimed that the man it had employed for almost five years had violated safety guidelines and a quarantine order. But the truth came out quickly. In a meeting with Bezos, according to a memo obtained by Vice News, Amazon's top lawyer had laid out a strategy for attacking Smalls as a part of a plan to distract media attention from the debate about the company's treatment of its workers. "He's not smart, or articulate, and to the extent the press wants to focus on us versus him, we will be in a much stronger PR position than simply explaining for the umpteenth time how we're trying to protect workers," Amazon general counsel David Zapolsky claimed in the memo.

But Smalls was smart, and articulate and a natural organizer. He founded the Congress of Essential Workers to advocate for working people, "particularly for those who have been subjected to retaliation by their employer and may have incurred expenses or may require legal guidance for potential civil rights grievances." He made his case in media interviews, on picket lines and in meetings with worker advocates. On April 6, just days after Smalls was fired, AFL-CIO president Richard Trumka told the union federation's Pennsylvania convention: "Coronavirus has pulled back the curtain on life-changing and in many cases life-saving power of collective action. We are standing shoulder-to-shoulder with Chris Smalls, the worker and organizer who planned strikes at Amazon facilities this week. One day later, Amazon fired him. They said it was for employee insubordination, but we knew it was employer retaliation. As is often the case with Jeff Bezos, the rhetoric does not match the reality."

At the same time, a coalition of major union groups—the AFL-CIO, the Retail, Wholesale and Department Store Union, the American Federation of State, County and Municipal Employees, the United Food and Commercial Workers International Union, the American Federation of Teachers, the Service Employees International Union and the International Brotherhood of Teamsters—joined more than thirty-five state and local elected officials from New York to call on Amazon to reinstate

Smalls. But they did more than that. They amplified the concerns that Smalls and other workers had raised.

"You claim to have adopted a number of practices to sanitize worksites and protect workers," the unions and their allies wrote. "But a compelling number of workers have come forward— and even run the incredible personal risk of walking off the job—to report that the actual situation in warehouses does not match Amazon's public relations statements. They report that the circumstances of their work make it impossible to comply with public health protocols—reporting crowded spaces, a required rate of work that does not allow for proper sanitizing of work spaces and empty containers meant to hold sanitizing wipes. Your workers deserve to have full protections and to be confident that they are not carrying Covid-19 home to their families. And the safety of your workers also impacts the safety of everyone who touches or receives packages once they leave your warehouses."

The nation's largest unions threw their support behind workers calling for warehouse closures with full pay until Amazon put into place a set of safety protocols. These included independent health and safety inspection and ongoing monitoring to ensure compliance with CDC and other governing health guidelines; 100 percent pay for all employees during sanitation closures; the cancellation of all rate and productivity requirements that limit employee time for proper sanitation; stricter protocols for six-foot distancing measures; a plan to cover childcare expenses for employees during school closures; full pay for all workers unable to return to work because of their own or family member illness or need to self-quarantine; retroactive pay for workers who had to take unpaid time off over the previous month due to Covid-19; and issuance of a public statement of improved protocols for the safety of workers and the public.

Senator Bernie Sanders, who was then a candidate for the Democratic presidential nomination, took up the issue. "Amazon's warehouse workers protested because people are getting sick on the job," Sanders said. "Their demands were not radical: a safer workplace, protective gear and paid sick leave. Amazon's response? Retaliate by firing a worker who helped organize the walk-out. That is absolutely immoral." Later, Sanders posted videos of Smalls telling his story and directed a message to Bezos. "Chris Smalls organized Amazon warehouse workers to demand protective gear, paid sick leave and workplace safety," Sanders said. "Rather than listen to him and change its policies, Amazon fired him and smeared his character. I say to Jeff Bezos: Enough! We will not tolerate CEO's who intimidate workers fighting for their human rights."

In the months that followed, Smalls kept speaking up as part of a chorus of Amazon workers around the world. In Alabama, workers would eventually force a historic unionization vote at a sprawling warehouse in the city of Bessemer. The union they worked with was one of the oldest working-class organizations in the country, the Retail, Wholesale and Department Store Union, which traced its history back to 1937 and also to the civil rights organizing of the 1960s. RWDSU kept a running tab of the dozens of its members who died from Covid-19 and made health and safety central to its campaign in Alabama. An Associated Press analysis of the organizing drive struck an optimistic note, reporting, "Stuart Appelbaum, the president of the Retail, Wholesale and Department Store Union, says the union's success in Bessemer is partly due to the pandemic, with workers feeling betrayed by employers that didn't do enough to protect them from the virus. And the Black Lives Matter movement, which has inspired people to demand to be treated with respect and dignity. Appelbaum says the union has heard from Amazon warehouse workers all over the country."

In response, Amazon spent millions on what was described as an "anti-union blitz." The company was ultimately successful in keeping the RWDSU from representing the workers in the warehouse. That was typical of the aggressive approach the company took to any worker organizing during the pandemic.

It was also typical of how Amazon pushed back against Attorney General James after she declared, "It's important that Amazon understands that if they are going to do operations in the state of New York, they've got to respect the rights of workers but, most importantly, they've got to attend to the health and welfare of their employees." James promised to investigate the company and followed through. When it became clear that the attorney general was going to act, Bezos and his lawyers grew increasingly agitated and litigious. Why? Because, as the head of what was widely seen as the most powerful law enforcement arm of any state government in the nation, James had the authority to crack down on a corporation that had a long history of avoiding accountability. She also had the stature to shine a light on how Amazon had cashed in on Covid-19.

When James and her team filed the state's lawsuit in February 2021, they charged: "Throughout the historic pandemic, Amazon has repeatedly and persistently failed to comply with its obligation to institute reasonable and adequate measures to protect its workers from the spread of the virus in its New York City facilities JFK8, a Staten Island fulfillment center, and DBK1, a Queens distribution center. Amazon's flagrant disregard for health and safety requirements has threatened serious illness and grave harm to the thousands of workers in these facilities and poses a continued substantial and specific danger to the public health."

That danger was created, the lawsuit argued, because the

company was more concerned about maximizing profits than about preventing the spread of the virus and saving lives. "Amazon has cut corners in complying with the particular requirements that would most jeopardize its sales volume and productivity rates, thereby ensuring outsize profits at an unprecedented rate of growth for the company and its shareholders," the attorney general's filing maintained.

Then it got specific about how and why that profiteering had occurred:

> Amazon has touted its efforts to protect employees during the Covid-19 pandemic, even creating a television advertising campaign to make this point. However, Amazon's many failures to take reasonable and adequate measures to protect its employees from Covid-19 by following regulatory guidance were a deliberate effort to evade the particular measures that would have hindered increased sales volume. Over the course of the pandemic, Amazon earned more than $160 billion in profits from its online sales. This figure represented approximately 44 percent year-to-year growth from pre-pandemic times, and increased growth of approximately 27 percent from its prior growth rate. Thus, Amazon earned approximately $30 billion in additional worldwide online sales that it would not have earned at its pre-pandemic growth rates. On information and belief, this increased sales volume amounts to approximately $28.5 million in additional profits from (New York's JFK8 and DBK1 warehouses) alone during the pandemic. Amazon's extreme profits and exponential growth rate came at the expense of the lives, health, and safety of its frontline workers.

James amplified this message in her own statements. "Since the pandemic began, it is clear that Amazon has valued profit over people and has failed to ensure the health and safety of its workers," she said. "The workers who have powered this country and kept it going during the pandemic are the very workers who continue to be treated the worst." In addition to asking a judge to require Amazon "to take all affirmative steps" to "adequately protects the lives, health, and safety of its employees"—and to award back pay and damages to Smalls and another former employee, Derrick Palmer—the attorney general's suit proposed to make Amazon "give up the profits it made as a result of its illegal acts."

That's the sort of legal language that scares even the most powerful CEO. Bezos and Amazon pushed back, in the courts and in the court of public opinion. But the company's attempts to sell itself as a model employer kept falling short. Under pressure from James and other attorneys general, the company reported in October that it had counted 19,816 presumed or confirmed Covid-19 cases among frontline employees at its Amazon and Whole Foods Market facilities across the United States. Making comparisons with the overall infection rate in the general population, the company's PR team declared the figure to be "lower than the expected number." It also suggested that the wide availability of data would "allow us to benchmark our progress and share best practices across businesses and industries." But Amazon did not update the case numbers as the pandemic surged in the fall of 2020 or in the winter of 2020–1.

Amazon was even less forthcoming when it came to discussing the death toll at its facilities. There was no question that Amazon workers had died. In May 2020, *USA Today* noted the deaths of at least eight Amazon warehouse workers from Covid-19. That story concluded with a cheery note: "Amazon has seen a spike in overall demand for its services as people stay at home due to coronavirus and have more necessities delivered. A recent projection shows Amazon CEO Jeff Bezos could reach trillionaire status by 2026."

As media outlets continued to speculate about Bezos's burgeoning wealth—and that of other coronavirus "winners"—Letitia James raised the essential question for essential workers: At what cost? But hers was not merely a rhetorical objection. It was a cry for justice from an official who was in a position to get justice. That's what scared Bezos and Amazon.

It is one thing to talk about the moral duty of companies to treat employees with dignity. It is something else to back that talk up with a knowing demand that the company pay the price for its illegal acts—even if doing so might prevent its biggest stockholder from becoming the world's first trillionaire.

CONCLUSION

The United States of Impunity

I never wonder to see men wicked, but I often wonder to see them not ashamed.
　　　　—Jonathan Swift, *Thoughts on Various Subjects*, 1706

The United States is the product of an accountability movement that was never fully realized. Thomas Paine called the country into being with *Common Sense*, a pamphlet that invited the beleaguered residents of thirteen British colonies of the eastern shore of North America to indulge their fury at the imperial abuses of King George III. He ridiculed the "men of passive tempers" who "look somewhat lightly over the offences of Great Britain, and, still hoping for the best, are apt to call out, 'Come, come, we shall be friends again for all this.'" Rejecting the prospect of reconciliation with "the power that hath carried fire and sword into your land," Paine encouraged Americans to ask themselves pointed questions: "Are your wife and children destitute of a bed to lie on, or bread to live on? Have you lost a parent or a child by their hands, and yourself the ruined and wretched survivor? If you have not, then are you not a judge of those who have. But if you have, and can still shake hands with the murderers, then are you unworthy the name of husband, father, friend or lover, and whatever may be your rank or title in life, you have the heart of a coward, and the spirit of a sycophant."

This was about more than refusing to shake hands with the murderers, however. It was, Paine recognized, about forging a new mentality that would see beyond the lie of reconciliation with those who abused positions of authority to the detriment of the people.

No excuses. No forgiveness. The stakes were too high for that. The American people needed to make a clean break with their imperial overlords, and with the foolishness that would suggest that a relationship so broken as that of the United Kingdom and the United States could be mended. A failure to do so would squander "the power to begin the world over again." When that revolution prevailed, Paine entertained the hope the new nation might "form the noblest purest constitution on the face of the earth."

Unfortunately, that never happened. King George and the petty royalists of Great Britain were repudiated. But then the petty royalists of the United States took over. Men in wigs, enslavers from the south and slave traders from the north, wrote a Constitution that embraced the sin of human bondage, denied the franchise to the vast majority of Americans and saddled the new republic with an economic system so crudely rapacious that it instantaneously made a lie of the founding premise that "all men are created equal." As Gore Vidal observed, "Long before Darwin the American ethos was Darwinian." The drafters of the Constitution, who excluded Paine and the truest revolutionaries from the process, set the United States on a course that would see genocide, civil war, systemic racism and sexism, economic inequality on a feudal scale and social divisions so stark that they would be exploited, decade after decade, century after century, by charlatans who capitalized on a system that invited their villainy. The worst of their kind, a royalist who worshipped the queen of England, came to power in 2017 after losing the popular vote for the presidency. Taking advantage of an Electoral College that permitted losers to become winners. Donald John Trump claimed a presidency for which he was wholly unfit, and proceeded on a ruinous course that would eventually see the country ravaged by disease, mass unemployment and seemingly irreconcilable division.

Trump's presidency was the ugliest manifestation of a system where the rot had grown so severe, so overwhelming, that when Covid-19 hit, when hundreds of thousands were dying, when millions were sickened, when tens of millions were left jobless, the stock markets soared to new highs. While nurses risked their lives with inadequate physical protections against a pandemic, while bus drivers fell ill because they were required to work as the disease spread, while immigrant workers in meat processing plants died because their employers failed to put adequate protections in place, billionaires retreated to second and third homes and monitored the steady increase in their fortunes from "emergency relief packages" that literally redistributed wealth upward. Trump's malfeasance was jarring, as Representative Pramila Jayapal, Democrat of Washington, noted in the midst of the crisis. "States have been sort of left to play out *The Hunger Games* on procuring swabs," she said. "I mean, literally, we have governors, my governor included, calling random people in China to try to get swabs off the back of a truck somewhere and get them here, only to find out then that perhaps they're not validated; they're not good for use. Same thing with PPE. I just think that the president has sort of come to this place where he's willing to sacrifice people's lives."

But it wasn't just the president. It was Cabinet members, senators, governors, media personalities and CEO's. The whole corrupt system was exposed. Yet it did not fall. It ran according to plan. In a moment of crisis, the rich and the powerful peddled the fantasy that no one was immune to the threat—even as they boosted their own immunity with fresh infusions of the wealth and privilege that had always protected them from the misery they imposed upon others. As the pandemic was being declared, Naomi Klein predicted how things would play out. "The Fed's first move was to pump $1.5 trillion into the financial markets, with more undoubtedly on the way," she explained. "But if you're a worker, especially a gig worker, there's a very good chance you're out of luck. If you do need to see a doctor for care, there's a good chance no one's going to help you pay if you aren't covered. And if you want to heed the public health warnings to stay home from work, there's also a chance that you won't get paid. Of course, you still need to pay your rent and all of your debts—medical, student, credit card, mortgage. The results are predictable. Too many sick people have no choice but to go to work, which means more people contracting and spreading the virus. And without comprehensive bailouts for workers, we can expect more bankruptcies and more homelessness down the road."

Klein knew what to look for because she wrote the book on how economic and political elites exploit crises to implement their cruelest agendas. "Look, we know this script," she explained in March of America's first pandemic year. "In 2008, the last time we had a global financial meltdown, the same kinds of bad ideas for no-strings-attached corporate bailouts carried the day, and regular people around the world paid the price. And even that was entirely predictable. Thirteen years ago, I wrote a book called *The Shock Doctrine: The Rise of Disaster Capitalism*, which described a brutal and recurring tactic by right-wing governments. After a shocking event—a war, coup, terrorist attack, market crash or natural disaster—they exploit the public's disorientation, suspend democracy, push through radical free-market policies that enrich the 1 percent at the expense of the poor and middle class."

Because Klein had sparked an understanding of how disaster capitalists and their neoliberal allies in positions of power employ the shock doctrine in times of crisis, and because Americans who remembered the exploitation of the 2008 meltdown were speaking up, there was a hope that 2020 would be different. But it was not to be. Despite the jarring circumstances into which the United States and countries around the world were thrust in the first months of 2020, the only change was that those who had robbed us before upped the ante. The public largesse was again grabbed up by the elites. More misery was imposed on the working class. More lies were told. More of the feeble systems for maintaining health and security in capitalist countries were undermined. More people got sick. More people died.

"How does that happen in the richest country in the history of the world?" Bernie Sanders asked when we first spoke about the pandemic in April of 2020.

Why does it always go this way?

A History of American Impunity

The answer is summed up in a word: impunity. The United Nations describes "impunity" as "the impossibility, de jure or de facto, of bringing the perpetrators of violations to account—whether in criminal, civil, administrative or disciplinary proceedings—since they are not subject to any inquiry that might lead to their being accused, arrested, tried and, if found guilty, sentenced to appropriate penalties, and to making reparations to their victims."

With only the rarest and most insufficient exceptions, economic and political elites in the United States have enjoyed a regal level of impunity for more than 230 years. The founders exempted themselves from their own promise that "all men are created equal" and reaped the benefits of an economic system built on slavery, child labor, wage theft and corruption. It took a civil war to undo the cruelest of their establishments: the institution of human bondage. When the war was done, former enslavers would, after a brief period of moral reconstruction, renew their fortunes by establishing a brutal system of Jim Crow segregation that was enforced by the night raids of the Ku Klux Klan, lynchings and chain-gang incarceration. So confident were they in their impunity that they erected statues honoring traitors that, only now, are being torn down by the brave champions of a new American revolution that begins with the basic premise that Black Lives Matter.

The cruelest compromises of our founding were written so deeply into the official record that well into the nation's third century, schoolchildren were taught that the delegates who forged the Three-Fifths Compromise and counted African-Americans as less than human were simply practical men who did what they had to do to get a country up and running. Those same children were taught that there was something "great" about the nineteenth-century compromises negotiated by Henry Clay, which doomed millions of men, women and children to continue in a condition of chained and whipped servitude.

There has been no real accountability for sins against humanity in American history. What accountability did the slave sellers and slave buyers face in a post–Civil War era when the United States failed even to deliver on the promise of forty acres and a mule?

They undid democracy, claimed statehouses and congressional seats through rigged "white primary" elections and ushered in a new age of American apartheid that enforced separate-but-equal racism, exploitation of sharecroppers and "right to work" profiteering.

What accountability did Strom Thurmond of South Carolina face for filibustering in favor of racism as a young legislator? He served in the United States Senate until he was 100 years old and was honored at the end of his tenure with a celebration at which the minority leader of the chamber warmly recalled a 1948 presidential campaign in which Thurmond declared, "All the laws of Washington and all the bayonets of the Army cannot force the Negro into our homes, our schools, our churches." Not in 1953, or 1963 or 1973, but in 2003 did the top Republican in the Senate, Trent Lott of Mississippi, gleefully announce: "I want to say this about my state. When Strom Thurmond ran for president, we voted for him. We're proud of it. And if the rest of the country had followed our lead, we wouldn't have had all these problems over all these years, either."

That's impunity, and—while Lott was ultimately eased out of his position—our political leaders continue to practice it with abandon. If you want to know how the United States ended up in the middle of a pandemic with a swindler president who could not be bothered to take the basic steps that were required to save lives, don't start with Trump. Start, perhaps, with Richard Nixon, the Republican president who skipped town before the House of Representatives could impeach him for the high crimes and misdemeanors of the Watergate scandal. Nixon collected a presidential pardon and a pension and lived the rest of his life in luxury, writing books, commenting on foreign affairs and trying to buff his reputation as an elder statesman. He could have been held to account with the completion of the House impeachment trial and conviction by the Senate. Instead, the Democrats who controlled those chambers conspired with the unelected Republican who succeeded Tricky Dick, Gerald Ford, to let Nixon off the hook with the cruelest lie of all: the promise of "healing."

No one was healed. No lessons were learned. Barely six years after Nixon flew off to his beachside mansion at San Clemente, another charlatan from California assumed the presidency and began steering the country into a scandal that made Watergate look like a pack of gum filched from the grocery store. "The Iran-Contra Affair was a secret US arms deal that traded missiles and other arms to free some Americans held hostage by terrorists in Lebanon, but also used funds from the arms deal to support armed conflict in Nicaragua," the History Channel tells us. "The controversial deal—and the ensuing political scandal—threatened to bring down the presidency of Ronald Reagan." But, of course, it didn't. Even with clear evidence of explicit and extended lawbreaking by Reagan and those around him, the Democrats who controlled the House and the Senate again let a Republican president off the hook. No impeachment, no trial, no constitutional consequences.

Well, yes, of course, Reagan broke laws. He violated his oath of office. He admitted as much. "Reagan himself acknowledged that selling arms to Iran was a 'mistake' during his testimony before Congress," we are told at history.com. "However, his legacy, at least among his supporters, remains intact—and the Iran-Contra Affair has been relegated to an often-overlooked chapter in US history." Intact, indeed.

When even the authors of presidential legacies stop trying to set things right, impunity locks in. The misdemeanors are neglected, unless they are salacious enough to stir the imagination of Ken Starr and Newt Gingrich. High crimes are charged, sometimes, but they are invariably dismissed by senators who embrace a political code of silence every bit as rigid as characters in a *Godfather* movie. The Constitution is a shredded document. The courts are packed with partisan judicial activists who protect their benefactors in the legislative and executive branches. The media can rarely be bothered with anything more than gossip.

The dumbing down of political morality in the United States didn't begin with Donald Trump; it ended with him. Not because the process was complete (rest assured that things can get worse) but because it seemed to have passed the point of no return. When a president presides over mass death and mass unemployment and remains politically viable enough to claim the nomination of a major party and to mount a re-election bid with even vaguely credible numbers, the rot in the system runs so deep that those who maintain it cannot be rehabilitated.

That's what makes this moment so haunting. We know that without accountability for the coronavirus criminals, the past will repeat itself, with a more despicable president mishandling a more daunting pandemic, with more reckless jurists striking down more necessary health orders, with greedier CEO's cashing in on starker misery.

This is the point when we have to break the pattern. The guilty men and women have to be removed. Where appropriate, and necessary, they can be punished.

But, above all, they must be banished—forever ejected from the politics and the economic future of the nation they have so crudely used and abused. They can't be rehabilitated as Nixon almost was. Or remembered fondly, as Reagan was. They can't be allowed to evolve into the "elder statesmen" that the miserable presidents of the last century's turning, Bill Clinton and George W. Bush, aspire to become. They have to carry the albatross of shame from this time forth and forevermore.

Why? Because if they are absolved and forgiven, their kind will rise again to murder us as Macbeth did Duncan. They will steal as casually as Sir John Falstaff did, when the Fat Knight told Prince Hal, "Why, Hal, 'tis my vocation, Hal; 'tis no sin for a man to labor in his vocation." They will debase us as surely as Iago did Othello. To imagine that there will be an improvement of social character without individual accountability for politicians and CEO's is to dream of that which has never been, and never will be.

Hunting the Guilty Men

The guilty must be named and shamed—not merely defeated at the polls but defeated in the memory of a country that can ill afford to forgive and forget. They cannot be allowed to exit into a comfortable retirement. Those whose actions filled refrigerator trucks with the bodies of Americans who did not need to die, who stood by as small businesses and farms were driven into insolvency, who stole the last shred of dignity from the jobless, cannot be permitted the revisionist's renewal. They must be marked as the beasts they are, immediately and permanently.

That's the point of this short text. My friend and comrade Tony Benn, who served for forty-seven years in the British Parliament, and whose activism bridged the period from the anti-fascist struggles of the 1930s to the anti-fascist struggles of the 2010s, taught me a few lessons about confronting power. "In the course of my life I have developed five little democratic questions," he said. "If one meets a powerful person—Adolf Hitler, Joe Stalin or Bill Gates—ask them five questions: 'What power have you got? Where did you get it from? In whose interests do you exercise it? To whom are you accountable? And how can we get rid of you?' If you cannot get rid of the people who govern you, you do not live in a democratic system."

Benn believed in the necessity of accountability, not for purposes of vengeance but for purposes of progress. He was an exceedingly gracious man, yet he refused to play the game of forgive and forget. A brilliant diarist, Benn believed that the great political and ideological battles of any time were waged in the field of recent history. The powerful connive to tell their own stories in the most self-serving manner, with an eye toward accentuating whatever virtues they may have possessed while erasing memories of their crimes.

"A historical perspective is the key to democratic politics, which if denied can bury the real issues and confine news coverage to high-level gossip about the rich and the powerful, reducing us to the role of spectators of our fate, rather than active participants," he explained. "The obliteration of the past strengthens the short-term calculations that pass for political thought, and for me the real heroes are those few who try to explain the world in order to help us to understand what we can best do to improve our lot."

Tony was old enough to recall a time when the left won a fight over recent history, and shaped perspectives for generations afterward. The fight came at the opening of World War II, in June 1940, after the "Phoney War" ended and the reality of the threat that Nazi Germany posed to Europe and the world was made abundantly clear. There were no longer any sane advocates for the appeasement of Hitler, who had taken full advantage of every opening that the weak-willed "diplomacy" of Prime Minister Neville Chamberlain and his aides had afforded fascism with their accommodation of a dictator.

The question was whether there would be any accountability for the sins of less than two years earlier: of September 1938, when Britain's groveling Conservative prime minister traveled to Germany, hat in hand, umbrella hanging from his arm, for the

Munich Conference, where he inked an agreement accepting Hitler's annexation of the Sudetenland region of western Czechoslovakia, then returned to London, met with King George VI and announced from the balcony of Buckingham Palace: "There has come back from Germany to Downing Street peace with honor. I believe it is peace for our time. We thank you from the bottom of our hearts. Now I recommend you go home, and sleep quietly in your beds."

When German foreign minister Joachim von Ribbentrop fretted about the agreement, Hitler said: "Oh, don't take it so seriously. That piece of paper is of no further significance whatsoever." Less than a year later, the Germans had invaded Poland, and W. H. Auden had written of how the "clever hopes" of a "dishonest decade" were expiring.

By May of the following year, the Germans had stormed across France and trapped the British Expeditionary Force on the beaches near Dunkirk in the north of France. A desperate rescue operation had achieved what Chamberlain's successor, Winston Churchill, referred to as the "miracle of deliverance," as an armada of more than 861 vessels ferried 338,226 soldiers—most of them British, but also French, Polish, Belgian and Dutch combatants—across the English Channel to safety. There was much to celebrate in the news of the rescue, and there were those who were determined to look forward from what Churchill described as "a colossal military disaster" toward the conflict to come.

Certainly, Chamberlain and the practitioners of appeasement were inclined to move on. These "Men of Munich" sought to retain their power, privilege and positions of influence. Despite having presided over what historian John Stevenson aptly described as "almost a decade of complacency and mismanagement which had brought the country to the brink of catastrophe and placed it in dire peril," Chamberlain's Tory ministers and whips presumed they would continue their political careers. And perhaps govern again.

Three British journalists had a different idea. Michael Foot, Frank Owen and Peter Howard pulled the files on the previous decade and, over a course of four days that literally overlapped with the evacuation of the troops from the beaches of Dunkirk, penned a fierce denunciation of the men responsible. They wrote anonymously as Cato, borrowing a name from the Roman senator who exposed Julius Caesar's corruption. Influenced by Foot's fascination with the Jacobin movements that arose at the time of the French Revolution, its seventy-six-word preface recalled the demand of an angry crowd for "a dozen guilty men."

The opening also featured a quote from Winston Churchill. Though the new prime minister was a Tory and Foot a socialist who would go on to a prominent political career of his own, they were united by their fury at damage done to the United Kingdom's defenses by Chamberlain and those who imagined compromises could be made with fascists. Such were the times, and such was the threat, that honest conservatives and socialists shared an understanding of the political power of pointing a finger of blame (one of Foot's co-authors, Owen, was a former Liberal MP; the other, Howard, was a Conservative). Churchill's line framed the value of memory well: "The use of recriminating about the past is to enforce effective action at the present."

That statement set the tone for the polemic, which with unrelenting fury identified the crisis, named the guilty men and charged the crimes. It concluded with the story of the German invasion of France, and an anguished recounting of the toll that might have been avoided. The last words were an all-caps damnation that read as a manifesto not just for the moment but for the future. Yes, with Churchill as premier, and a new government in place, there was hope. "But," Foot and his compatriots wrote:

OUR FINAL AND ABSOLUTE GUARANTEE IS STILL IMPERATIVELY DEMANDED BY A PEOPLE DETERMINED TO RESIST AND CONQUER: NAMELY, THAT THE MEN WHO ARE NOW REPAIRING THE BREACHES IN OUR WALLS SHOULD NOT CARRY ALONG WITH THEM THOSE WHO LET THE WALLS FALL INTO RUIN. THE NATION IS UNITED TO A MAN IN ITS DESIRE TO PROSECUTE THE WAR IN TOTAL FORM: THERE MUST BE A SIMILAR UNITY IN THE NATIONAL CONFIDENCE. LET THE GUILTY MEN RETIRE, THEN, OF THEIR OWN VOLITION, AND TO MAKE AN ESSENTIAL CONTRIBUTION TO THE VICTORY UPON WHICH ALL ARE IMPLACABLY RESOLVED.

Guilty Men was published one month after the writing was completed. Despite the fog of war and the reluctance of traditional booksellers to peddle so potent a prescription for what ailed the UK, Foot recalled rather indelicately that "it sold like a pornographic classic." More than 200,000 copies were bought, and the book went into twenty-seven editions in a few months and remains available to this day—with a charming preface by Foot, who eventually revealed himself, was elected to Parliament and became leader of the British Labour Party.

Foot was always the first to acknowledge the weaknesses of a book written so quickly, but he made no apologies. "Being one of the authors," he said, "I can testify that the whole affair was contrived in a rush and a rage: our aim was to secure changes in the men running the war." *Guilty Men* achieved that end because, as Foot noted, "*Guilty Men*'s argument became the Churchill argument." In fact, it became much more than that. Chamberlain biographer Graham Macklin observed that "*Guilty Men*, which excoriated Chamberlain for leading a woefully unprepared not to mention ill-equipped Britain to the 'edge of national humiliation,' caught the national mood."

Macklin concluded, "It is hard to exaggerate the importance of *Guilty Men*, which functioned as a literary people's court publicly delivering a verdict that the lack of a general election since 1935 had prevented the public from doing." Writing six decades after Chamberlain's death, historian David Dutton observed: "Whatever else may be said of Chamberlain's public life his reputation will in the last resort depend upon assessments of this moment [Munich] and this policy [appeasement]. This was the case when he left office in 1940 and it remains so sixty years later. To expect otherwise is rather like hoping that Pontius Pilate will one day be judged as a successful provincial admin- istrator of the Roman Empire." The same went for the clique that surrounded Chamberlain, whose own obituaries identified them as the "Men of Munich" and often referenced *Guilty Men*.

The Hellhound of Wall Street

These are different times, with new sensibilities and distinct political demands. Yet, the answer to the guilty men and women of our interregnum must necessarily be as robust as it was in that previous moment of accountability. A president of the United States has not merely appeased dictators (although, to be clear, he did a lot of that during his four years in office), he has for his own political purposes presided over a death cult that witnessed refrigerator trucks filling up with dead bodies on the streets of American cities. United States senators have turned a blind eye to the suffering of tens of millions of jobless Americans, while enriching themselves and their campaign donors. Cabinet members who swore sacred oaths to use the awesome power of the world's wealthiest nation in the interest of its people have connived, in the midst of a pandemic, to force workers back onto unsafe assembly lines and children back into unsafe schools. Central bankers have again bailed out Wall Street, while allowing Main Street to curl up and die. CEO's have sacrificed their employees' lives on the altar of profit.

None of their sins can be forgotten, none of them forgiven.

Nothing should be off the table in this country's response to coronavirus criminals and pandemic profiteers: electoral humiliations, impeachments, investigations, indictments, seizures of assets and jail terms. But we should recognize in seeking all of these legitimate remedies that there is a point to the accountability process that has only a little to do with the present and quite a bit more to do with posterity. Churchill was wrong about a lot of things, but he was right that "the use of recriminating about the past is to enforce effective action at the present." And it is effective action in the present that can transform the future.

Accountability is often confused with retribution. That's understandable. People whose loved ones died in nursing homes ravaged by preventable outbreaks of the virus can be forgiven for wanting to see officials penalized for their failure to place health and safety above politics and profits. Families that buried parents and grandparents who died because irresponsible leaders failed to lead in imposing mask mandates and social distancing, or because political hacks in judicial robes blocked responsible leaders from imposing those mandates, may well be inclined to demand specific punishments for the reprobates who rejected science and human decency. And workers who have been exposed to illness and death by billionaires who built their fortunes during a pandemic will be excused for entertaining vengeful sentiments.

But there is a danger in narrowing the scope and character of the mission to the imposition of fines and jail time for individual wrongdoers. While many might be satisfied to see Trump behind bars or Bezos bereft, the measure of justice must be greater. Ultimately, the point of punishing the wrongdoers of our time is to save our children and grandchildren from the fates that we experienced. Instead of settling for the temporary satisfaction of a powerful figure exposed to transitory chastisement, we have to keep our eye on the prize of transformational justice.

The achievement of that justice requires us to stand at the intersection of punishment and policy. What we recognize when we are in this position is that accountability, done right, drives change.

The best lesson in this regard comes from a few years before Michael Foot and his associates wrote *Guilty Men* in London. This story played out in Washington, as Americans wrestled with the question of who was to blame for the Great Depression. Much like the pandemic of the 2020s, the depression of almost a century earlier was global in scope and character. Banking systems and industries collapsed in multiple countries. The masters of the economic universe were quick to suggest that this was a natural catastrophe for which no one could or should be blamed.

But that lie, like the lie that says *the pandemic was going to be horrible, no matter who was in charge, no matter what decisions were made,* was absurd on its face. Of course, there were guilty men then, as there are now. Of course, things could have turned out differently if the right people were in charge, and the right actions were taken. That was understood in the 1930s, when Franklin Delano Roosevelt began his presidency by announcing that "the rulers of the exchange of mankind's goods have failed, through their own stubbornness and their own incompetence."

FDR declared on that cold Inaugural Day in 1933 that the "practices of the unscrupulous money changers stand indicted in the court of public opinion." But the thirty-second president and those around him were not satisfied with a public relations victory. "There must be an end to a conduct in banking and in business," Roosevelt said, "which too often has given to a sacred trust the likeness of callous and selfish wrongdoing."

First, the wrongdoers needed to be named. Then, they needed to be held to account. To this end, an effort was made to identify the criminals, not merely in the pages of muckraking newspaper and magazines, but in the formal sessions of the United State Senate. Roosevelt and his allies in the Congress were not willing to settle for the thin gruel of a "blue-ribbon commission" of inquiry, or even the "truth and reconciliation commission" that we heard proposed as a response to the high crimes and prodigious profiteering of the coronavirus pandemic.

Rightly so. It was true then, as it is true now, that the defenders of a corrupt and relentlessly cruel status quo count time and bureaucracy as their great allies. If the investigation of a crisis is fobbed off to a commission of grandees or a secretive special counsel its scope can easily be limited, and the energy for accountability and change can be dissipated.

But in 1933, the energy was switched on by the Hellhound of Wall Street. That was the nom de guerre headline writers attached to Ferdinand Pecora, an immigrant from the Comune di Nicosia on the island of Sicily who grew up on the mean streets of Hell's Kitchen, collected a law degree in 1911 and made a reputation for himself as the most honest prosecutor in New York City. Pecora made his name as the Manhattan assistant district attorney who cracked down on Wall Street's "bucket shops," fly-by-night stock brokerages with clear conflicts of interest that preyed on small investors and often left them penniless. During the 1920s, Pecora forced the closing of more than a hundred of these brokerages and became a favorite of working-class New Yorkers at a time when crusading prosecutors were covered by the city's tabloid papers as superheroes.

Pecora would almost certainly have been elected as Manhattan district attorney in 1929, when the job came open. But his political trajectory was blocked by the Tammany Hall political machine, which feared that the prosecutor would use the position to crack down on the many corruptions that benefited Democratic elected officials in New York City. So he went into private practice. But Percora's reputation as a ferocious inquisitor was well recalled—so much so that after FDR's election in 1932, Senator Peter Norbeck of South Dakota, the Republican chair of the Senate Committee on Banking and Currency, offered Pecora $255 a month to take charge of a bungled inquiry into the causes of the stock market crash of 1929. The Republicans who controlled the committee in the last months before the New Deal came online were under pressure to crack down on the bankers and speculators who continued to operate on Wall Street. But their intervention, which began before the election, had been a desultory affair that seemed to be going nowhere. Two chief counsels had been fired and a third resigned before Norbeck finally turned to Pecora.

As soon as the New Yorker arrived in Washington, the scope and character of the investigation expanded. Pecora demanded more time, and more authority to go after records of wrongdoing. When he had gathered his evidence, Pecora started calling bankers and stockbrokers as witnesses, putting them under oath to tell the truth, the whole truth and nothing but the truth. When they held back, the veteran prosecutor opened up.

"Under Pecora's expert and often withering questioning, the Senate committee unearthed a secret financial history of the 1920s, demystifying the assorted frauds, scams and abuses that culminated in the 1929 crash," recounted historian Ron Chernow. "The riveting confrontation between Pecora and the Wall Street grandees was so theatrically apt it might have been concocted by Hollywood. The combative Pecora was the perfect foil to the posh bankers who paraded before the microphones."

Pecora was brilliant. He knew what one of his aides described as "the intricate mazes of banking, syndicates, market deals, chicanery of all sorts." More importantly, he knew how to guide senators and the American people through those mazes in pursuit of damning truths. When bankers and stockbrokers appeared before the committee, they were shaken to learn just how much information on their nefarious activities had been dug up by the chief counsel—and by how confident he was in grilling the millionaires whose speculative scheming had ruined lives and robbed the country of any sense of economic security.

"Bankers had been demigods in the 1920s, their doings followed avidly, their market commentary quoted with reverence," Chernow explained. "They had inhabited a clubby world of chauffeured limousines and wood-paneled rooms, insulated from ordinary Americans. Now Pecora defrocked these high priests, making them seem small and shabby." Chernow recounted how, on Black Thursday of 1929, the nation applauded a seemingly heroic attempt by major bankers like Albert Wiggin of Chase and Charles Mitchell of National City, to stem the market decline. But at the hearings "Pecora showed that Wiggin had actually shorted Chase shares during the crash, profiting from falling prices. He also revealed that Mitchell and top officers at National City had helped themselves to $2.4 million in interest-free loans from the bank's coffers to ease them through the crash.

National City, it turned out, had also palmed off bad loans to Latin American countries by packing them into securities and selling them to unsuspecting investors. By the time Pecora got through with the bankers, Senator Burton Wheeler of Montana was likening them to Al Capone and the public referred to them as 'banksters,' rhyming with gangsters."

The prosecutor from New York was a sensation, so much so that the Senate Committee began to be referred to as "the Pecora Commission." When Roosevelt assumed the presidency and Democrats took charge of the Senate in the spring of 1933, Pecora turned up the heat. *Time* magazine headlined its report on the inquiry "Wealth on Trial." When bankers and their echo chamber in the business press complained that Pecora was undermining confidence in the financial system, FDR himself argued that the speculators "should have thought of that when they did the things that are being exposed now."

The exposés kept coming, week after week, month after month. Pecora put the head of the New York Stock Exchange under oath, along with the most prominent stockbrokers and investors of the era. "To their shock, pompous financiers, unaccustomed to having their actions or integrity questioned by anyone, much less some pipsqueak legalist making $255 a month, were no match for his cross examination," observed author and commentator Bill Moyers.

Pecora eventually turned the attention of the committee to the banking empire of John Pierpont "Jack" Morgan Jr. Calling the partners and finally Morgan himself, Pecora revealed that the wealthiest men in America had paid no taxes in 1931 and 1932, and that the House of Morgan maintained a "preferred list" of politically prominent figures, including Supreme Court Justice Owen Roberts and former President Calvin Coolidge, who were given access to insider information and allowed to buy new stocks for a fraction of what the average investor paid.

Working without the constraints that so frequently limit the reach of special commissions and special counsels, and with the full force of Congress and the Roosevelt White House at his back, Pecora operated on a simple premise. "Had there been full disclosure of what was being done in furtherance of these schemes," he recalled in his memoirs, "they could not long have survived the fierce light of publicity and criticism. Legal chicanery and pitch darkness were the banker's stoutest allies."

In the end, some of the "banksters" were charged with crimes based on the revelations of wrongdoing. Others were forced to resign in shame. Such was the story of Charles Edwin Mitchell, the president of National City Bank (now Citibank), who had built the institution into a dominant force in American finance with an elaborate scheme in which the investment section of the operation counseled clients to buy stocks with money they borrowed from the banking section. After the 1929 crash, investors were ruined, and banks collapsed. Under intense scrutiny by Pecora, Mitchell admitted that he knew National City Bank was pushing shaky investments. That admission ruined Mitchell, explained Michael Perino, the law professor and adviser to the Securities and Exchange Commission who authored the book *The Hellhound of Wall Street: How Ferdinand Pecora's Investigation of the Great Crash Forever Changed American Finance.*

"When Mitchell strode into that hearing room on February 21st, 1933, bankers had taken their fair share of lumps over the course of a few years," Perino told Moyers in an interview in 2009. "But, he was still the pre-eminent banker of his day. Just a few weeks earlier, he had been quoted in the *New York Times* telling the shareholders of National City, 'The economy is sound.' And five days later, he resigned from City Bank, and as a matter of fact, there's this famous scene where Pecora and the chairman of the committee are looking out the Senate window and they see Mitchell who had strode into the hearing room surrounded by his retinue of staffers and lawyers walking alone to Washington Station in D.C. carrying his own suitcase. His career was over."

Ultimately, "Sunshine Charley" Mitchell was charged with tax evasion. He escaped jail time but had to pay a $1 million civil fine. Far more importantly, the revelations about the criminal activities of the bankers, and about their collaborations with "preferred list" politicians, led to a radical transformation of banking and politics.

"What Pecora did was to take complex, corporate maneuverings, complex transactions on Wall Street and really turn them into simple morality plays," explained Perino. "That was his genius. He was a smart lawyer. And he knew that the game plan that he had to follow was to quite frankly whip some populist outrage. . . . And once that anger was in place, once that clamor for reform was in place, Congress essentially fell in line."

By the time the hearings wrapped up in the spring of 1934, they had "paved the way for remedial legislation," according to Chernow. "The Securities Act of 1933, the Glass-Steagall Act of 1933 and the Securities Exchange Act of 1934—all addressed abuses exposed by Pecora. It was only poetic justice when Roosevelt tapped him as a commissioner of the newborn Securities and Exchange Commission."

The greater poetic justice, however, came in the long-term restructuring of how people thought about bankers and banking. Just as Foot and his colleagues fingered the guilty men who had appeased Hitler and wrote them out of the political future of the United Kingdom, Pecora hauled the bankers and stockbrokers down from the pedestals they stood upon in the 1920s, so altering the discourse that when he sought re-election in 1936, Roosevelt made the story of the previous decade's stock market speculation and the economic collapse that followed central to his appeal, as in this October speech:

> For twelve years this nation was afflicted with hear-nothing, see-nothing, do-nothing government. The nation looked to the government but the government looked away. Nine mocking years with the golden calf and three long years of the scourge! Nine crazy years at the ticker and three long years in the breadlines! Nine mad years of mirage and three long years of despair! Powerful influences strive today to restore that kind of government with its doctrine that that Government is best which is most indifferent.
>
> For nearly four years you have had an Administration which instead of twirling its thumbs has rolled up its sleeves. We will keep our sleeves rolled up. We had to struggle with the old enemies of peace—business and financial monopoly, speculation, reckless banking, class antagonism, sectionalism, war profiteering. They had begun to consider the Government of the United States as a mere appendage to their own affairs. We know now that Government by organized money is just as dangerous as Government by organized mob.

As able on the campaign trail as Pecora was in the hearing room, Roosevelt invited Americans to recognize the struggle between financial power and democracy as a morality play that had fundamental consequences for their lives:

> Never before in all our history have these forces been so united against one candidate as they stand today. They are unanimous in their hate for me—and I welcome their hatred.

I should like to have it said of my first Administration that in it the forces of selfishness and of lust for power met their match. I should like to have it said of my second Administration that in it these forces met their master.

That fall, Roosevelt won his second term with the most sweeping electoral mandate in modern American history. FDR's Democratic Party retained its congressional majorities, and the opposition Republicans were forced to accept much of the New Deal agenda as the new normal of American politics and governance. The man Roosevelt defeated that year, Kansas governor Alf Landon, would never again hold elected office. The same was true of the president Roosevelt defeated in 1932. In his own way, Herbert Hoover became an American version of Britain's disgraced Neville Chamberlain.

Hoover would carry the stigma of having failed the country in its time of peril for the rest of his long life—so much so that, when he died in 1965, his *New York Times* obituary began with a recounting of the Great Depression. Even after Hoover and the other guilty men of the 1920s and early '30s were dead and gone, the rules and regulations put in place in response to their deeds remained. Only decades later, when a new generation of guilty men and women—some of them Republicans, some Democrats—formed a shamefully bipartisan league of corruption were the protections finally dismantled. And the country again imperiled.

For more than a half century, the homeland was protected—not so much by laws and armies but by an understanding of history as it had been written by the Hellhound of Wall Street. By the time the Pecora hearings ended in May 1934, they had generated 12,000 printed pages of testimony. "These documents have served generations of historians," according to Chernow.

"Our national narrative of stock market mayhem in the 1920s is largely composed of characters and anecdotes gleaned from their pages."

A New Crusade Against Impunity

National narratives need to be renewed on a regular basis. The dismantling of New Deal safeguards by Democratic president Bill Clinton and his Republican congressional collaborators in the "greed is good" 1990s offers a revealing footnote to the story of the past and the present. Even the Pecora-inspired regulatory reckoning of the 1930s was insufficient to stand the full test of time on its own. That was not because of his weakness, but because of ours. Even if we do not forgive, we tend to forget. And when we do, impunity creeps back.

But that does not mean that we cannot learn from the Hellhound of Wall Street. What Pecora taught us is the same lesson that Foot and his compatriots taught, and that Churchill and Roosevelt understood. When a country has been undermined, weakened and traumatized by those who choose political advantage or personal profit over human life and shared prosperity, truth and reconciliation is insufficient. Forgiving and forgetting becomes dangerous. There must be a reckoning and it must be sweeping in its scope and character or the crimes of the past will be repeated.

The shadow of a pandemic that killed hundreds of thousands who should never have died, that sickened millions who should never have fallen ill, that impoverished tens of millions who should never have been dislocated will not lift until there has been a full accounting. It is for the purpose of that accounting that investigations are necessary, charges are required and convictions must be attained. It is in the pursuit of that accounting that Senate hearing rooms must again be turned into chambers of inquiry and recrimination, that transformative legislation must be drafted and a new age must be signed into law.

We have a duty, to the dead, to the ailing, to the damaged and the endangered, to be as pugnacious as Michael Foot and as fierce as Ferdinand Pecora. Each inquiry that is launched into a pandemic profiteer, each conviction that is recorded for a coronavirus criminal, each defeat that is handed a guilty man or woman matters because it forms a part of a new national narrative.

In the fall of 2020, as a pandemic raged during the course of a presidential campaign, the stakes were every bit as high as in 1932 or 1940. But the wisest political observers recognized that the election result, even if it was positive, would not be sufficient to repair the damage done. "Our democracy is at a faint heartbeat; it was broken even before Trump," said Representative Alexandria Ocasio-Cortez of New York. "And after we work to command victory in November, I need folks to realize that there's no going back to brunch."

That was a crucial warning. Impunity never takes a break. It always reasserts itself. This is why the writers and the prosecutors of the past recognized that recriminations were necessary. Some of those recriminations come on the campaign trail and at the ballot box.

But it is not enough to defeat an insurrectionist president while his minions continue to run roughshod in the Senate. It is not enough to trade a Donald Trump in 2020 for a Trump 2.0 in 2024. It is not enough to expose a profiteering pharmaceutical company and let it continue to profiteer, or to note that billionaires got richer during the pandemic and then to sit back and watch them become trillionaires.

There can and should be many indictments—legislative, criminal and civil. They should hold coronavirus criminals and pandemic profiteers to account wherever laws have been broken and sacred oaths have been abandoned.

Ultimately, however, we must concern ourselves with the deeper indictment that only time can impose. The "guilty men" of our time must retire—or be retired. But they must also be consigned to the ash heap of history. They must go there so they will haunt us no more. They must go there because we cannot afford to allow their kind to continue charting a ruinous course for our country and for our world. They must go there because the names of those who sinned against human decency in the long dark age that extended from early 2020 to early 2021 must never again be accorded the honors of high office or the comforts of high station.

They must go there so that the United States of Impunity is no more, forever.

A Note on Sources

This book was written as a pandemic gripped America. It was completed during a lull in that pandemic. It relies on interviews with officials and activists who sought to address the crisis, on studies and reports that accessed the health care and economic issues that extended from it, and on news reports from the period. It is informed, as well, by historical writing that offered insight into times of crisis, and on the deeper question of how accountability might be achieved in such moments and in their aftermath.

Americans who lived through the most turbulent days of 2020 and 2021 will understand that the period was intense, confusing, cacophonous and often overwhelming. These notes reflect on the sources of information that helped me to put this interval in perspective. I am especially grateful to the members of Congress, legislators, academics, doctors, nurses, frontline workers and union activists who took time from their work to guide me through complicated discussions about infectious diseases, public health, economic instability and morality. I am, as well, appreciative of the journalists who, in one of this country's most challenging moments, embraced their twin duties to comfort the afflicted and to afflict the comfortable.

Preface

I interviewed New York State Assemblyman Ron Kim in April 2021, at a point when he was in the thick of his fight to hold Governor Andrew Cuomo to account. Kim's insights informed several sections of this book. My thoughts on the role that accountability can play in inspiring and achieving transformative change were informed by discussions with Rebecca Solnit, Noam Chomsky and the late Gore Vidal, as well as my research and writing over many years on the subject of impeachment. An example of that writing can be found in my 2006 book *The Genius of Impeachment: The Founders' Cure for Royalism* (The New Press), for which Gore wrote the introduction. It is one of many books I have worked on with my longtime editor, Andy Hsiao. The copy of *Guilty Men*, which I relied on throughout the writing of this book, is the 2010 edition published by Faber and Faber Ltd. It includes a typically erudite, witty and self-deprecating preface by Michael Foot, and an authoritative introduction by John Stevenson. I also referred, frequently, to Foot's writing on Tom Paine, including his fine introduction to *Rights of Man and Common Sense* (Everyman's Library, 1994). Kenneth O. Morgan's *Michael Foot: A Life* (HarperCollins, 2007) is an exceptional biography of an exceptional journalist, author, political agitator and human being.

Introduction

Labor activists highlighted the issues that arose from Mike Jackson's death, and I was able to follow their work. I am especially appreciative of the information and insight provided by Christine

Neumann-Ortiz and the brilliant activists with Voces de la Frontera. I also appreciated information I got from United Steelworkers Local 2-232's reports, and the union local's blog. The *Bellows* produced vital coverage of the reaction to the company's handling of the pandemic, including a fine interview with union organizer Chance Zombor under the headline "They are doling out bonuses for billionaires while employees are literally worked to death," published on June 26, 2020. I turned to several *Milwaukee Journal Sentinel* articles, including ones headlined "A Briggs & Stratton employee who pushed for more coronavirus restrictions in the workplace died from the virus" (June 16, 2020) and "Protesters go to Assembly Speaker Robin Vos' home to lay a wreath; Milwaukee won't move to next phase of reopening" (June 18, 2020), as well as the *Milwaukee Independent*'s "Marchers Condemn Briggs & Stratton for Giving Millions to Executives as Mike Jackson Worked to Death" (July 8, 2020), by Joe Brusky. Also, *UpNorthNews* published an outstanding article on the reactions of family members and friends to the Jackson's death: "Father of 8 Dies of Covid-19 After Collapsing at Work. Coworkers Describe the Pressure to Work Sick" (June 14, 2020). The CBS News report "Factory worker's death highlights debate over GOP-backed coronavirus liability shield" appeared on August 4, 2020. Reactions to the rising Covid-19 death rate can be found in the Associated Press report of May 27, 2020, headlined "US death toll from coronavirus surges past 100,000 people." Trump's "medical war" comments can be found in *Time*'s report "'Our Big War.' As Coronavirus Spreads, Trump Refashions Himself as a Wartime President" (March 19, 2020). *Axios* National Political Correspondent Jonathan Swan's interview with Trump was released August 3, 2020. The Don Winslow Films piece "#ConsequencesForTrump" appeared on August 5, 2020. The *La Crosse Tribune* article "On Wisconsin's worst day of the pandemic, thousands pack in at West Salem race track for Trump Rally" appeared on October 30, 2020. The same day, Wisconsin Public Radio reported, "Trump Draws Thousands to Rally as Wisconsin Sees Record High Covid-19 Cases, Deaths." Video of the rally can be found on YouTube under "Live: Trump Hold Campaign Rally in Wisconsin / NBC News." Wisconsin Public Radio ran a report on October 27, 2020, "At Memorial to 600 Milwaukeeans Dead From Covid-19, Organizers Urge Action." The *Milwaukee Journal Sentinel* headline that same day read, "'There are lives at stake': 600 empty chairs displayed in Milwaukee to represent county's coronavirus deaths."

Chapter 1. *The Killing Presidency of Donald Trump*

I covered Trump's first and second impeachment trials for the *Nation* magazine. The reports are archived at thenation.com under "authors, john-nichols." *USA Today* wrote about reactions to the death toll passing 400,000 in a January 19, 2021, article headlined "'Blood on his hands': As US surpasses 400,000 Covid-19 deaths, experts blame Trump administration for a 'preventable' loss of life." Bob Woodward's book *Rage* was published by Simon & Schuster on September 15, 2020. The *Washington Post* reported on it in a September 9, 2020, article headlined "Woodward book: Trump says he knew coronavirus was 'deadly' and worse than the flu while intentionally misleading Americans." The *Lancet*'s Covid-19 reports are found at "coronavirus, collection, thelancet. com." The *Guardian* reviewed on the Lancet report and other studies in a February 11, 2021, article headlined "US could have averted 40% of Covid deaths, says panel examining Trump's policies." The *Washington Post* report headlined "How many coronavirus deaths are truly attributable to Trump?" appeared on October 23, 2020. *FactCheck.org* called out Trump's false equivalencies regarding Covid-19 and the flu on September 9, 2020, in "Trump's Deceptive Comparison of the Coronavirus to the Flu." I wrote about Trump's fabrications in the *Nation* on September 10, 2020, in the piece "Trump Lied, Americans Died." Kristin Urquiza addressed the Democratic National Convention on August 17, 2020. The *Arizona Republic* reported on the speech in an August 18, 2020, article headlined "Kristin Urquiza, who blistered Gov. Doug Ducey in viral Covid-19 obituary, speaks at Democratic National Convention."

Chapter 2. Mike Pence: Yes-Man of the Apocalypse

Mike Pence's article "There Isn't a Coronavirus 'Second Wave': With testing, treatments and vaccine trials ramping up, we are far better off than the media report" appeared on June 16, 2020, in the *Wall Street Journal*. For information on Covid-19 death tolls and infection rates, I relied on the CDC's Covid Data Tracker, as well as the *New York Times* "Tracking Coronavirus" dashboard, both of which provided daily updates that were verified and generally considered to be thoughtful, even conservative, in their assessments. *Time* magazine's report "Alarming Data Show a Third Wave of Covid-19 Is About to Hit the US" appeared on September 28, 2020. Pence addressed the Republican National Convention on August 26, 2020. The *New Yorker* report of August 27, 2020, was headlined "Mike Pence's Big Lie About Trump and the Coronavirus at the Republican National Convention." *PolitiFact*'s assessment of Pence's speech, "Fact-checking Mike Pence, night 3 of the 2020 RNC," appeared August 26, 2020. I wrote extensively about Pence's record in my book *Horsemen of the Trumpocalypse: A Field Guide to the Most Dangerous People in America* (Nation Books/Bold Type Books), published in August 2017. Pence's ruminations on the Great American

Smoke Out were featured on his 2000 congressional campaign website. *Vox* reported on Pence's tobacco stance in an October 4, 2016, article headlined "Mike Pence claimed 'smoking doesn't kill' as late as 2000." The *Chicago Tribune* examined Pence's anti–reproductive rights zealotry in David Rutter's groundbreaking June 6, 2015, report headlined "Little Indiana town paid for war on Planned Parenthood." *HuffPost* explained the same issues in its September 22, 2015, piece "Indiana Shut Down Its Rural Planned Parenthood Clinics and Got an HIV Outbreak." Tom Frieden's devastating comments on Pence's policies can be found in an October 7, 2015 *Indianapolis Star* article titled "Needle sharing decreases among Indiana addicts." Gregg S. Gonsalves and Forrest W. Crawford published "Dynamics of the HIV Outbreak and Response in Scott County, Indiana, 2011-2015: A Modeling Study" in *Lancet HIV* in September 2018. They also wrote an excellent piece for *Politico*, "How Mike Pence Made Indiana's HIV Outbreak Worse," published on March 2, 2020; this important article explained: "The vice president claims success tamping down HIV. Now he's leading Trump's coronavirus response. We studied what he did as governor, and it's not encouraging." Oregon Senator Jeff Merkley expressed his concerns about Pence taking over the coronavirus task force on February 26, 2020, as did New York Representative Alexandria Ocasio-Cortez. Dr. Craig Spencer reacted to Pence's failure to wear a mask on April 28, 2020. The *Politico* article headlined "How Mike Pence slowed down the coronavirus response," by Dan Diamond and Adam Cancryn, appeared on August 26, 2020. The article titled "Pence absent from Covid-19 planning calls for more than a month," by Cancryn and Dan Goldberg, appeared in *Politico* on October 29, 2020. I covered the 2020 debates for the *Nation*; those articles are archived at thenation.com. Bess Levin's *Vanity Fair* report "Undecided Voters Thought Donald Trump Came

Off as a Deranged Twatwaffle, Still Might Vote for Him" appeared on September 30, 2020. I wrote an assessment of Harris's debating skills, "Kamala Harris Will Shred Mike Pence in the Vice Presidential Debate," which appeared in the *Nation* on August 11, 2020. My report on the debate, "Kamala Harris Called Out Covid Lies and Guilty Men," appeared in the same magazine on October 8, 2020. A transcript of the vice presidential debate is posted on debates.org /debate-history/2020-debates. Suzette Hackney's *USA Today* article titled "Pence's political future hinges on how he leads the White House Coronavirus Task Force: Vice president could be committing the biggest political misstep of his career if he keeps sitting on the sidelines as Covid-19 cases and deaths soar" ran on December 4, 2020.

Chapter 3. *The Grounding of Jared Kushner*

I interviewed Senator Sherrod Brown of Ohio, a leading voice on trade policy, several times about the role deindustrialization played in leaving the United States unprepared for the pandemic. An article based on those conversations, "Sherrod Brown: Covid Shows How Corporate 'Free Trade' Policies Threaten Public Health," appeared in the *Nation* on October 29, 2020. The *Independent*'s report on nurses and medical gear headlined "Coronavirus: Nurses forced to wear trash bags at hospital where worker died from Covid-19: After the death of a colleague, nurses at Mount Sinai hospitals in New York say they are running out of equipment" ran on March 26, 2020. The findings of the National Nurses United study were published in "Covid-19 survey of registered nurses shows little improvement and worsening availability of personal protective equipment" by that group and by the California Nurses Association/National Nurses Organizing Committee on March 20, 2020. I monitored these reports and kept in contact with National Nurses United throughout the pandemic. For background on Kushner's mangled real estate deals, see "Deal Gives Kushners Cash Infusion on 666 Fifth Avenue," *New York Times*, August 3, 2018. I write extensively about Ivanka Trump and Jared Kushner in *Horsemen of the Trumpocalypse*. Judd Legum's "7 jobs Jared Kushner is now doing for the United States of America," was published on March 31, 2017, by *Think Progress*. Andrea Bernstein's WNYC reporting on the Trumps and the Kushners was required reading during Donald Trump's presidency. She discussed her work with *Vox* in a fine extended article, "The most powerful person in the White House not named Donald Trump," which appeared on June 13, 2020. CBS News reported on Kushner's view of his responsibilities in "What Is Project Airbridge?" on March 30, 2020. Gabriel Sherman's look behind the scenes at the White House, "'There's No Boogeyman He Can Attack': Angry at Kushner, Trump Awakens to the Covid-19 Danger," appeared in *Vanity Fair* on March 16, 2020. Katherine Eban also wrote a revealing piece for *Vanity Fair* on Kushner's role, "'That's Their Problem': How Jared Kushner Let the Markets Decide America's Covid-19 Fate," which ran on September 17, 2020. A video of the April 7, 2020, briefing where Trump talked up Project Airbridge can be found on YouTube under "4/7/20: Members of the Coronavirus Task Force Hold a Press Briefing." Questions about Project Airbridge arose quickly; Jake Brewster wrote well about them on June 9, 2020, in a *Forbes* article headlined "'Incompetence, Confusion': Democrats Seek Probe Into Trump Pandemic Relief Initiative 'Project Airbridge.'" Fox News featured Kushner on April 26, 2020, in the report titled "Jared Kushner on securing US supply chain amid coronavirus: We can never rely on foreign supplies again." ABC News covered the concerns of members of Congress in an April 27, 2020, report. "'Little or no transparency': Warren

wants data on White House medical supply program." The
network featured reaction from House members like Florida's
Ted Deutch and Minnesota's Angie Craig on April 23, 2020, in
a report headlined "Kushner-backed program chartering
flights to address hospital shortages raises questions in Congress."
Governor J. B. Pritzker of Illinois appeared on the April 6, 2020,
edition of the *PBS NewsHour*, in a piece titled "Federal government has delivered less than 10 percent of PPE Illinois requested."
The *Washington Post* article headlined "White House's pandemic
relief effort Project Airbridge is swathed in secrecy and exagger-
ations" appeared May 8, 2020. The NBC News story titled
"Government orders 100,000 new body bags as Trump mini-
mizes death toll" aired on April 30, 2020. The State of
Washington has archived Governor Jay Inslee's letters about PPE
at governor.wa.gov/news-media under "Inslee letter to Pence calls
for national PPE mobilization." On May 11, 2020, NBC News
reported on the impending end of Kushner's project in a story
titled "Jared Kushner's highly scrutinized 'Project Airbridge' to
begin winding down." The American Federation of Teachers
union announced its TV ad buy in an April 14, 2020, press
release titled "AFT Launches Six-Figure Ad Campaign Targeting
Trump Over PPE Lies, Inaction." A detailed report on the Michigan protests, "Healthcare workers, supporters rally to demanding
'PPE over profit' outside of UM Hospital," was published by
mlive.com on April 16, 2020. Reactions from various senators,
including Elizabeth Warren of Massachusetts and Richard
Blumenthal of Connecticut, can be found in a June 9, 2020,
statement on Warren's senate.gov site under "Warren, Schumer,
Blumenthal Release New Findings and Documents from Invest-
igation of Trump-Kushner 'Project Air Bridge' Coronavirus
Response." The House Oversight and Reform Committee memo
"Information Provided by Medical Distribution Companies on

Challenges With White House Supply Chain Task Force and Project Airbridge" was released on July 2, 2020. Vice President Pence's claims about the "success" of the administration response can be found in "There Isn't a Coronavirus 'Second Wave,'" *Wall Street Journal*, June 16, 2020. The House Committee on Homeland Security hearing, on the subject of "Examining the National Response to the Worsening Coronavirus Pandemic," took place on July 8, 2020. Elizabeth Spiers's article "I worked for Jared Kushner. Of course he says his Covid-19 failure is a success" ran in the *Washington Post* on May 8, 2020.

Chapter 4. *The Unmasking of Mark Meadows*

In researching responses to the 1918 influenza pandemic, I relied on materials from the Wisconsin Historical Society. I was also informed by Polly Price's forthcoming book *Plagues in the Nation: How Epidemics Shaped America* (Beacon Press). Price's March 19, 2020, article for the *Atlantic*, "How a Fragmented Country Fights a Pandemic," was an invaluable resource. The *Saturday Evening Post* of May 6, 2020, reported on "The Mask Slackers of the 1918 Influenza Pandemic." Becky Little wrote about the "Spanish flu" and responses to it on May 6, 2020, in "When Mask-Wearing Rules in the 1918 Pandemic Faced Resistance" for history.com. Nancy Bristow's book *American Pandemic: The Lost Worlds of the 1918 Influenza Epidemic* was published by Oxford University Press in 2017. World Health Organization statements on mask mandates can be found at the World Health Organization website under "Mask use in the context of Covid-19." The *Lancet* assessment, headlined "Physical distancing, face masks and eye protection to prevent person-to-person transmission of SARS-CoV-2 and Covid-19: a systematic review and meta-analysis," was published on June 1, 2020. The *Conversation* published an article titled "New Zealand hits zero active coronavirus cases. Here are five measures to keep it that way," by Michael Baker and Nick Wilson, on June 7, 2020. The *New York Times* story, "As US Deaths Surpass 300,000, Obituaries Force Reckoning With Covid," is a strikingly sensitive piece by Julie Bosman; it appeared on December 13, 2020. On December 18, 2018, the *Tampa Bay Times* disclosed a case of résumé fixing in an article headlined "As Trump mulled chief of staff pick, US Rep. Mark Meadows's USF degree was fixed on Wikipedia." The *New York Times* reported on how Meadows undermined mask-mandate proposals in "Trump's Focus as the Pandemic Raged: What Would It Mean for Him?" published on December 31, 2020. A very fine *Times* summation of Trump's resistance to masks was published on October 2, 2020, as "In His Own Words, Trump on the Corona-virus and Masks." Pence appeared on the CBS News program *Face the Nation* on June 28, 2020. Retired history professor Milton Ready's assessment of Meadows, "Man of the Hour: The Rise of Mark Meadows," was published on June 4, 2019, by the *Mountain Xpress* of Asheville, North Carolina. I wrote extensively for the *Nation* on the rise of the Freedom Caucus and the battles within the Republican Party during the latter stages of Barack Obama's presidency and Trump's years in office. For more on Meadows and the Freedom Caucus, read "A House Divided: How a radical group of Republicans pushed Congress to the right," by Ryan Lizza, in the *New Yorker* of December 6, 2015. Tina Nguyen reported on John Boehner's impression of Meadows in her October 30, 2017, article for *Vanity Fair*, "'Idiots,' 'Anarchists' and 'Assholes': John Boehner Unloads on Republicans in a Post-Retirement Interview." I talked with John Dean several times about his vital book *Conservatives Without Conscience*, which was published by Viking in 2006. The *Washington Post* produced a number of articles on the dysfunctional relationship between

Trump and Meadows, including "Meadows under fire as Trump chief of staff for handling of pandemic and other crises" (October 26, 2020, by Josh Dawsey) and "The inside story of how Trump's denial, mismanagement and magical thinking led to the pandemic's dark winter" (December 19, 2020, by Yasmeen Abutaleb, Ashley Parker, Josh Dawsey and Philip Rucker). The MIT/University of British Columbia paper on mask mandates was titled "Causal Impact of Masks, Policies, Behavior on Early Covid-19 Pandemic in the US" For background, see "Masks mandates have major impact, study finds," MIT News Office, August 5, 2020. The *Nature Medicine* article "Modeling Covid-19 scenarios for the United States" appeared on October 23, 2020. Nancy Cook and Meredith McGraw produced a fine review of Meadows's loyalty to Trump during the president's last days in office, "'I'd be pretty pissed off': Meadows angers staff as he cozies up to Trump," in the *Politico* of October 8, 2020.

Chapter 5. Mike Pompeo's Cold War against Science and Solidarity

I have written extensively about Mike Pompeo throughout his career. He rated a chapter in my book *Horsemen of the Trumpocalypse*. When he took over as secretary of state, I wrote about the move for the *Nation* on March 13, 2018, in the article "The Koch Brothers Get Their Very Own Secretary of State: Trump's pick to replace Rex Tillerson is an errand boy for billionaires." Pompeo's remarks on Cuban doctors fighting Covid-19 can be found in the transcript from his press briefing on the State Department website under "Secretary Michael R. Pompeo at a Press Availability, April 29, 2020." AFP reported on Pompeo's statements about Cuban doctors and South Africa in the April 29, 2020, article headlined "Pompeo criticizes S. Africa, Qatar for taking Cuban doctors." The *Washington Post* reported on Pompeo and Cuban doctors in the January 21, 2020, article titled "The US is pushing Latin American allies to send their Cuban doctors packing—and several have." The Associated Press reported on the reaction to Cuban medical aid for South Africa in the article "Cuban Doctors Arrive to Help South Africa Fight Coronavirus" on April 27, 2020. President Obama delivered his remarks to the Cuban people on the role of Cuban health care providers on March 22, 2016. Prensa Latina reported on the reaction of the Cuban president, Miguel Díaz-Canel, to Pence's remarks in the June 12, 2020, article headlined "Cuban president denounces US immoral and arrogant rhetoric." NBC News reported on Cuba's international effort to fight Covid-19 in a story titled "Cuba sends 'white coat army' of doctors to fight coronavirus in different countries: Nearly 40 countries across five continents have received Cuban doctors during the pandemic," on September 14, 2020. The *Economist*'s article headlined "Cuba's doctors are in high demand" was published on April 4, 2020. Reuters reported on another initiative in a March 21, 2020, story titled "Cuban doctors head to Italy to battle coronavirus." On September 14, 2020, a Reuters headline announced, "Cuba punches above weight with 'white coat army' during pandemic." A Harvard International Review study, "An Army of White Coats: Exploring the Implications of Cuban Medical Diplomacy," was published on December 23, 2020. The report by Miguel González Palacios headlined "Pan American Health Organization in intensive care," appeared on August 11, 2020, in Open Democracy. The late Albor Ruiz's article "Pompeo's Sick Obsession: The United States criticizes Cuba for sending doctors, while its main export is soldiers" was published on June 17, 2020. Senator Patrick Leahy denounced the redesignation of Cuba in a statement issued on January 11, 2012. Sébastien Roblin's assessment of that action, headlined "Biden undermined on Cuba, Iran by last-minute Pompeo terror designations," was published by NBC News as part of its "Think" series on January 13, 2021. Elise Labott's "No Amount of Swagger Can Dress Up Pompeo's Legacy" was published on January 21, 2021, by *Foreign Policy*. The *Washington Post*'s December 2, 2020, report on Pompeo's late-term social calendar was headlined "Pompeo invites hundreds to indoor holiday parties after subordinates are warned against hosting 'non-mission critical events.'" NBC News headlined its October 9, 2020, report on the notorious White House gathering "Fauci calls Amy Coney Barrett ceremony in Rose Garden 'superspreader event.'" Senator Robert Menendez, the Ranking Member of the Senate Foreign Relations Committee, called for Pompeo to cancel the indoor holiday party in a statement issued on December 4, 2020. John Hudson's December 16, 2020, report for the *Washington Post* was headlined "Pompeo cancels final holiday party after he comes into contact with coronavirus." The World Health Organization's statement on the Covax Facility, titled "172 countries and multiple candidate vaccines engaged in Covid-19 vaccine Global Access Facility," was issued on August 24, 2020. The *New York Times* piece "If Poor Countries Go Unvaccinated, a Study Says, Rich Ones Will Pay" was published on January 23, 2021. The ABC News report titled "US declines to join global Covid-19 vaccine effort because of WHO's role: The Trump administration will also withhold $62M it owes the agency" appeared on September 2, 2020. Bloomberg's report "Next Africa: Falling Behind in the Race for Covid-19 Vaccines" was published on January 8, 2021. NPR reported on January 22, 2021, "'Until Everyone Is Safe, No One Is Safe': Africa Awaits the Covid-19 Vaccine." I have written a good deal about Ellen Johnson Sirleaf and Russ Feingold over the years, often focusing on their insights regarding infectious diseases and health care. John Campbell's piece "US Africa Policy Needs a Reset" appeared on October 12, 2020, in *Foreign Affairs*.

Chapter 6. How Betsy DeVos Tried to Leverage a Pandemic to Privatize Public Education

The *Orlando Sentinel* reported on the governor's remarks on July 9, 2020, in an article headlined "Gov. DeSantis seeks to speed up testing in Orange, says schools need to open." A Tampa TV station, WTSP, reported on school reopenings in a July 14, 2020, story titled "'Teachers are preparing lesson plans and living wills': Florida teachers union pushes for delayed start to school year." WFLA 8's coverage included a piece titled "St. Pete law firm offering free living wills for teachers returning to school amid coronavirus surge," which aired on July 14, 2020. The Kaiser Family Foundation report "How Many Teachers Are at Risk of Serious Illness if Infected With Coronavirus?" was issued on July 10, 2020. The National Education Association titled its 2019 study of the secretary of education's tenure "Betsy DeVos has been a disaster for public education from day one." AFT president Randi Weingarten wrote about her work on these issues in a *Washington Post* column headlined, "This summer, we can test-drive best practices for safely reopening schools," on May 26, 2020. Weingarten tweeted "Their goal isn't safety, it's politics" on July 12, 2020. The Center for Disease Control and Prevention's "Operational Strategy for K–12 Schools Through Phased Prevention" can be found at cdc.gov. *Politico* reported on the secretary's pressure campaign in a July 7, 2020, article headlined "DeVos blasts school districts that hesitate at reopening." I wrote about rising concerns over DeVos's statements for the *Nation* in "Ayanna Pressley to Betsy DeVos: 'I Wouldn't Trust You to Care for a House Plant Let Alone My Child,'" which was published on July 14, 2020. CNN covered rising concerns about DeVos's approach in a July 15, 2020, report headlined "'Normally, people don't play with kids' lives': Trump's push to reopen schools becomes another partisan fight." DeVos spoke about "fearmongering" in an appearance on Fox News's *Tucker Carlson Tonight* on July 7, 2020. She spoke with Fox's Chris Wallace on July 12, 2020. I wrote about representatives Bowman and Pressley in the July 14, 2020, article for the *Nation*.

Chapter 7. Elaine Chao Let Them Die

I wrote extensively about the deaths of workers in the transportation sector for the *Nation* in the spring of 2020. The articles are archived at the magazine's website. While reporting, I spoke with leaders of the various transportation unions for the article "'We Will Not Sit Back and Let Transit Workers Be Treated Like Cannon Fodder,'" which was published on April 3, 2020. One of America's ablest labor reporters, Mike Elk, wrote about Scott Ryan's death in the Payday Report article "ATU Shop Steward, Who Warned of Covid-19 Dangers, Dies From It," which appeared on March 27, 2020. An Amalgamated Transit Union statement on Ryan's death, "Amalgamated Transit Union Mourns Passing of First Member from Covid-19, Brother Scott Ryan of Local 1576-Lynnwood, WA," was issued on March 27 2020. The *Everett Herald* article headlined "Bus driver who worried early about coronavirus dies of it" was written by Zachariah Bryan and appeared on March 28, 2020. The *Seattle Times* report titled "After driver dies, Community Transit workers question whether the agency is protecting them from coronavirus," by Heidi Groover, was published on March 27, 2020. The *Governing* magazine article "What Does Safe Public Transit Look Like During Covid-19?" appeared on August 24, 2020. I have written a good deal about Elaine Chao over the years, including a chapter in my book *Horsemen of the Trumpocalypse*. The joint TWU-ATU statement "America's Largest Transit Worker Unions Vow 'Aggressive Action' if Transit Systems Don't Protect Frontline Workers" was issued on April 3, 2020. The *Washington Post* report headlined "Transit workers are paying a heavy price during the pandemic" was published on March 17, 2020. The TWU's "Save Lives Now" letter was sent on April 17, 2020. The "Protect Crew and Passengers" letter from Sara Nelson of the flight attendants union was sent on April 23, 2020. Representative Peter DeFazio wrote his letter to Chao on February 26, 2020. Readers can find Heather Krause's June 23, 2020, testimony, "Air Travel and Communicable Diseases: Status of Research Efforts and Action Still Needed to Develop Federal Preparedness Plan," at science. house.gov. The AFL-CIO Transportation Trades Department's "Petition for Rulemaking of the Transportation Trades Department, AFL-CIO: Mandatory Passenger Mask Usage to Address Covid-19" was delivered on July 27, 2020. *Politico*'s report, "Chao cool on 'heavy-handed' pandemic regulations for airlines," appeared on June 3, 2020. The *New York Times* report "41 Transit Workers Dead: Crisis Takes Staggering Toll on Subways" appeared on April 8, 2020. The *Washington Post* wrote about Danny Cruz's efforts to track the deaths of transit workers in a May 17, 2020, article titled "Transit workers are paying a heavy price during the pandemic"; the *Times* also chronicled the effort in several reports. When the US House Transportation and Infrastructure Committee held a hearing June 9, 2020, on the impact of Covid-19 on transportation workers, reports on Cruz's tally were submitted to the official record. Sujatha Gidla's brilliant essay, "'We Are Not Essential, We Are Sacrificial': I'm a New York City subway conductor who had Covid-19. Now I'm going back to work," was published by the *New York Times* on May

5, 2020. The *Forbes* article "US Airlines Can't Really Get Tough on Requiring Face Masks Without Action by Trump Administration" was published on June 17, 2020. The letter from Chao's DOT rejecting pleas for a mask mandate was dated October 2, 2020. The union response, "On the Day POTUS Tests Positive for Covid-19, US DOT Rejects Mask Mandate for All Commercial, Public Transportation," was issued the next day. Senator Richard Blumenthal, Representative Jesus "Chuy" Garcia and the Transportation Trades Department's Larry Willis wrote an excellent article for the *Hill*, headlined "As frontline workers contract Covid-19, we're not doing enough to protect the traveling public," which appeared on October 20, 2020. The same publication reported on December 11, 2020, about concerns over spikes in positive tests for flight attendants in an article headlined "United Airlines flight attendants asked to keep working after Covid-19 exposure: report." An Amalgamated Transit Union letter noting the 100th death among its members was sent to members of Congress on December 18, 2020. President Biden's executive order on mask wearing was issued on January 20, 2021. The Department of Homeland Security announced its new approach in a January 31, 2021, statement titled "TSA to implement Executive Order regarding face masks at airport security checkpoints and throughout the transportation network." Transport Workers Union President John Samuelsen reacted to the Biden administration's moves on January 20, 2021, while the Association of Flight Attendants President Sara Nelson spoke up on January 21, 2021. An online link to the Metropolitan Transit Authority memorial can be found on the MTA website new.mta. info, under "Covid memorial." A poignant video featuring former US poet laureate Tracy K. Smith's "Travels Far" can be found on YouTube under "Travels Far" and "mtainfo."

Chapter 8. Mitch McConnell's Fatal Bargain

I covered the debate over the Heroes Act, as well as the dynamics in the Senate, for the *Nation*. One piece that summed up many of the issues was "Democrats Will Be Lost Without the Senate," which appeared in the July 27/August 3, 2020, issue of the magazine. Peter King explained his vote in a number of interviews; they are summed up in this piece for the *Hill*, "GOP Rep. Pete King to buck party, vote for Democrats' coronavirus relief bill" (May 13, 2020), and in this Fox News interview, "GOP Rep. Peter King says he has 'no choice' but to vote for Democrats' $3T coronavirus relief bill" (May 15, 2020). ABC News reported on the Pelosi and Schumer comments on expected Senate action in the article titled "House passes $3 trillion relief package, bill 'DOA' in Senate" (May 15, 2020). I interviewed Schumer several times during this period, and his comments informed my perspective. The Louisville *Courier-Journal* reported on the Heroes Act on May 14, 2020, in a story headlined "Do we need HEROES? Yarmuth, McConnell at odds over $3T coronavirus relief bill." McConnell delivered his perspective in a speech on the Senate floor, "This Half of the Capitol Is Doing Our Job," on May 14, 2020. The *ABA Journal* reported extensively on the liability shield debate and McConnell's approach to it; one article was headlined "McConnell says Covid-19 aid bill must include liability shield for businesses and hospitals" (April 29, 2020). *PolitiFact* assessed McConnell's fundraising in an article headlined "Does Mitch McConnell receive more money from lobbyists than any other member of Congress?" (March 27, 2014). *Market-Watch* discussed the same subject in a story titled "America's top CEOs are opening up their wallets for Mitch McConnell's re-election campaign" (October 30, 2020). McConnell's "red line" comment came in a Fox News interview on April 28, 2020.

The US Chamber of Commerce letter "Coalition Letter on Coronavirus Liability Protections" was sent on July 30, 2020. The letter from Nader and other activists was sent on April 18, 2020. *Newsweek* reported on McConnell's broad view of how liability shields should work in the article "Mitch McConnell Says Senate Won't Pass Further Coronavirus Relief Unless Businesses Protected From Lawsuits" (April 29, 2020). Steve Ellis wrote "Blanket Covid-19 liability shield will cost taxpayers," for *Roll Call* (August 21, 2020). I wrote "Mitch McConnell's Ghoulish Plan to Exploit Covid Desperation to Shield Corporate Crime," for the *Nation* (December 7, 2020). Public Citizen's statement "Proposal Would Immunize a Wide Range of Employer Wrongdoing" was issued on August 3, 2020. Bernie Sanders spoke about the Manchin–Romney Covid-19 proposal on December 4, 2020.

Chapter 9. How Rand Paul Got Covid-19 Wrong, Wrong and Wrong Again

The Quinnipiac University Poll on opinions regarding Dr. Fauci surveyed 2,077 self-identified registered voters nationwide from April 2–6, 2020. The *Washington Post* wrote about Senator Paul's clash with Fauci on May 12, 2020, in an article headlined "Fauci responds to Rand Paul and his skeptics: He's not trying to be the 'end-all' on coronavirus response." The YouTube video of the clash can be seen on the site under "Senator Paul to Fauci: 'As Much as I Respect You, I Don't Think You're the End-All' on Decisions." The *New York Times* reported on the hearing in a May 12, 2020, article, "At Senate Hearing, Government Experts Paint Bleak Picture of the Pandemic." Virginia Heffernan's stinging column "Rand Paul isn't a subliterate yawper like Trump. But he's spreading the same deadly coronavirus lies" appeared on May 15, 2020, in the *Los Angeles Times*. Laura Ingraham tweeted her praise of Paul on May 12, 2020. The *New York Times* report "Coronavirus Cases Spike Across Sun Belt as Economy Lurches Into Motion" ran on June 18, 2020. Bloomberg reported on the concerns of scientists in "Oregon Joins Florida, Texas in Confronting Covid-19's Resurgence," published on June 17, 2020. The Associated Press did the same in the June 24, 2020, article headlined "'Coming back and biting us': US sees virus resurgence." C-SPAN featured the Fauci testimony on June 30, 2020; video and a transcript can be found at c-span.org under "Covid-19 Response and Reopening Schools." Senator Elizabeth Warren's review of her questioning of Fauci was released on June 30, 2020, as "Dr. Fauci to Senator Warren: US Could See 100,000 Covid-19 Cases a Day." The *Washington Post* report "'We just need some more optimism': Rand Paul's crusade against Anthony Fauci takes a curious turn" was published on June 30, 2020. *The Boston Globe* headlined its report on Fauci's March 18, 2021, appearance on Capitol Hill "In a heated exchange, Senator Paul accuses Dr. Fauci of wearing masks after being vaccinated 'for show.'" The C-SPAN video of the Senate hearing is found at c-span.org under "Senator Rand Paul Clashes With Dr. Fauci Over Mask-Wearing." Fauci appeared on CNN's *Cuomo Prime Time* program on March 18, 2021, and explained his concern that people might not wear masks after hearing Senator Paul's comments.

Chapter 10. Have Another Shot of Hydroxychloroquine, Ron Johnson

I have covered Ron Johnson since 2010. My piece for the *Progressive* on his conspiracy theories, headlined "The Heir to Joe McCarthy: Wisconsin's Ron Johnson is following in the footsteps of the disgraced former Senator," appeared on April 13, 2021. The Associated Press article titled "Sen. Johnson on others getting shots: 'What do you care?'" was published on April 23, 2021. Johnson discussed his vaccine skepticism on a Wisconsin radio program, *The Vicki McKenna Show*, on April 23, 2021. CNN reported on the GOP's anti-vax tendency in an April 24, 2021, piece headlined "Vaccine hesitancy among Republicans emerges as Biden's next big challenge." The *Washington Post* article "'I'm still a zero': Vaccine-resistant Republicans warn that their skepticism is worsening" appeared on April 20, 2021. A very good Monmouth University poll on vaccine hesitancy among Republicans was released on April 14, 2021. The *PolitiFact* analysis titled "What Ron Johnson gets wrong about the Covid-19 vaccines" was released on April 23, 2021; it was written by science writer Madeline Heim of the Appleton *Post-Crescent* newspaper. Johnson's "No, I had Covid . . ." interview was telecast on CBS 58 Milwaukee, March 10, 2021. The *Washington Post* fact check headlined "Ron Johnson's unscientific take on the coronavirus vaccine" was published March 15, 2021. Johnson's Senate Homeland Security and Government Affairs Committee hearings on the topic of "Early Outpatient Treatment" were held November 19, 2020, and December 8, 2020. "The Snake-Oil Salesman of the Senate" appeared November 24, 2020, in the *New York Times*. The *Milwaukee Journal Sentinel* article on Johnson's feeling of being let down by the government, headlined "Doctors slam Sen. Ron Johnson over hearing on Covid-19 treatments," appeared on

November 20, 2020. The FDA statement, "FDA cautions against use of hydroxychloroquine or chloroquine for Covid-19 outside of the hospital setting or a clinical trial due to risk of heart rhythm problems," was released on July 1, 2020. The *Vanity Fair* piece "Quack Cures Lose Their Appeal Now That Trump Himself Is Sick With Covid-19" appeared on October 5, 2020. It noted that "instead of hydroxychloroquine, oleandrin, or any of the other 'shiny objects' his administration has pushed, the president is mixing cutting-edge experimental treatments with a familiar drug that the Pentagon has been studying: famotidine, better known as Pepcid AC." The *Journal Sentinel* article titled "Doctors slam Ron Johnson over hearing on Covid-19" was published October 5, 2020. Dr. Ashish Jha commented on the "testament to how politicized science has become" on November 19, 2020. He testified to the Committee on Homeland Security and Governmental Affairs on the same day. Sarah Godlewski's article "Ron Johnson Brings Fringe Science to the US Senate" appeared on the *Nation*'s website on December 14, 2020. Dr. Avorn's comments were featured in a *Journal Sentinel* piece headlined "'What he is doing is outrageous': Doctors slam Sen. Ron Johnson over hearing on Covid-19 treatments," published on November 20, 2020. Tom Nelson commented on the "scientifically illiterate beliefs" of Senator Johnson on April 23, 2021.

Chapter 11. The Kristi Noem Nightmare

I used the CDC's "Covid Data Tracker" and the *New York Times*'s "Tracking Coronavirus in South Dakota: Latest Map and Case Count" to follow patterns in the state. On December 21, 2020, KELO-TV, the CBS affiliate in Sioux Falls, reported on the state's predicament in a story titled "South Dakota's Covid-19 death rate highest in the nation according to health professionals."

The 2021 Conservative Political Action Conference took place February 25 to February 28 in Orlando, Florida. The American Conservative Union posted a video of Governor Noem's remarks on YouTube under "CPAC 2021—Remarks by Kristi Noem, South Dakota." Fox News ran a story headlined "DeSantis, Noem are breakout stars at CPAC, but Trump maintains grip on party" on March 1, 2021. The Sioux Falls *Argus Leader* announced the death of a key state representative in an April 4, 2020, article headlined "Coronavirus claims life of South Dakota lawmaker Bob Glanzer." Noem tweeted several times about the death of the veteran legislator. The *Washington Post* article titled "South Dakota's governor resisted ordering people to stay home. Now it has one of the nation's largest coronavirus hot spots" appeared on April 13, 2020. The *Native Sun News* of Rapid City covered coronavirus on Indigenous lands in a May 22, 2020, story titled "Covid-19 checkpoints on reservations to remain." The Sioux Falls *Argus Leader* ran the story headlined "Mayor TenHaken calls on Gov. Noem to order shelter-in-place for Sioux Falls area," on April 14, 2020. Many media outlets reported on Trump's Mount Rushmore fantasies, including the *Argus Leader* two years earlier, while Noem served in Congress, in an April 9, 2018, article titled "Mount Trumpmore? It's the president's 'dream,' Rep. Kristi Noem says." On June 30, 2020, NBC News detailed Noem's approach to the Mount Rushmore event in a piece headlined "S. Dakota Gov. Noem says 'we will not be social distancing' at July 3 celebration with Trump at Mount Rushmore." The Associated Press told the story of Noem's gift to Trump in a January 21, 2021, report titled "SD governor gave Trump bust with face on Mount Rushmore." The Associated Press report on Noem's exposure to Covid, headlined "South Dakota governor, exposed to virus, joined Trump on jet," was published on July 6, 2020. Noem attacked the "elite class of so-called experts" in her August 27, 2020, address to the Republican National Convention. The CDC report on the Sturgis fiasco, "Covid-19 Outbreak Associated With a 10-Day Motorcycle Rally in a Neighboring State; Minnesota, August–September 2020, was released November 27, 2020. An NBC News report titled "Coronavirus cases linked to Sturgis Motorcycle Rally now found in Minnesota, 2 other states" appeared on August 22, 2020. On September 2, 2020, the same network ran a follow-up story titled "Weeks after Sturgis motorcycle rally, first Covid-19 death reported as cases accelerate in Midwest." KELO-TV featured an assessment of Noem's criticism of studies of Sturgis as a "superspreader event" in a September 9, 2020, piece headlined "South Dakota professors provide insight on Sturgis Rally Covid-19 report." Another KELO-TV report on the dispute, which appeared on August 31, 2020, was headlined "Governor Noem speaks about Covid-19 active case increase in South Dakota." Experts such as former Harvard Medical School professor William Haseltine commented on the crisis in South Dakota in a November 15, 2020, *USA Today* piece titled "The Dakotas are 'as bad as it gets anywhere in the world' for Covid-19." KELO-TV ran a November 17, 2020, story titled "South Dakota doctor's group supports statewide mask mandate." AP's piece, "As Deaths Spiral, South Dakota Governor Opposes Mask Rules," appeared on November 16, 2020. The *Argus Leader* reported on the spiraling crisis in a December 4, 2020 piece headlined "Some Covid-19 patients flown out of state as S.D. hospital ICU capacity dwindles." The *Washington Post* noted Fauci's response in a February 28, 2021, piece headlined "S.D. Gov. Kristi Noem says she nailed the pandemic response. Fauci: The numbers 'don't lie.'" I wrote about Jonathan Reiner's assessment for the *Nation* in "South Dakota Governor Kristi Noem Is a Deadlier, More Delusional Alternative to Trump," on March 5, 2021. The *Mitchell Republic* reported on the school masking kerfuffle in an August 3, 2020, piece headlined "State education association blasts Noem campaign email encouraging school 'without masks.'" The *Argus Leader* carried news of Sharon Schuldt's death in an October 28, 2020, article headlined "Sonia Sotomayor Elementary nutrition worker dies of Covid-19 complications." *Indian Country Today* told the story of Ethel Left Hand Bull's death as part of its excellent series, "Portraits From the Pandemic"; the piece about Left Hand Bull's death, "Covid devastates South Dakota family," was published on November 6, 2020. KELO-TV reported on the death of Blanca Margarita Ramirez Gonzalez on May 29, 2020, in "Young Huron mother died of Covid-19; most cases of virus in state among those under 40." The *Argus Leader*'s Makenzie Huber wrote a moving piece on the death of Agustín Rodriguez, headlined "'I lost him because of that horrible place': Smithfield worker dies from Covid-19," which appeared on April 16, 2020. A video of Noem's April 13, 2020, Fox News appearance can be found at video.fox.news.com under "South Dakota food plant temporarily closes after workers test positive for Covid-19." *People's World* wrote critically of Noem on April 17, 2020, in a piece titled "S.D. Gov. Noem has blood on her hands after Smithfield outbreak." Readers can follow Kooper Caraway, president of the South Dakota Federation of Labor, on Twitter, @KooperCaraway.

Chapter 12. Ron DeSantis's Imperial Overreach

Ronald Reagan's election eve address, "A Vision for America," was delivered on November 3, 1980. The South Florida *Sun-Sentinel* reported on DeSantis's suspension of local officials in an article headlined "'You're suspended.' How Gov. Ron DeSantis differs from Rick Scott in ousting local officials" (January 28,

2019). DeSantis signed legislation prohibiting state and local governments from having sanctuary policies on June 14, 2019. The *Miami Herald* reported on other possible measures in a September 21, 2020, article headlined "DeSantis proposes crackdown on protesters, penalties to cities that 'defund' the police." The *Tampa Bay Times* report on the reaction of local officials, "Ron DeSantis: Any municipality that 'defunds' police will lose state funding," appeared on the same day. A detailed *Orlando Sentinel* piece on the YouTube fight, "After YouTube pulls DeSantis video for mask fallacies, governor holds another Covid-19 talk with same docs," was published on April 12, 2021. On May 3, 2021, DeSantis issued his executive order "Suspending All Remaining Local Government Mandates and Restrictions Based on the Covid-19 State of Emergency." On June 16, 2021, the governor issued an even more aggressive executive order, announcing, "Ron DeSantis Protects Floridians From Unscientific and Unnecessary Covid-19 Mandates by Local Governments." The *Miami Herald* report headlined "DeSantis declares Covid 'state of emergency' over, overrides local restrictions" appeared on May 3, 2021. The Associated Press report on reactions to the DeSantis move was published the same day in an article headlined "Florida governor signs law preempting local Covid edicts." WPLG/Local 10 News in Miami reported on reaction from local government officials on May 3, 2021, as did WPBF-TV 25 in West Palm Beach.

Chapter 13. Andrew Cuomo's Broken Halo

I discussed the nursing home scandal with a number of New York political figures and union activists as it played out. I especially appreciate the insights I got from Assembly member Ron Kim and veteran Working Families Party activist Dan

Cantor. *City and State New York* produced a detailed timeline of the controversy; readers can view it at cityandstateny.com under "A timeline of Cuomo's handling of Covid-19 in nursing homes." The New York *Daily News* reported on the rising death figure in an article headlined "N.Y. releases Covid nursing home death data," which appeared on February 10, 2021. The Associated Press report titled "Not just Covid: Nursing home neglect deaths surge in shadows," ran on November 19, 2020. The PBS *NewsHour* detailed Dawn Best's story and comments in a piece headlined "As Covid deaths soar, nursing home deaths caused by neglect surge in the shadows" (November 19, 2020). An investigation by *City Limits*, "A Nursing Home Had One Covid Case. Then Came the New, Infected Patients," was published on May 4, 2020. A Fox News report ran on May 19, 2020, under the headline "Rep. Stefanik calls for probe of Cuomo's nursing home order: There was 'zero transparency.'" The Siena College Research Institute poll was released on April 27, 2020. Cuomo's book *American Crisis: Leadership Lessons From the Covid-19 Pandemic* was published by Crown in October 2020. Ron Kim spoke to *Jacobin* magazine for a February 20, 2021, interview, "Andrew Cuomo Declared War on Ron Kim for Telling the Truth." The Associated Press reported on anger over Cuomo's decisions in a piece headlined, "AP count: Over 4,500 virus patients sent to NY nursing homes," which appeared on May 22, 2020. The *Wrap* featured video of Cuomo saying he wouldn't put his own mother in a nursing home, on May 27, 2020. A CBS News report ran on May 18, 2020, under the headline "Cuomo says no one should be prosecuted for coronavirus deaths in New York, including those in nursing homes." CNN published an explainer titled "Cuomo downplayed and deflected questions about nursing home data during daily press conferences last spring" on March 11, 2021. CNN assessed Cuomo's false assertions in an October 2, 2020, piece headlined "Fact checking Gov. Cuomo's false claim about Covid-positive patients and nursing homes." New York Attorney General Letitia James released her report "Nursing Home Response to Covid-19 Pandemic" on January 28, 2021. The *New York Times* article "N.Y. Severely Undercounted Virus Deaths in Nursing Homes, Report Says" appeared on April 22, 2021. On April 28, 2021, the *Times* reported "Cuomo Aides Rewrote Nursing Home Report to Hide Higher Death Toll." The *New York Post* article, "Cuomo aide Melissa DeRosa admits they hid nursing home data so feds wouldn't find out," was published on February 11, 2021. A *Times* piece on Cuomo and accountability, "Cuomo Accepts Some Blame in Nursing Home Scandal but Denies Cover-Up," appeared on March 5, 2021. On February 17, 2021, the *Daily News* ran an article headlined "Cuomo slams Assem. Ron Kim over nursing home criticism." A *Times* article, "Cuomo Attacks a Fellow Democrat Over Nursing Home Criticism," appeared on April 28, 2021. The letter from New York State Assembly Democrats seeking to strip Cuomo of his emergency powers was sent on February 16, 2021. Ron Kim wrote a piece for the *Guardian* titled "Why did Governor Cuomo give nursing homes immunity from Covid deaths?", which appeared on February 23, 2021. David Sirota's important investigative piece, headlined "Cuomo gave immunity to nursing home executives after big campaign donations," was published by the *Guardian* on March 26, 2020. An *Open Secrets* analysis titled "Hospital lobby tied to Cuomo wields influence in Washington" was released on February 18, 2021. The *Daily News* ran a story on February 24, 2021, titled "Ron Kim questions health care donations to Cuomo coffers amid Covid, immunity push." Kim's epic Twitter thread—including the declaration: "Now, we must hold Andrew Cuomo accountable for his abuse of

power and deadly decisions that led to countless deaths . . ."—
unspooled on April 9, 2021.

Chapter 14. *The Deadly Delusions of Wisconsin Supreme Court Justice Rebecca Bradley*

SCOTUSblog reported on the Supreme Court decision in a post titled "Divided court allows indoor worship services to resume in California" on February 6, 2021. The high court's decision in the case of *South Bay United Pentecostal Church et al., v. Gavin Newsom, Governor of California, et al.*, was issued on February 5, 2021. Chris Cillizza wrote a CNN analysis headlined "How the Wisconsin Supreme Court threw the state into coronavirus chaos" on May 14, 2020. For the *Nation*, I wrote, "Wisconsin's In-Person Voting Threatens Health and Democracy," on April 6, 2020, and "Wisconsin's Pandemic Election Is a Red Alert for Democracy in America," on April 9, 2020. The *Wisconsin Examiner* on May 13, 2020, reported on reaction to the court order in an article headlined "Wisconsinites respond to Supreme Court tossing out Safer at Home." Ruth Conniff's article headlined "The GOP tests 2020 campaign theme: 'Some of you will have to die'" was published May 11, 2020. The groundbreaking Brennan Center for Justice communique, "New Report Finds $39.7 Million Spent on Campaigns for State Supreme Court Judgeships in 2017–2018, $10.8 Million of It by Special Interest Groups," was released on December 11, 2019. State Senator Tim Carpenter issued his statement, "Republican Senators Convene to Pass the Buck," on September 23, 2020. The *PolitiFact* assessment headlined "Steineke's actions, words don't match on Covid-19 bill" was issued on January 27, 2021. The Associated Press discussed out-of-state funding in the Wisconsin Supreme Court election campaigns in a February 3, 2016, story titled

"Outside spending begins in Wisconsin Supreme Court race." The Brennan Center's "Buying Time 2016—Wisconsin" review of campaign spending in the Supreme Court race was posted on April 19, 2016. I wrote about Bradley's referencing of the *Korematsu* decision in the piece headlined "Justice Rebecca Bradley's terrible, horrible, no good, very bad historical analogy" in the *Capital Times* on May 19, 2020. The *Korematsu* decision was discussed at length in a thoughtful December 2, 2019 article featured by the American Civil Liberties Union, "During Japanese American Incarceration, the ACLU Lost—and Then Found—Its Way," written by Elaine Elinson and Stan Yogi, co-authors of *Wherever There's a Fight: How Runaway Slaves, Suffragists, Immigrants, Strikers and Poets Shaped Civil Liberties in California*. PBS Wisconsin featured a report on the Wisconsin Supreme Court deliberations, "Supreme Court Hears 'Safer at Home' Challenge," on May 5, 2020. Norman Y. Mineta, the chair of the Board of Trustees for the Japanese American National Museum, released a statement denouncing Bradley's comments on May 8. The Japanese American Citizens League statement "JACL Rebukes 2020 Wisconsin Justice's Comparisons to Japanese American Experience" was issued on May 6, 2020. Readers can review Rebecca Bradley's concurring opinion at wpr.org under "Wisconsin Legislature, Petitioner, v. Secretary-Designee Andrea Palm, Julie Williams Van Dijk and Lisa Olson." George Takei tweeted about Justice Bradley, from May 14, 2020.

Chapter 15. *That Time Rahm Emanuel Offshored America's Ability to Fight a Pandemic*

I have written extensively about Rahm Emanuel since the 1990s for the *Nation* and other publications. The PBS *Frontline* program "The Virus: What Went Wrong?" aired June 16, 2020. Scott

Becker was featured in the *Frontline* documentary and an excellent *New Yorker* piece titled "The Plague Year: The mistakes and the struggles behind America's coronavirus tragedy," by Lawrence Wright, which was published on December 28, 2020. In the early days of the pandemic, Emanuel wrote an opinion piece titled "Let's make sure this crisis doesn't go to waste" for the *Washington Post* on March 25, 2020. The *Policy Matters* study "Promises unfulfilled: Manufacturing in the Midwest" was issued on September 28, 2020. Dan Breznitz and David Adler wrote about these issues for the *New York Times* in a January 4, 2021, op-ed piece headlined "America Can't Even Produce the Things It Invested." I wrote about Emanuel's pursuit of a place in the Biden administration in several *Nation* articles, including "Do Not Hire This Man" (December 3, 2020) and "Ambassador Rahm Emanuel? No, No, a Thousand Times No" (March 23, 2021). Lori Wallach described Emanuel as "corporate hack extraordinaire" on her fine podcast, *Rethinking Trade*. The *Huff-Post* article "The Left Promises a Bruising Battle if Biden Taps Rahm Emanuel," which featured criticism of Emanuel from the NAACP and other groups, appeared on December 1, 2020. Roots Action highlighted opposition to an Emanuel nomination with its March 16, 2021, statement, "Coalition Opposes Rahm Emanuel for Ambassador Post, Citing Absence of 'Ethics, Integrity and Diplomatic Skills.'" WMAQ's report "White House Memos Reveal Emanuel's Agenda on Immigration, Crime" came out on June 20, 2014. I wrote about Trump's exploitation of trade issues for the *Nation* in a story published February 23, 2016: "President Donald J. Trump—It Could Happen: His promise to protect jobs and change trade policies could win over blue-collar workers, especially in the industrialized swing states." The *Politico* article headlined "Chi-town opens arms to China," which featured critiques of the former mayor's trade stance, was published on December 17, 2014. *Nikkei Asia* reported on Emanuel's trip to Japan in a July 14, 2018, story titled "Top Obama aide to pursue open trade amid protectionist turbulence: Rahm Emanuel, now Chicago mayor, says joining TPP is still in America's interest." The Economic Policy Institute's assessment, headlined "We can reshore manufacturing jobs, but Trump hasn't done it," appeared on epi.org on August 10, 2020. Lori Wallach discussed "the wide-scale export of US jobs" on April 15, 2008. Noam Chomsky discussed the shortages in an interview with *TruthOut* headlined "Ventilator Shortage Exposes the Cruelty of Neoliberal Capitalism," published on April 1, 2020. I interviewed Sherrod Brown a number of times in 2020 and 2021, for articles in the *Nation* and for this book.

Chapter 16. Pfizer's Vaccine Profiteering

The Rev. Martin Luther King Jr. spoke to the second convention of the Medical Committee for Human Rights on March 25, 1966. The Rev. William Barber II's essay "The Real Epidemic Is Poverty" appeared in the *Progressive* on March 30, 2020. The latest update of the CDC's "Health Equity Considerations and Racial and Ethnic Minority Groups" report appeared on April 19, 2021. The *Lancet* assessment "Covid-19 pandemic highlights racial health inequities" was published on July 10, 2020. Brookings published its report titled "Mapping racial inequity amid Covid-19 underscores policy discriminations against Black Americans" on April 16, 2020. *Science* released an important analysis, headlined "Deaths of health workers in Africa highlight vaccine inequity," on February 19, 2021. The Associated Press analysis "Racial disparity seen in US vaccination drive" appeared on January 30, 2021. The *Barron's* report, "Pfizer CEO Says Companies Should Make Profit on Covid-19 Vaccines," appeared on

July 28, 2020. The *Guardian* reported on pharmaceutical company profits in a November 10, 2020, article headlined "Pfizer and BioNTech could make $13bn from coronavirus vaccine: Johnson & Johnson and AstraZeneca pledged to make their vaccines available on a not-for-profit basis." *Fierce Pharma*, the pharmaceutical industry daily monitor, noted profit projections in its July 30, 2020, report titled "Pfizer CEO says it's 'radical' to suggest pharma should forgo profits on Covid-19 vaccine." Reuters reported on the subject on July 20, 2020, in an article headlined "Pfizer says it will charge other developed countries on par with US for vaccine deals." John Quelch wrote an opinion piece titled "Pfizer's vaccine maximizes profit, not the greater good" in the *Tampa Bay Times* on December 23, 2020. A US Department of Health and Human Services announcement from that same day declared, "Trump Administration purchases additional 100 million doses of Covid-19 investigational vaccine from Pfizer." *Quartz* ran an analysis on February 4, 2021, headlined "Pfizer's Covid-19 vaccine is set to be one of the most lucrative drugs in the world." *Pharmaceutical Technology*'s report, headlined "Pfizer forecasts $26bn of Covid-19 vaccine revenue after first-quarter success," appeared on May 5, 2021. *HealthExec* published an article titled "Pfizer CEO: Expecting pharma to fight Covid for free 'very fanatic and radical,'" on July 30, 2020. Michael Hiltzik's *Los Angeles Times* column "Pfizer, Moderna expect billions in profits from Covid vaccines. That's a scandal." was published on January 4, 2021. ACT UP's "Pfizer Greed Kills" action took place on April 2, 2016. *Out* magazine reported on the renewal of activist David Wojnarowicz's message in an article, "ACT UP Is Still Fighting 33 Years Later—Now It's Coronavirus," published on March 24, 2020. ACT UP New York's social media accounts maintained a lively and thoughtful discussion on coronavirus. The @actupny Twitter account featured terrific videos on March 11, 2021, of the "Free the Vaccine" protests. *Common Dreams* reported "#Peoples Vaccine Day of Action Calls for Big Pharma to 'Drop the Patents'" on March 11, 2021. Bernie Sanders issued his statement on vaccine profiteering on March 10, 2021.

Chapter 17. Drowning Grover Norquist's Anti-Government Delusion in the Bathtub of His Own Hypocrisy

I've written a good deal about Grover Norquist over the years for the *Nation*, as did my late colleague, the brilliant William Greider. Bill's classic piece, "The Republican Party's Goal Is to Destroy the Federal Government: For years, their driving ambition has been to get government 'down to the size where we can drown it in the bathtub,'" appeared on April 24, 2003. *Politico* ran a story headlined "Both parties pile on Massie after effort to force recorded vote flops" on March 27, 2021. My interview with Sanders, "Bernie Sanders Is as Frustrated as You Are," appeared on April 7, 2020, in the *Nation*. *Forbes* ran a report on July 6, 2020, headlined "Vocal Opponents of Federal Spending Took PPP Loans, Including Ayn Rand Institute, Grover Norquist Group." That same day, *Bloomberg* reported, "Grover Norquist's Americans for Tax Reform Fdn. Got PPP Loan." The communique "Americans for Tax Reform and Americans for Tax Reform Foundation Statement on PPP Loan" is archived at the groups' website, americansfortaxreformfoundation.org. The *Roll Call* story titled "Groups critical of taxes, spending not opposed to PPP loans" was published on July 6, 2020. The Taxpayers for Common Sense statement and video of July 9, 2020, is archived at the group's website, taxpayer.net, under "Statement on the Paycheck Protection Program." William F. Buckley's reflection on Ayn Rand can be viewed in delicious video form on YouTube under "William Buckley on Ayn Rand and *Atlas Shrugged*." "Big Sister Is Watching You," Whittaker Chambers's scathing critique of Rand's *Atlas Shrugged*, appeared in *National Review* on December 28, 1957. The CBS *60 Minutes* episode on Norquist aired November 20, 2011. The *New York Times* article "A German Exception? Why the Country's Coronavirus Death Rate Is Low," was published on May 6, 2020.

Chapter 18. *The Pandemic Profiteering of Jeffrey Preston Bezos*

I wrote about Jeff Bezos's burgeoning fortune for the *Nation* in "As Pandemic Profits Put Bezos on Track for Trillionaire Status, Tish James Asks: At What Cost?" on February 23, 2021. The Americans for Tax Fairness/Institute for Policy Studies report "US Billionaire Wealth Surges Past $1 Trillion Since Beginning of Pandemic—Total Grows to $4 Trillion" was written by Chuck Collins and published on December 9, 2020. The *Guardian* piece featuring comments from bankers, headlined "Billionaires' wealth rises to $10.2 trillion amid Covid crisis," ran on October 6, 2020. *Business Insider*'s article titled "Jeff Bezos has taken back the title of the world's richest person after a drop in Elon Musk's wealth" appeared on February 17, 2021. Check out *Comparisun*'s list of the world's richest companies at comparisum.com under "The Trillion Dollar Club." *MarketWatch* published a report on May 14, 2020, headlined "Amazon's Jeff Bezos was trending on Twitter as users debated the possibility of him becoming a trillionaire." New York State Attorney General Letitia James announced on February 17, 2021, that she was suing Amazon; read her statements and filings at ag.ny.gov under "Attorney General James Files Lawsuit Against Amazon for Failing to Protect Workers During Covid-19 Pandemic." *Politico* reported on the lawsuit the same day in an article titled "New York sues

Amazon, accusing company of unsafe pandemic conditions." Chris Smalls appeared on CNBC on March 29, 2020. Smalls wrote the opinion piece "Dear Jeff Bezos, instead of firing me, protect your workers from coronavirus," in the *Guardian* of April 2, 2020. The Vice News report "Leaked Amazon Memo Details Plan to Smear Fired Warehouse Organizer: 'He's Not Smart or Articulate'" appeared the same day. Readers can follow the Congress of Essential Workers on Twitter at: @TCOEW. Richard Trumka addressed the Pennsylvania AFL-CIO Convention on April 6, 2020. The union statement "America's Top Unions Demand Amazon Do Better," was issued on April 1, 2020. Bernie Sanders addressed the issue the same day on social media and in interviews. The Associated Press story headlined "Amazon is facing the biggest unionization push in its history" appeared on March 29, 2021. Read the full New York lawsuit on the ag.ny. gov website under "The People of the State of New York by Letitia James, Attorney General of the State of New York, Plaintiff against Amazon.com Inc., Amazon.com Sales, Inc., and Amazon. com Services LLC, Defendants." Amazon posted its updates about Covid testing and related issues at aboutamazon.com. An NBC News report on September 30, 2020, was headlined "Lack of oversight and transparency leave Amazon employees in the dark on Covid-19." The *USA Today* article headlined "Another Amazon warehouse worker dies from Covid-19 bringing total to 8" ran on May 21, 2020.

Conclusion: *The United States of Impunity*

Thomas Paine's *Common Sense* was published by the author on January 10, 1776. I have written often about Paine's influence on the American experiment over the years. I have, as well, maintained a conversation over many years with the great Paine scholar Harvey Kaye. Kaye's book *Thomas Paine and the Promise of America* (Hill & Wang, 2006) is required reading for patriots and revolutionaries of all countries. Gore Vidal wrote about America's Darwinian character in "Homage to Daniel Shays," his greatest essay, which was published in the *New York Review of Books* on August 10, 1972. Representative Jayapal spoke about *The Hunger Games* character of the pandemic moment in an interview with *Politico's Women Rule Podcast*, released on May 20, 2020. *Democracy Now* aired its interview with Naomi Klein, headlined "'Coronavirus Capitalism': Naomi Klein's Case for Transformative Change Amid Coronavirus Pandemic," on March 19, 2020. Tony Benn and I knew each other from the early 1990s until his death in 2014. He outlined his questions about power in a speech to the British Parliament on March 22, 2001. I wrote about Benn and the questions for the *Nation*, "Tony Benn and the Five Essential Questions of Democracy: The British parliamentarian, who has died at age 88, was one of history's great champions of giving power to the people," published on March 14, 2014. The term "Phoney War" refers to an eight-month period at the start of World War II, when Allied actions in response to German aggression were limited. Neville Chamberlain delivered his remarks on September 30, 1938, while the Hitler quote is recounted in David Faber's *Munich, 1938: Appeasement and World War II* (Simon & Schuster; 2010). Auden's great poem was "September 1, 1939." John Stevenson wrote a valuable introduction to the 1998 edition of *Guilty Men* (Penguin). Graham Macklin's *Chamberlain* was issued by Haus Publishers Ltd. in 2006. David Dutton's *Neville Chamberlain* was published by Bloomsbury Academic in 2001. FDR delivered his first inaugural address on March 4, 1933. In writing this chapter, I relied on archived newspaper and magazine accounts from the 1930s regarding Ferdinand Pecora, as well as conversations with

Representative Marcy Kaptur, Democrat of Ohio, who has made a serious study of Pecora's work. The *New York Times*, which covered Pecora extensively for five decades, featured a thorough obituary when he died: "Ex-Justice Ferdinand Pecora, 89, Dead" (December 8, 1971). Michael Perino's excellent biography, *The Hellhound of Wall Street: How Ferdinand Pecora's Investigation of the Great Crash Forever Changed American Finance*, was published in paperback by Penguin Books in 2011. Perino appeared on *Bill Moyers Journal* on April 24, 2009. Ron Chernow's op-ed "Where Is Our Ferdinand Pecora?" was published by the *New York Times* on January 5, 2009. Pecora's memoir, *Wall Street Under Oath: The Story of Our Modern Money Changers*, was published in 1939 and republished in 1973 by A. M. Kelley. Franklin Roosevelt's "I welcome their hatred" address was delivered in New York on October 31, 1936. Alexandria Ocasio-Cortez made her "it was broken even before Trump" comment on September 19, 2020.

Index

.